Too Many Reasons to Live

Too Many Reasons to Live

My Autobiography

ROB BURROW

With Ben Dirs

MACMILLAN

First published 2021 by Macmillan
an imprint of Pan Macmillan
The Smithson, 6 Briset Street, London EC1M 5NR
EU representative: Macmillan Publishers Ireland Ltd, 1st Floor,
The Liffey Trust Centre, 117–126 Sheriff Street Upper,
Dublin 1, D01 YC43
Associated companies throughout the world
www.panmacmillan.com

ISBN 978-1-5290-7324-9

1 3 5 7 9 8 6 4 2

A CIP catalogue record for this book is available from the British Library.

Typeset in Fairfield LT Std by Jouve (UK), Milton Keynes
Printed and bound by CPI Group (UK) Ltd, Croydon, CR0 4YY

Visit **www.panmacmillan.com** to read more about all our books
and to buy them. You will also find features, author interviews and
news of any author events, and you can sign up for e-newsletters
so that you're always first to hear about our new releases.

To Lindsey, Macy, Maya and Jackson

Shoot for the moon. Even if you miss,
you'll land among the stars

Love always, Hubby/Daddy

Foreword

BY KEVIN SINFIELD

I'll never forget the first time I saw Rob on a rugby field. I was fourteen, he was twelve and we were training with Leeds Rhinos, including the first team. As you can imagine, we were both starstruck. And it was boys against men. But Rob was zipping all over the place, terrifying all these giants and making them look stupid. He looked like a mouse in a cartoon, causing absolute mayhem.

That isn't really supposed to happen in rugby league, a sport in which big men almost always have the upper hand. But Rob was utterly unique, which meant he was able to flip the rules on their head. He might have been tiny, but he had lightning speed, all the skills, wonderful agility and was extremely fit. But most of all, he had incredible determination and courage.

I was Rob's captain for thirteen years and never stopped feeling like his big brother. In fact, all his Rhinos teammates felt protective of him. But despite his size, he never needed looking after. Opponents would try to run over the top of him, but he was a good defender who never shirked a tackle. If an opponent took a liberty, he wasn't afraid to stand up for himself. Even when he was playing pranks on his biggest, hardest teammates in the changing room, I knew he could handle himself. He loved caffeine, whether it was coffee or Red Bull, which meant he hardly ever shut up. But he was too likeable to get mad at. Cheeky, always making people laugh, made the place fun.

That Leeds Rhinos team won everything there was to win and Rob was integral to its success. But it wasn't just that he scared defenders to death and produced moments of magic to win big games, time and time again. He also personified everything that was special about that side's culture. He was a great friend, respectful, honest, selfless, loyal, worked so hard and cared so much. Even during the tough times, when things weren't going quite as he wanted, he never stopped loving Leeds or his teammates.

People need to understand that every successful team, in whatever sport, goes through dark times. Besides the glorious victories, there are soul-destroying defeats. Players get dropped or injured. They get sick of the sight of the training field; of those dark mornings running up hills; of those gruelling pre-seasons that seem like they'll never end and make playing rugby league feel like a very unpleasant job. But it's during those dark times – when players are working themselves into the ground, fighting for each other tooth and nail, proving they have each other's backs, want to get better and win more trophies – that the tightest bonds are forged and friendships taken to another level.

When we all retired from playing, we were no longer in each other's pockets, day in and day out. But that closeness never left us. Whenever we met, there was always a twinkle in our eyes, in recognition of all the great times we had together. So when Rob was diagnosed with motor neurone disease, it wasn't a surprise how everyone rallied. We were all floored by the news, as was everyone connected with Leeds Rhinos and rugby league in general. But as soon as that Bat-Signal went up, the call was answered by many.

We couldn't even begin to imagine what Rob was going through. But we wanted to be the best friends possible and support him in whatever way we could. We were all certain of one thing: if it had happened to any of us, the reaction would have been the same – and Rob would have been right at the front of the queue, giving everything he had for his mate, just as he did on the rugby field.

Rugby league isn't the biggest sport in the world, but it's a very special one. What it's doing now for Rob is what it's always done and what it always will do. So many members of the rugby league family have pitched in and done wonderful things. But Rob's courage has touched thousands of people beyond the sport we both love. He's inspired an army, which is doing everything it can to raise money and awareness of MND, so that one day a cure will be found.

Rob's a shy bloke, was never one for the limelight. So for him to open up his life for all to see was a remarkable thing to do. Lots of people are going through tough times at the minute, what with Covid. But I hope Rob's story makes people reflect and provides some perspective. However dark things seem, there are people who care and want to take some of the burden. When a friend hits a rough patch, it can bring out the best in you. And time is precious, so it's best to be positive, as nice as possible and fit in as much as you can.

Every time I talk about Rob on camera, I get emotional. But every time I see him, he's got a big smile on his face. He still gives off so much energy and I feel like a better person for being in his company. When I remind him of some funny story, his eyes sparkle, his shoulders shake and tears of laughter stream down his face. All these years later, and despite how tough his life has become, he's still revelling in those old pranks he played. I was lucky to have Rob as a teammate. I've never been prouder to call someone a friend.

Prologue

GRANDDAD BOB NEVER MISSED A GAME WHEN I WAS growing up. He'd stand on the touchline in all weather – usually grey, often raining – and clap every time I got the ball. Mum says he always thought I'd be something special. Truth be told, even if I'd ended up working in a warehouse, Granddad Bob probably would have turned up to watch. While I was stacking boxes, he'd have been cheering me on, telling everyone I was the best warehouse worker there was.

I was quick, with a wicked swerve and sidestep. When you see me in old home videos, I look like a wind-up toy, or a spinning top. If it seems like I'm slightly out of control, that's because I was. My brain didn't always know where my legs were taking me. Luckily, my opponents didn't know either. I'd pop up all over the field, as if by magic, and cause mayhem. I beat a lot of tackles and scored a lot of tries. Dear old Granddad Bob did a lot of cheering.

The problem was my size. Every week, I was the smallest player on the pitch. Some kids, the real lumps, were twice as big as me. Even I thought it looked quite comical. But when I say it was a problem, it only was for other people. It wasn't for me, and certainly not for Granddad Bob. During a game, he'd often overhear coaches and parents talking about me: 'That Burrow lad's very quick and very skilful, but he'll never make it. Far too small.' And Granddad Bob would pipe up with, 'Just you watch, you'll have changed your mind by the end of the game.' After I'd scored another hat-trick, Granddad Bob would give them a big wave and a hearty cheerio, before chuckling all the way home.

Granddad Bob never doubted me, but other people continued to, throughout my career. When I was scouted by Leeds Rhinos, people said I was too small. When I joined the Rhinos academy, people said I was too small. When I made my Rhinos first-team debut, people said I was too small. When I was first picked for my country, people said I was too small (one headline writer in Australia called me a 'Pommy squirt'!). Even after I won my eighth Grand Final with Leeds, there was probably still at least one naysayer, keeping the lack of faith. I can picture him now, sitting on his sofa, scowling at his TV and muttering, 'How did that Rob Burrow ever make it? He's far too small . . .'

But the funny thing is, I completely understand. If someone else my size had tried to make it in rugby league, I'd have written them off in a heartbeat: 'Not a chance. Ridiculous. Try becoming a jockey.' Which makes me think, it wasn't so much that I ignored the naysayers, it's more that I didn't really hear them. In one ear, out the other. Because if you took it all in, you'd curl up and die. I suppose you'd call that focus. And that's how I am now, 100 per cent focused. Every day, motor neurone disease (MND) tries to convince me to quit – tells me I'm too small, that I don't have what it takes – but I simply refuse to listen.

You know what my dad calls me? The Black Knight, from *Monty Python and the Holy Grail*. When my voice started to go and he asked me how I was, it was a case of 'Tis but a scratch!' When I couldn't get around on my own any more, it was a case of 'It's just a flesh wound!' You know what they should stick on my headstone? 'All right, we'll call it a draw.' MND picked on the wrong bloke, just like opponents on the rugby field always picked on the wrong bloke. Thought they'd run over me, trample me to dust. I can't keep dodging the disease forever, but I won't stop trying. I'm not thinking about the full-time hooter, I'm still out there fighting tooth and nail. That's how it has to be.

★

From my perch on the sofa, I can see my two daughters, Macy and Maya, running riot in the garden. My little boy, Jackson, is playing by my feet. I'd say he was burbling, but that would be rich coming from me. It's a beautiful late summer's day, by Yorkshire standards. Sunny but not too warm, a slight breeze knocking the heat off. Just right for kicking a ball around with your son. But I'll never kick a ball around with Jackson, like my dad did with me. I'll never be Granddad Rob to Jackson's kids. I can't even reach out and touch him, let alone leap from my perch, toss him over my shoulder and charge headlong into the garden. And I can't even burble, let alone tell him I love him.

But I don't want to upset anyone. That's not the idea of this book. Do you want to know the truth? I feel tremendously lucky. The other day, my wife Lindsey asked if I'd change anything about my life, if it meant not getting MND. I told her I wouldn't change a thing. Lindsey found that comforting, powerful even, but I'm not sure she understood it. I suppose a lot of people would be racking their brains, trying to think of things they could have done differently. But how could I not feel lucky? I've achieved so much. I have a wonderful wife and three beautiful children. What more does a man need?

Since being diagnosed, people keep asking me about my bucket list. Do you fancy jumping out of a plane? Don't you want to see the Grand Canyon? But this is my bucket list: watching my children grow up, for as long as I can. I've done everything else I need to do, now I have a responsibility to stick around. Not only to my family, but also to everyone else living with this horrible disease. I need to prove that if your doctor says you've only got two years left to live, you can double it. By fighting as hard as I can, I hope others can find strength. I hope they can see that there are too many reasons to live.

★

When you're diagnosed with MND, normality suddenly becomes incredibly important. Everyday things I might otherwise have missed – like a sly smile on Jackson's face, or seeing one of the girls from a different angle and noticing how much she's grown – give me a tremendous lift. That's all that counts. Not money or material things. Not what's going on in the news. Just the kids and their happiness. As such, I try to live in the present as much as possible. Savour each moment, like swilling fine wine. But I can't help looking back. I spend so much time sat on my perch, it would be strange not to.

Sometimes, I picture myself as I was, that speedy kid with the wicked swerve and sidestep. Almost impossibly agile, almost impossible to grab hold of, like a bar of soap on legs. And I find it difficult to comprehend that my body was ever able to do those things. The same body that struggles to get off the sofa, feed itself or send a text. And then I picture Granddad Bob. If he was still with us, he'd be cheering me on. He'd think that what I'm doing now is the most special thing I've ever done.

1

IT ALL STARTED WITH THE WORD 'CONSISTENCY'. OR IT would, if you were making a film about me. It was September 2019, I was presenting an award at a Rhinos dinner and had to make a little speech. I'd never exactly been Stephen Fry on the microphone, but this was meat and drink to me. It was the sort of thing I'd done plenty of times before, with no problems whatsoever. This academy lad who'd won the award was a very consistent player, but I couldn't get the bloody word out. I've always been a bit short-tongued, but this was different. The word 'consistency' was like a drunk on roller-skates, sliding sideways across my lips, bashing into my teeth and repeatedly failing to find the exit.

Kev Sinfield, my old captain, asked if anything was up with me. A couple of the other lads thought I'd been drinking. If I had been drinking, it would have made sense. I hadn't, so it didn't. But I was more embarrassed than worried. And I felt bad for the lad that I'd fluffed his special moment.

The book version of the story is a bit longer. A month or so before that awards ceremony, in August 2019, I was on holiday in Scotland, where my mum noticed I was having trouble articulating some of my words. It wasn't obvious, probably something only a mum would spot. Then, when I went to Florida with Lindsey and the kids, I felt tired all the time, devoid of energy.

When I was still playing rugby, I needed six espressos before leaving the house in the morning and stayed topped up with regular cans of Red Bull. But that was a necessity, to get me through the grind of training. And it's not something I started doing at the end, I was doing it from when I was a teenager. Now, I was struggling to get out of bed and nodding off on the sofa at 6 p.m., like an old fella. In between, poor Lindsey was doing all the donkey work, getting Jackson up in the morning, changing his nappies and lugging him about all day. Lindsey had always told me how useless I was, but this was something else completely.

After the awards dinner, my neighbour picked up on my slurring, asked if I was on drugs. I still didn't think much of it, even when my arms started twitching. I was under quite a lot of stress. Things were a bit rocky with my coaching job at Leeds and we were in the process of moving, selling one house and buying a new one. I thought it might have had something to do with my medication. I'd broken two collarbones during my career and was always chopping and changing pills for the aches and pains. But when I couldn't pronounce the word 'solicitor' (while I was on the phone to my solicitor, which was a bit embarrassing), Lindsey insisted I ask the Rhinos doctor about it. Kev suggested I do the same. Having been my skipper, he was now the Rhinos' director of rugby and my boss. He had a duty of care, but he was also a friend.

I was going for a jab on my shoulder anyway, so mentioned the slurring as an aside. The doctor didn't seem alarmed but referred me to a neurologist in Leeds. That's when I started doing a bit of reading, because just the word 'neurologist' sounds serious. I'd had a lot of bangs on the head, and there had been a few stories in the news about former rugby players suffering from early onset dementia. But, according to the dreaded Dr Google, one of the illnesses that matched my symptoms most closely was motor neurone disease. Then again, the internet will tell you lots of awful things, most of them untrue.

At the clinic, I had some nerve conduction tests done and failed three of them. Lindsey thought my reflexes seemed a bit brisk, so she asked the consultant if it might be MND. Lindsey's a physiotherapist and had treated people with MND, among lots of other horrible diseases, so knew more than most. She'd also been doing her own reading. But you know what medical people are like, they can be a bit defensive. Like cabbies when you question the route they're taking, or rugby coaches when you question their tactics. So the consultant replied, 'Why are you asking that? Are you a doctor?', before telling us off for Googling. He assured us it was unlikely to be MND, because it was just so rare. Instead, he thought it might be something called myasthenia gravis, which is a treatable problem that affects the speech muscles.

When the MRI scan and blood tests came back clear, we were quite optimistic. So much so that Lindsey wasn't going to come with me for the second consultation. The girls had a swimming lesson that night, so it would have made more sense for her to go straight home after work. But for whatever reason, she decided to come with me. I think Lindsey knew, deep down inside.

I'd been coaching that day – 12 December 2019, a date I'll never forget – so Lindsey met me off the train in Leeds. We were laughing and joking on the way into the clinic. We expected them to say, 'It's nothing to worry about, Mr Burrow, here are some tablets. You'll be right as rain in no time.' I'd settled on it being a viral infection, which would explain the tiredness, why I felt like an old fella. But when we walked into the room, the consultant and his nurse weren't laughing and joking, they were sat there looking very serious.

The consultant asked how I was, and I said I felt fine. Then he said, 'It's not good news. I'm sorry to tell you it's motor neurone disease.'

'Are you sure?' I replied.

'We wouldn't be telling you unless we were.'

The rest of that consultation is a blur. I don't remember Lindsey asking how long I had to live. I don't remember the consultant saying I had a year or two. I do remember asking if Lindsey was OK. She had a bit of a cry and we cuddled. Then I said, 'Thank God it's me and not you or the kids.' That wasn't me trying to be a tough guy. I'm sure most husbands would feel the same.

When I phoned my parents to tell them the news, Dad hit the deck. My eldest sister Joanne tells me his legs gave way like fag ash. I could hear Mum sobbing uncontrollably in the background. Poor old Joanne had no choice but to keep a stiff upper lip. When me and Lindsey walked through the front door, Lindsey also collapsed in the hall-way. It wasn't a pretty scene. There's not much pretty about MND. Then we took the girls swimming and tried to act normal.

The awards dinner where I couldn't pronounce 'con-sistency' had been less than three months earlier. From mentioning it in passing to the Rhinos doctor to being diag-nosed took three weeks. Riding high one day, shot down the next.

★

Nothing can prepare you for that moment. Nobody can tell you how you're meant to react. But I didn't expect things to be so vague. It was pretty much a case of, 'You've got MND, there's no treatment, no cure, and you've probably got a couple of years to live. Off you toddle.' I wanted to know more. Why did I have MND? Why did some sufferers live longer than others? What about Stephen Hawking? Why the hell have I only got two years when he had fifty-odd? Who could I speak to, to find out what this disease would do to me?

As I've said, Lindsey knew far more than me about the devastation MND could wreak. She'd dealt with MND patients who weren't able to get out of bed or feed them-selves or breathe unaided. So she knew all too well what I was in for. And she knew what she was in for. No wonder she was in a bit of a state.

That first week or so after being diagnosed was grimly surreal. Other than my voice, which was getting more and more slurred and gravelly, I felt fit as a fiddle. I'd only just turned thirty-seven. I'd played in a Super League Grand

Final only two years ago. I could still drive, run and lift the kids onto my shoulders. It didn't make sense. I wondered if the consultant had made a terrible mistake. Maybe he was new at this stuff? Maybe he'd mixed me up with someone else?

I kept thinking about my family's life after I'd gone. Lindsey as a widow, without a man about the house, and the kids not having a daddy. Who'd take the girls swimming? Who'd teach Jackson to catch and kick a ball?

My mum and dad are such sweet people and I worried the news might crush them. How could their dynamic little boy, who had defied all the odds on the rugby field, be reduced to this? Once he'd peeled himself off the carpet, Dad was a mixture of guilt and defiance. He wondered if rugby was responsible, blamed himself for letting me play. All those knocks on the head, which had once seemed like badges of bravery, now suddenly just seemed daft. But Dad wasn't ready to stop believing in his little superhero. He thought I'd beat it, like nobody else had. Make the disease look foolish, like I'd made all those big, ugly men look foolish on the rugby field. I did it then, I'd do it now.

The hardest task was telling the kids. Macy was eight, Maya four and Jackson turned one a few days after my diagnosis. How do you break it to three small children that their dad has an incurable disease and won't be around for much longer? That's something else we weren't told. Lindsey and I were still struggling to wrap our heads around it. We didn't have the answers, so weren't sure we'd be able to cope with any questions they might have.

We wanted to tell them before Christmas, in the hope that it might clear some of the gloom. When Lindsey started explaining that Daddy was ill, Maya looked up from her toys and said, 'What are you telling us this for? It's boring.' With that, she went back to playing with her toys. Talk about breaking the ice. Absolutely perfect. It felt like a big weight had been lifted off my shoulders, and Lindsey felt the same. A couple of days later, Macy said to Lindsey, 'Mummy, I feel sad that Daddy was told what he was.' She asked a few questions and Lindsey told her that the doctors and nurses were doing everything they could but that Daddy wasn't going to get better. There's no textbook way of dealing with this stuff, but our policy was to be honest.

I thought telling the kids might clear the fog. It did, but it soon descended again, trailing behind me wherever I went. One evening, I gathered Macy and Maya in my arms and hugged them against my chest, harder than I'd ever done, before taking Jackson upstairs for a feed. While he chattered away contentedly in the dark bedroom, I pictured him on his first day of school, looking smiley and proud as punch in his smart new uniform. I pictured him on a rugby field, darting here and there, leaving defenders clutching at thin air. I pictured us walking hand in hand towards Headingley Stadium, both decked out in the blue and amber of Leeds. It was a collage of the impossible, my own personal movie reel of things that would never happen. Tears rolled down my cheeks as I rocked Jackson to sleep.

★

You'd think that dealing with friends would be easier, but that wasn't really the case. My initial approach was a mixture of black humour – which probably made some people feel uncomfortable – and evasion. The day after my diagnosis, a mate texted to see how I'd got on at the clinic. My instinct was to make a joke about it. At Leeds's training ground, there's a big mural of club legends who have died. So I texted back, 'Bad news. Got motor neurone disease. Save a place on the mural.' That was probably a bit mean of me. What was he supposed to say to that? Then again, how was I supposed to tell him?

I sent long messages to a few of my closest teammates, including Kev Sinfield, Danny McGuire, Jamie Peacock, Keith Senior and Jamie Jones-Buchanan, with whom I'd shared a dressing room at Leeds for the best part of two decades. They'd already twigged that something was badly amiss. Like they say about washed-up boxers, they're always the first to know, deep down, but the last to admit it. Meanwhile, close friends can see the stark truth.

As my boss, Kev had had a ringside seat for my deterioration, which is why he was so keen to get to the bottom of things. But I actually think my decline was easier to detect from a slight distance, that old friends I saw from time to time were better placed to gauge the changes in me. Jamie Jones-Buchanan noticed I was getting thinner. I'd always been short, but years of intensive training had thickened me up, made me almost bulbous, especially around the thighs and backside. A few weeks after the dinner where I couldn't pronounce the word 'consistency', he gave me a call and I struggled to pronounce his name. Then, in November, me and Danny McGuire did a gentlemen's evening in Cumbria, which consisted of about two hundred blokes getting leathered and wanting entertaining rugby stories. I could barely talk and Maggsy had to cover for me. We somehow managed to get through it, but that must have been quite disconcerting for him and I know he was worried.

When I met Jonesy for a coffee on the Kirkstall Road in Leeds, the questions kept coming. It wasn't an interrogation, more an hour's gentle probing, but Jonesy's concern worried me. You know what it's like when friends start making a fuss. You can bury the truth, but when mates pull out their shovels and start digging, sensors get tripped. That those sensors didn't trigger alarm bells was down to wishful thinking, or not thinking at all.

When texts started trickling in from people I hadn't told, I realized news of my diagnosis had leaked and started spreading through the Rhinos grapevine. One hardcore Leeds fan, a great guy called Richard Stockdale, who had seen almost every game I'd played since I was a teenager, sent me a direct message on Twitter, asking if I was OK. I said I was fine, and why was he asking? When he said he'd been told some bad news about my health, I came clean. That's when I decided to take control of the situation. Far better to hit people with the truth, however brutal and difficult to stomach, than have them walking on eggshells around me and whispering behind my back.

*

Jamie Peacock, Rhinos teammate

I'd heard Rob was having one or two problems with his health. But I thought it was just some aches and pains, like a lot of former rugby players have to put up with. When someone told me he was slurring his words, I did wonder if it might be something more serious. But Rob was still a young man, didn't drink, kept himself fit. There had to be an innocent explanation.

I'd been to New York for four days, drinking non-stop with a mate. Driving home from the airport, I was jet-lagged and full of the post-booze blues. That's when I got the call from Kev. When he told me Rob had MND, I broke down behind the wheel. It felt like my heart was breaking. I already knew how bad MND was, because Sam Burgess's dad had died of it. Sam, an old England teammate, had spoken to me about his dad's illness a few times, how quickly it had taken hold of him, how quickly he'd deteriorated.

In 2011, I was on holiday in Florida when my dad rang to tell me he had stage four cancer and only three months to live. My world fell apart. And I had the same sense of overwhelming sadness when I heard about Rob. Rob was the world's nicest bloke. He had three young kids. He was a great friend. I kept asking myself the same question, over and over again: Why him?

Barrie McDermott, Rhinos teammate

I'd heard something might be up with Rob from one of his assistant coaches, Jonny Wainhouse. I knew it was unlikely to be drink or drugs, because that was never Rob. Then Kev told me Rob was having conversations with his family and seeking medical advice. So I gave him a call and said, 'Come on, Rob, let's have a coffee. I'm worried about you.'

I remember Rob walking in and me tapping my watch and saying, 'Come on, dickhead, you're late.' That man was never on time. I gave him a hug, asked him how he was and he said he was fine. When I asked him how he really was, and what was going on with his speech, he said he was going through a bit of stress, that's all. Aside from the slurring, he was as sharp as ever. But I had this awful feeling in the pit of my stomach. I'd seen how much Rob got knocked around on the pitch. And there'd been a lot of stuff in the news about brain injuries in rugby union. So while we were drinking our coffees and eating our muffins, I was thinking, 'God, I hope he hasn't got something terrible like that.' When it was time to say goodbye, I gave him another hug and said I'd see him after Christmas.

A couple of weeks later, Rob sent me a text to say he'd seen a doctor and been told it was nothing serious. Big sigh of relief. But a week or so after that, he sent me another text that I'll never, ever forget: 'I've got motor neurone disease. I don't know how long I've got, but I feel great and I'm going to give it a good crack. Don't worry.' I was sat in a chair in my bedroom sobbing uncontrollably. I just couldn't bring myself out of it. When I tried to tell my kids, they thought one of their granddads or grandmas had died. That's how bad I was. They didn't understand why I was so upset. I didn't really understand it. I think it was the speed of it. One minute my mate was fine, the next he had a life-threatening disease. And I suppose you don't really know how close you are to some people until something goes wrong.

★

Every time someone gets MND, it's like a grenade going off. Yes, the person who has the disease takes the biggest hit, but it causes widespread collateral damage. Jamie Peacock (or JP to his mates) and Barrie Mac were two of the hardest lads I ever played with. They're two of the hardest lads ever to play rugby league, full stop. I suppose I should be flattered, and I am in a way. But the thought of JP and Barrie in tears at my plight just adds to the sense of guilt. And while writing this book, I've discovered that they weren't the only tough-as-teak blokes to break down on learning of my diagnosis.

Keith Senior was at a wedding when he got my text, and he tells me it hit him like a ton of bricks. Danny McGuire was in Australia, and he tells me he was overcome by a feeling of helplessness. It wasn't just that Maggsy was at the other end of the world, which meant he couldn't pop round, put his arm around me and offer some words of reassurance, it was also that he didn't really know what to say anyway. When Maggsy rang, he told me he was sorry. What more could anyone offer? I was sat with my dad when my old St Helens rival Sean Long phoned, and he was very emotional. Although maybe he still hadn't got over the three Grand Finals he lost against Leeds? Sorry, Longy, I couldn't resist.

*

All the best books have a dashing hero, someone who comes flying to the rescue when all seems doomed. This book has loads of them. But in those early days after my diagnosis, two blokes stood out. Kev Sinfield was like a big brother to me, displaying many of the qualities that marked him out as a great captain of Leeds, including being calm in a crisis and having the organizational skills of a general.

The other one was a half-man, half-giraffe in a yellow tartan suit. Three days after my diagnosis, I was watching *BBC Sports Personality of the Year* and Doddie Weir was presented with an award. I didn't know much about Doddie – I was vaguely aware he'd played rugby union for Scotland, but I've never really been interested in the other code – but it turned out we had a lot in common. Doddie, who had been diagnosed with MND in 2016, gave an amazing speech about his charity work and trying to find a cure for the disease. I was struck by how positive he seemed. Doddie didn't strike me as a dead man walking, he seemed very much alive. It gave me a glimmer of hope. And when you're groping in the dark, a glimmer can seem like a lightning bolt.

The following day, I watched a BBC documentary about Doddie and was blown away by his attitude to life. Unbeknown to me, Kev had been in touch with Bryan Redpath, a former Scotland teammate of Doddie's, who coached Kev during his stint in union with Leeds Carnegie. And a week before Christmas, me and Kev met Doddie and his old Scotland teammate Gary Armstrong at the Holiday Inn in Carlisle. It was like a summit: me with my faithful wingman, Doddie with his. Hoping to make some sense of MND.

Just as I didn't know much about rugby union, Doddie didn't know much about rugby league. He certainly didn't know much about me. But we clicked immediately. The first thing I noticed about Doddie – apart from his yellow tartan trousers, which are probably visible from the moon – was that he seemed happy, proud and serene. Doddie didn't look beaten up, like a man who was sagging on the ropes. He looked like he was still holding his own.

Doddie's headline lesson was that you can still live a good life despite MND. You can still do things with your family, cram lots of great memories in. He treated living with MND as an extension of his rugby career, almost as a game. If you embrace the game and play it hard, like both of us played rugby, you can win little skirmishes within the greater battle. He gave me the example of putting his shoes on: when Doddie could no longer tie his laces, he got himself some rubber no-tie laces. Every time he slipped into his shoes after that, he was putting two fingers up at MND. When he could no longer lift a glass to his lips, he got himself a long straw. Just being able to change the TV channel was a victory over MND. Unlike a game of rugby, which only lasts eighty minutes, MND has no set time limit. The battle can go on for years. But if you make each day a new game, those little victories become incredibly important.

Kev was probably dreading that meeting, thought we'd be crying in each other's arms and shouting, 'Woe is me!' But we laughed a lot. It's impossible not to in Doddie's presence. He told us how difficult it had been to tell his mates, which struck a chord with me. Apparently, when he told Gary Armstrong, the first thing Gary said was, 'I hope you get the potholes in your driveway filled up.' Doddie replied, 'Gary, I've just told you I've got a life-threatening disease and all you're worried about are my potholes.' And Gary shot back, 'I don't want a call from your wife, to say your wheelchair's stuck.'

Doddie didn't sugar the pill. He told me how devastating the disease had been, for him and his family. How his wife had to clothe, shower and feed him. How it was difficult for a proud, stubborn, fiercely independent former sportsman like him to accept help. How not knowing how long he had left was a constant torment. He also showed flashes of anger, especially when talking about the lack of progress in terms of treatment: there had been no major breakthroughs in the twenty-first century and no new MND medication for twenty-eight years.

But Doddie also told me how MND had made him re-evaluate life. When you're slogging along, working all hours to save enough money for your retirement, it's easy to forget how life should really be lived. But when Doddie got that knock on the door, followed by that terrible news – 'Sorry, mate, you've got MND' – the important things in life, principally family and friends, were brought into sharper focus, at least after the shock had worn off.

That day in Carlisle, I felt like I'd joined a new team. It's not a team I would have chosen to play on; it picked me. But at least I had an inspirational skipper, just like in my Rhinos days. Doddie taught me the rules, showed me the path I needed to follow. No, there weren't any drugs that could help, but the greatest weapon I had was between my ears. Yes, MND was a terrible illness, but humour and positive thinking could make it more bearable.

Doddie wasn't embarrassed by his illness, hadn't pulled down the shutters. Instead, he'd invited the public in and given them a ringside seat for the fight. Not because he wanted pity, but because he wanted to raise awareness and money in the fight against MND. I had a responsibility to do the same, so that they might find a cure. They might not find it tomorrow, they might not find it in time to save me and Doddie, but they'll find it one day.

My fight with MND wasn't all about me, it was also about the brickie, the postman, the factory worker. I never took a backward step on the rugby field, and I wasn't going to start now. My team needed me to tackle it head on, just like I'd tackled all those eighteen-stone props in my rugby days. They needed to see that even a little fella like me could give MND a bit of a ding-dong.

I don't think Doddie saw himself as doing anything particularly inspirational that day, he was just chatting about his experiences with someone who was desperately seeking some answers. But that meeting with the big man changed everything for me. I'm not particularly religious, and neither is Doddie. But I went into that meeting blind, and now I could see. If anyone from the Holiday Inn is reading this, stick a plaque on the front of your Carlisle hotel: 'Doddie Weir performed a miracle here. 18 December 2019.'

★

The day after meeting Doddie, I decided it was time to face the media. Rhinos press officer Phil Daly asked BBC Look North reporter Tanya Arnold to come down to Headingley Stadium with a camera, as well as the *Mirror*'s rugby league correspondent Gareth Walker and Pete Smith from the *Yorkshire Evening Post*. When I walked into the executive box for the interviews, there were two cameras pointed at two chairs, placed under two blazing lights. There was no backtracking now, it was time to tell the country my secret.

I thought I did pretty well for the first few minutes, described my symptoms and told the story of my diagnosis without any hitches. But when Tanya asked about the impact the diagnosis had had on my family, Doddie's magic momentarily wore off. A big-man hug from Kev put me back on track, before I had another wobble down the stretch. But there was never any question about the interview not being broadcast. Kev and Phil had their doubts, but I was adamant. There was no point in me going on TV and pretending MND was a bit of a breeze. People needed to see how it had affected me, physically and emotionally. Yes, Doddie had worked a miracle. But the miracle didn't mean I was cured. The miracle didn't mean I wasn't going to have some wobbles. The miracle simply meant that, however devastating MND was, I was going to face up to it with spirit and dignity.

Rhinos arranged a private consultation with an MND specialist called Professor Chris McDermott, from the University of Sheffield. Professor McDermott confirmed the diagnosis but provided me with a bit more hope. He told me about trials that were taking place in the UK, which I could maybe be a part of. He told me how lucky I was to be diagnosed so early, because some people don't find out what's wrong with them for ages. He said that being young and fit would help me and that maybe I'd defy the initial prognosis and stick around for longer than a couple of years. I did ask Professor McDermott how it would all end, and he told me that most people with MND die in their sleep. But I wasn't afraid of death, I was afraid of not making the most of however long I had left.

The diagnosis confirmation was another hammer blow for Lindsey. As it was, she hadn't been eating and was having trouble sleeping. One day, she went to the bank, forgot her PIN and broke down in front of the cash machine. But that was no good for me, her or the kids. So I said to her, 'When you're down, you make me feel down. And if we're both down, the kids will get upset. There's no point asking yourself, "Why Rob? What's he done to deserve this?" It is what

23

it is. I haven't done anything to deserve it, it's just rotten luck. Getting upset isn't going to change anything. We just have to roll our sleeves up.'

That was a big turning point for Lindsey. If I could be positive, then so could she. From that moment on, we had a strict no-crying policy at home, at least for the adults. If my dad's bottom lip started to quiver, I'd have a little word with him, like Gary Lineker with Gazza at the 1990 World Cup. I just wanted everyone to be normal. I knew that would be difficult, because there's nothing normal about MND. There's nothing normal about your husband suddenly struggling to put his shoes on. There's nothing normal about your dad suddenly struggling to kick a ball. There's nothing normal about your mate suddenly sounding like he's gargling gravel. But you've got to take the rough with the smooth. As I used to say to my Rhinos teammates: 'If you want the rainbow, you've got to put up with the rain. Do you know which "philosopher" said that? Dolly Parton. And people say she's just a big pair of tits.'*

---

* Don't worry, Ricky Gervais is not going to sue a man with motor neurone disease. But if this book does end up being pulped, then you'll know why.

2

A FEW MONTHS AFTER MY DIAGNOSIS, MUM AND DAD were helping me to my car when this bloke drove past and waved. A couple of minutes later, while I was still parked up, this bloke wandered over, fished fifty quid from his pocket and insisted I take it, to put towards my fund. The funny thing was, he was wearing a Castleford Tigers shirt, and Castleford fans hate Leeds with a passion.

Whenever I played against Cas, their fans would spend most of the game chanting, 'We hate Leeds scum!' (Leeds fans would chant back, 'There's only one Rob Burrow! The only man in Cas who's got a full-time job!') So I thought what that Tigers fans did was lovely. But I shouldn't have been surprised. That's just what people are like round our way. Salt of the earth, would give you the shirt off their back, even if you're a local boy who ran away to play for the Rhinos.

Me and the family live in Pontefract, an old market town in West Yorkshire. Me and my two sisters were born there, but raised in Castleford, just a few miles away. Like most rugby league players, I haven't travelled far. Rugby league players aren't footballers, we don't pack up and move to a big pile in Harrogate as soon as we've made a few quid (I should add that a footballer's definition of making a few quid is a bit different to ours). That's what sets rugby league apart from other sports, its connection to the community. For the most part, professional rugby league players are no different from the fans, it's just that we're lucky enough to have a bit of talent.

My dad was originally from Leeds but met my mum at the Burberry factory in Castleford, just across from the station. Dad was a big Leeds fan and Mum was mad on Cas, which meant they had a few fallings-out while they were courting (back in those days, Cas were often more than a match for Leeds, winning consecutive Challenge Cups in 1969 and 1970). But Mum eventually conned Dad into marrying her and they've been in Castleford ever since.

Castleford was a mining town then, and there are stories about players doing a shift down the pit on a Saturday morning before playing eighty minutes in the afternoon. The pits closed in the 1980s, as they did in towns across the region. But the one thing they couldn't take from us was rugby league.

In Yorkshire's big cities, like Leeds, Huddersfield and Hull, rugby league has plenty of competition from football. But in the area around Wakefield – the so-called Five Towns – rugby league has always been the only sport worth knowing. Walk through Castleford town centre the day after a game and you'll see people standing in small clusters, all of them wearing Tigers shirts, discussing what went right or wrong. And why they all still hate Leeds. And it will be the same in Wakefield and Featherstone, places you might never have heard of if it wasn't for rugby league.

Joanne came first, followed by Claire and then me. After I arrived, Dad did a little dance around the delivery room, because he'd so wanted a boy to go with his two daughters. When a nurse gave him a voucher for the canteen, he used that as an excuse to slip out to the working men's club. When he left the hospital it was a lovely, sunny September day. When he got back after a couple of pints he was wet through, because he'd been caught in a thunderstorm. Strangely, my mum didn't believe his story that the canteen had sprung a leak.

I was always very sporty and determined. When I was a kid, we'd go on caravanning holidays to a place called Primrose Valley, on the North Yorkshire coast. There was a big pub there with a beer garden and some steep steps leading up to the entrance. One day, Granddad Bob nudged my dad and said, 'Have a look at Rob.' I was squatting and jumping up the steps, like you see proper athletes doing, or Rocky in the movies. And I was only about three. Everyone in the beer garden was chuckling away and Granddad Bob was proud as punch, wanting them all to know that I was his grandson.

Granddad Bob thought the world of me, and the feeling was mutual. He had loads of grandkids, but I was his golden grandchild. He used to say to me, 'I think the sun shines out of your backside.' When I got a bit older, he updated it to, 'I'd use your shit for toothpaste.' He was full of funny old sayings like that, a proper Yorkshire character, and like a mate as well as a granddad.

Granddad Bob loved his horseracing and was constantly studying the form. Picture one of those old fellas with a copy of the *Racing Post* permanently stuffed under his arm. We'd sit and watch the horses together on the telly and before every race he'd say, 'Son, I'm gonna win big . . .' He never did, but he had that same sunny optimism about everything. Including me.

I was a good kid, no trouble at all. Actually, that's not entirely true. I was cheeky and a bit of a joker, always playing pranks on people. We'd play in the street a lot, and I'd constantly be knocking on doors and running away. Or hitting people on the back of the head and running away. And whenever my sisters came near me, I'd try to run away as well. And you wonder why I was so elusive on a rugby pitch. My sisters tormented me something rotten. They'd call me 'golden boy', because they reckoned I was the favourite child. And they soon worked out that being kissed by them was the worst thing I could possibly imagine. They'd pin me down, tickle me, pucker their lips and say, 'Would you like us to give you a kiss, Rob?' And I'd be wriggling and thrashing around like a fish in a net, desperately trying to escape their clutches. No word of a lie, the first time I kissed them both voluntarily was on my wedding day.

But I can't have been that bad, because the first time my dad can remember shouting at me was when I dropped a ball on the rugby field. My first real memory of rugby league was being taken to a game between Leeds and Leigh. I don't remember much about it, apart from being very confused. Because they sounded similar, I thought Leeds and Leigh were the same team. Dad had a season ticket seat in

Headingley's North Stand, while I didn't have to pay. I'd sit on Dad's knee, or on a spare seat if there was one going.

Over time, I started asking tactical questions: 'Why did such and such player do that? Why didn't such and such player do this instead?' I became obsessed with Garry Schofield, the Great Britain legend who was one of the few shining lights in that Leeds team. I had posters of Garry on my wall and desperately wanted to be him.

Whenever we were at the caravan, I'd spend every waking hour playing touch and pass. I'd make all the other kids join in, whether they wanted to or not. Looking back, it probably wasn't much fun for some of them, watching me run around for hours. Our house back in Castleford was at the top of a cul-de-sac, and all the local lads would play touch and pass until it was dark. That cul-de-sac has produced a lot of talent. Apart from me, there was Michael Shenton, who went on to captain Castleford; Ben Crooks, the son of Hull legend Lee who also became a professional; and James Clare, who went on to play for a number of Super League teams. An interviewer once asked Lee Crooks where I learned my skills and he replied, 'I'll tell you where he learned his bloody skills, right outside my house. I was constantly having to pick the ball out of my flower beds, because Rob kept kicking it into touch.'

I'd even play rugby against Dad in the lounge. If Mum was trying to watch something on the telly, we'd play in the kitchen instead. We'd use one of those floppy rugby balls, but otherwise it was quite full on. We'd be bouncing off doors, banging into walls, rolling around on the floor, with all sorts falling on top of us. And the whole time, Dad would be doing his best impersonation of the BBC rugby league commentator Ray French: 'Here comes Rob Burrow, trying to make some space . . . skips past one . . . skips past two . . . he's just got his old man to beat! He's going to go the full length! That is a sensational try!'

When I was seven, a lad from over the road, Scott Carter, asked if I wanted to watch him play. His team was Travellers Saints, who played their games behind Featherstone Rovers' ground and even wore the same shirts. When we turned up, the game had been cancelled, so I ended up joining in training. That's how Travellers, or Featherstone Lions as they were later known, became my amateur team. After a few games, Scott's dad knocked on our door and said to my parents, 'You need to come and watch. Your lad's pretty good.'

I was tiny, not much bigger than a speck of dust, so it's not as if there were any thoughts of me making a career of it. The ball would look like a boulder in my hands, I'd be wearing a scrum cap that was miles too big for my head and you wouldn't be able to see my knees, because my shorts would be almost down to my ankles. In those early days, the coach would only put me on when the team were well ahead. But there were glimpses of what was to come. I wasn't exactly Garry Schofield (although I did wear my socks around my ankles like him), but I was always one of the quickest on the pitch. And I could naturally step off both feet, which is not something most people can do. But Mum and Dad weren't brash, pushy parents anyway. They didn't have stars in their eyes, they were just happy I'd found something I liked doing.

I enjoyed my time at Airedale High School, even though people kept trying to burn it down – one building was lost just after I joined and it's been set fire to a couple of times since. I'd never been particularly academic (whenever I was asked to write a story in primary school, I'd always make it about rugby, usually accompanied with a drawing of a ball and a set of posts) but, as long as the arsonists steered clear of the rugby field and my grades were good enough to keep my sisters from taking the piss out of me, I was happy.

Airedale's rugby coach was a Castleford scout called Mr Banks, and the school had a reputation for breeding quality players. Airedale old boys included Cas legends Bob and Kevin Beardmore, who also played for Great Britain. I was decent at cross-country and football, but rugby was always my first love. I enjoyed that feeling of running free, as well as the sense of jeopardy. I knew that if anyone caught me, I was going to get a shoeing.

Dad thought I'd get fed up with rugby when things started getting more physical. I don't think Mum would have been too fussed if I'd jacked it in, because she found watching me quite harrowing. But I liked the rough and tumble almost as much as I liked the feeling of making a clean break. Because of my size, I had to develop good tackle technique. I learned to go low and chop people down at the legs, rather than stand in front of them and get run over.

One game for Featherstone, I started on the bench and kept badgering the coach, a fella called Bob Woodhead, to put me on. Eventually, Bob gave in. A few minutes later, the biggest lad on the other team was galloping down the wing and I came out of nowhere and tackled him into touch. Bob ran over and gave me a hug. It was like he'd had an epiphany: I wasn't a defensive liability; I was a brave little bugger and strong with it. After that, Bob was always saying to me, 'There's something special about you, Rob. I think you're going to make it.' Bob played professionally in the 1970s, so his opinion meant something.

There were a lot of good players around at the time, and the inter-school rivalries were fierce. But I never stopped standing out. Opposition players knew I had a wicked side-step, but there was nothing they could do about it. I didn't know which foot I was going to step off, so what chance did they have? And if I had two or three defenders blocking my path, I'd duck underneath them instead. Whenever I got the ball, I looked like I'd been launched by the plunger of a pinball machine.

On Sundays, I played football for Featherstone Colliery. After one game, a Manchester City scout invited me along for a trial. I did pretty well, scoring three goals in two games. They also gave me a bag of coins as expenses, which I suppose was meant to impress a kid from Castleford. But I remember saying to Granddad Bob, 'Get me away from this place, I just want to play rugby.' I also had a trial at Leeds United, while Barnsley were very interested. But I didn't want to be the next Billy Bremner, I wanted to be the next Garry Schofield. To be honest, I wasn't even that good at football, just quicker than most. Luckily for me, rugby league clubs had already started sniffing around.

It was around this time, when I was eleven or twelve, that other players' parents started raising doubts about me. They'd often say nice things followed by a 'but'. Such as, 'Your lad were brilliant today, Geoff, but he could do with putting some weight on.' Or, 'Your lad's certainly a bag of tricks, Geoff, but it's just a shame he's so small.' There was probably jealousy involved, because I was being eyed up by clubs and their lads weren't. And Granddad Bob thought they were talking nonsense. But they were only being realistic. Just as the youth coach at Castleford was only being realistic when Mr Banks took me to see him. He took one look at me and said, 'What's he doing here? Too small.'

★

Danny McGuire, Leeds Rhinos teammate

I first met Rob when we were both ten, when he was playing a season for Castleford Panthers and I was playing for East Leeds. I was small for my age, but Rob was absolutely tiny. I remember him wearing every piece of protective equipment known to man: scrum cap, shin pads, shoulder pads, those thigh pads you stuck down your cycling shorts. It's a wonder he wasn't wearing safety goggles. He looked like the kid the coach felt sorry for and was worried might get hurt if anyone did as much as blow on him. But as soon as the whistle went, nobody could lay a finger on him. He was just so quick and elusive, like a whippet running all over the pitch.

I didn't play against him much back then because I played up a year and he left Castleford and rejoined Featherstone, who were in a lower division. But we got to know each other when we started playing together for Yorkshire age groups. We hit it off straightaway. And I'd stand next to him in photos, so that everyone knew I wasn't the smallest in the team.

I had a bit of a growth spurt when I was thirteen or fourteen, around the time we both signed for Leeds, but Rob stayed the same size. And that's when it became clear that there was a lot more to his game than speed, footwork and the ability to beat people and score tries. He was very good at reading a game, but the thing that really stood out was his toughness. Every time he played, he was the smallest on the pitch. But he was also the bravest and most determined. Whenever he got whacked, he'd jump straight back up and off he'd go again.

At the same time, I think most people still had their doubts about him. You've got to remember that Jason Robinson, one of the best British rugby players of all time, in both codes, was rejected by Leeds for not being big enough. And Jason Robinson can't possibly have been as small as Rob. On top of that, people were looking at Rob's mum and dad, who were both small as well, and thinking, 'He's not going to get much bigger, it's just in the genes. And if they let him play men's rugby, he's going to get hurt.'

★

Even before the Super League era started in 1996, rugby league was no sport for small men. Roger Millward, another Castleford lad who became a legend playing for Hull Kingston Rovers and Great Britain, was considered tiny at five foot four inches, and he was playing in the 1960s and 1970s. And Roger, great as he was, didn't have to play against eighteen-stone wingers from Samoa, people like Wigan's Va'aiga Tuigamala, who could run the 100 metres in eleven seconds while pulling a fridge. Great Britain scrum-half Andy Gregory and Australia's Alan 'Alfie' Langer, who were both only five foot five, were stars in the 1980s and 1990s (Alfie was a guilty hero of mine, always ripping Great Britain apart despite being so small), but successful players of that size were few and far between.

One thing I had on my side was an affinity for people called Bob, and it was yet another Bob who kept the faith when others were wavering. Bob Pickles was the chief scout at Leeds and had already spotted a few of what would become the Rhinos' 'golden generation', most notably Kev Sinfield. One weekend, Bob turned up to watch Featherstone play in a Cup Final. I knew he was coming and I was a bit nervous beforehand, but managed to put in a good performance. The way Bob tells the story, he started watching the game through the window of the clubhouse and all he could see was a scrum cap, bobbing up and down, disappearing and reappearing. When he came outside to take a closer look, he discovered the scrum cap was attached to me.

Bob had a chat with my dad, discovered we were both big Leeds fans and arranged for us to meet the head coach Dean Bell and his assistant Hugh McGahan. They took one look at me and thought Bob was taking the mick. That might have been that, as far as my dreams of playing for Leeds went, but Bob kept coming back. Week after week, he'd report back to Dean and Hugh, try to convince them to sign me. But their response was always the same: 'Not big enough, Bob. Not by a long shot.' Then Bob would have to tell my dad, 'They keep telling me he's too small to make it, Geoff, but I keep telling them he will.' Bob had this incredible belief that wouldn't be shaken.

Then, the Monday after I'd played in a Yorkshire Under-13s v. Lancashire Under-13s game, which was a curtain-raiser for Bradford–Leeds at Odsal Stadium, Dean called Bob into his office and said, 'Me and Hugh watched that Rob Burrow on Saturday. He was bloody sensational.'

Dean and Hugh still weren't entirely convinced and spent a lot of time agonizing over whether to sign me or not. But eventually they decided to trust Bob's judgement and take a punt. Apparently, Dean said to Bob, 'He's gonna need a bloody big heart to make it.' I don't know whether Dean, deep down, thought my heart would be big enough in the long run. Probably not. But I have to tip my hat to him. How many gifted little kids have been thrown on the scrapheap, purely based on their size? How many gifted little kids could have been another me, if only adults making the decisions had shown more imagination? That's the key word, imagination. Because hardly any little kids have made it in rugby league, they can't imagine it happening. They can't see how that little kid might offer something different. They only see the problem.

*

When Bob phoned Mum and Dad to give him the good news, they were chuffed. They even took Bob out for Sunday lunch in Castleford, to say thank you. Even at the time, I knew that being signed at thirteen was a long, long way from running out at Headingley for the first team. My signing wasn't even official, because of my age (Mum and Dad have got a photo of Bob and me clutching a mysterious envelope, containing a cheque for £1,500, which was all hush-hush). But when you're that young, you think your future is set in stone.

All I wanted to do was play rugby league for Leeds. Nothing else mattered. School was just something going on in the background, white noise. I wasn't a bad lad, I was just a bit cheeky. I talked too much in class and was always at the heart of any nonsense that was going on (apart from burning down buildings, that had nothing to do with me). I did enough work to get by, but I've no idea what I would have done had I not made it at rugby. And the cruel truth is that, however desperately you want something, you don't always get to choose your path in life. Often, other people choose it for you instead.

When I was sixteen, Leeds had to decide whether to sign me officially. A couple of years earlier, Dean Bell had stepped down as head coach and become head of youth development, running the academy. I hadn't grown a great deal in the intervening three years and probably weighed less than nine stone. Dean is on record as saying he could have tossed a coin on whether to sign me or not. But, for whatever reason, he decided to double down on his initial gamble.

I think the consensus was that at some point, I'd hit a natural ceiling. It was all very well me running rings around kids at the recreational level, but what about when all thirteen opposition players were big, athletic and skilful? There were no weak links in academy rugby; everyone was pretty handy. I knew I was up against it when Dad asked Bob Pickles why Leeds hadn't picked up Chev Walker. Chev was built like a tank, seriously quick and hard as nails, but Bob still wasn't sure he had what it took. Leeds did eventually sign him, and he made his first-team debut at sixteen, but that shows you how fine the line is.

Shortly after officially signing, in 1999, there was a trial match, involving a mix of academy lads and possible signings. That was the most nervous I'd ever been. For the first time in my life, I was about to go up against the best of the best, a bunch of kids who wanted the same as I did – to pull on the blue and amber and run out at Headingley. And every single one of them was bigger than me. I remember sitting in the dressing room, looking up at all these giants – some of them over six feet tall, some of them over sixteen stone, with muscles on top of muscles – and feeling terrified. And they were probably looking at me and thinking, 'This is big boys' rugby now, he's not gonna last five minutes.'

Early in the first game, a giant on the other team received the ball on the wing and ran straight at me. For my poor parents, it must have been like watching a slow-motion car crash. I waited until the big lad was a couple of metres away from me, dipped as low as I could, rammed my shoulder into his shins, lifted him up and dumped him on his head. Nowadays, they'd call that a spear tackle and send me off. Back then, it had everyone cheering and slapping each other on the back. For Dean, and everyone else, that was a moment of truth. I hadn't just proved that I could cope with the physical side of the game, I'd shown that I relished it. And I was never scared after that.

When the senior team reached the Challenge Cup Final in 1999, the academy boys were taken along to Wembley to support them. We were sat in the corner, where most of Leeds's second-half tries were scored, going wild with excitement. Leroy Rivett scored four tries as Leeds hammered London Broncos 52–16 to win their first trophy since 1978. And while we didn't do anything apart from make a racket, we felt part of something very special that day.

That same year, I toured Australia with Great Britain and Northern Ireland schoolboys. Rugby league down under is on a different level. Some of their lads had beards.

Nevertheless, I still managed to impress. I won man of the match in Kingaroy and the guy who presented me with the award wanted to scout me for Brisbane Broncos. He said I was the best scrum-half he'd seen since Alfie Langer. Dad had to tell him I'd already signed for Leeds, but that was a huge compliment and confidence boost. To fudge a line from Sinatra, if you can hold your own in Australia as a rugby league player, you can hold your own anywhere.

I do sometimes wonder where my talent and determination came from. Dad likes to joke that it didn't come from him. He did play an amateur game, alongside the great John Holmes. But while Holmes went on to make 625 appearances for Leeds and win a World Cup with Great Britain, Dad never got picked again. Mum played hockey, but reckons she wasn't that good either. My sisters were never interested in sport, although they competed in ballroom dancing, winning trophies all over the country. And I suppose that shares some similarities with rugby, in that it's all about coordination and footwork.

You have to go right back into the mists of time to find the Burrow I have most in common with, sport-wise. Dad's granddad was a boxer, who went his whole career without ever once being knocked down or stopped. He wasn't a professional in the proper sense, but he would have boxed in fairground booths all over Yorkshire and been paid a cut of the gate. Apparently, he was even smaller than me: five foot four, and nine stone wet through. He must have taken a hell of a lot of hits and been incredibly brave and tough.

★

It's time to buckle up for a bit of history, because it will help put my story into context. Readers not too familiar with rugby league might assume I'd joined the sport's equivalent of Manchester United. They'd be right, but maybe not in the way they think. Like Manchester United before they started winning things under Alex Ferguson in the early 1990s, Leeds were for many years rugby league's great underachievers. Some might say a laughing stock.

Rugby league has always been a working-class sport, ever since its split from rugby union in 1895, but Leeds were the closest thing it had to a well-to-do club (admittedly, these things are relative up north). While rugby league was mainly played in gritty northern towns – places like Castleford, St Helens and Wigan – Leeds were supposedly big city slickers. Fans of other teams thought they were arrogant, and I remember watching them on TV and Sky commentator Eddie Hemmings describing them as 'aristocrats'. Not that it made much difference on the pitch. But don't take it from me, take it from my old pal Richard Stockdale, who had to suffer almost two decades of Leeds-inflicted agony . . .

★

Richard Stockdale, Rhinos superfan

I started watching Leeds in 1980. For my whole childhood, Leeds were all I cared about. My dad took me to watch them home and away, at grounds all over the north. I never missed a game, reserves or first team. But I had to put up with an awful lot of rubbish. Leeds even made me cry some weeks.

Leeds had a reputation for spending big on the wrong players. It would be harsh to say they didn't care, but I'm not sure they were at Leeds for the right reasons. The owners never seemed to have a long-term plan and didn't grow enough of their own talent. There was no real spirit or culture at the club. The attitude seemed to be, 'Let's just sign another big player, that'll shut the moaners up.' At one stage in the 1980s, we had ten Aussies or Kiwis in our squad, and I'm sure many of them were only there to make a quick buck.

Leeds were supposedly this grand old club with a great history, but we never used to win any trophies. Not only did we never win any trophies, we used to get tonked quite regularly. I saw Warrington beat us by fifty points at Headingley in the mid-1980s. I was also at Wigan in 1992, when Martin Offiah scored ten tries against us in a 74–6 defeat. Yes, you did read that correctly. To be completely honest, we were a complete joke. Everywhere we went, whether it was Halifax, Widnes, Whitehaven or Workington, rival fans would sing, 'What a waste of money!' And they were absolutely right.

I never stopped going or left a game before the final hooter. I knew that if I stuck with it, something would change eventually. Leeds were just too big a club to keep failing. But, my God, that club put me through the wringer . . .

★

By the time I arrived at Headingley, Leeds had won only three league titles in their history, the last in 1972. While Wigan were winning eight consecutive Challenge Cups and seven consecutive league titles in the 1980s and 1990s, Leeds supporters were having to make do with one Yorkshire Cup triumph. Leeds had some bloody good players during that time, including my childhood hero Garry Schofield and the great Ellery Hanley, but not enough of them to keep the crowds from dwindling. By the mid-1990s, the Loiners, as Leeds were nicknamed back then, were getting as few as 4,000 through the gate for some home games, in a stadium that held over 15,000. And in 1996, the first year of Super League, Leeds narrowly avoided relegation and almost went bankrupt.

Enter a couple of businessmen from Castleford, Gary Hetherington and Paul Caddick. Gary had set up Sheffield Eagles in the early 1980s, when he was still in his twenties. That was a bold move, considering hardly anyone in Sheffield had the faintest interest in the sport. But Gary somehow got the Eagles promoted to the top flight in 1989, and they were part of the first season of Super League. Paul was in engineering and property development and worth a fortune. Gary and Paul came with cash and a plan, exactly what Leeds needed.

One of the first things they did, other than change the club's name to Leeds Rhinos, was spend £350,000 on a kid from Oldham called Iestyn Harris. On paper, that looked like classic Leeds, trying to spend their way out of trouble. But Iestyn turned out to be very handy. In fact, he soon overtook Garry Schofield in my affections. In 1998, Leeds reached the Grand Final, losing to Wigan. And in 1999, they won their first Challenge Cup for twenty-one years (that game at Wembley where I was making a racket in the corner). Not many fans were leaving Headingley before the final hooter any more, and diehards like Richard – and me – were finally getting a few rewards for our patience.

You might say Iestyn was to the Rhinos what Eric Cantona was to Manchester United – the bloke who sparked a revolution. But, just like Alex Ferguson and his so-called

Class of '92 (Beckham, Scholes, Giggs and the rest), Gary Hetherington and Paul Caddick realized that the seeds of long-term success needed to be sown in their own back-yard. By the time I arrived at Leeds's academy in 1999, it was regularly churning out players who were able to make the step up to the first team almost seamlessly. Bob Pickles has to take a lot of credit for that. It was Bob who brought Kev Sinfield and Adrian Morley to the club as kids, from Oldham and Salford respectively. Adrian made his debut at the age of seventeen in 1995, Kev at the age of sixteen two years later.

Most of the lads in and around my age were from even closer to home. And when you have local lads, you have local pride. Danny McGuire, Chev Walker, Richie Mathers, Ryan Bailey and Jamie Jones-Buchanan were all from Leeds. Coming from Castleford made me exotic. Like me, all they'd ever wanted to do, since they could walk and talk, was pull on the blue and amber.

There was so much local talent to choose from, you almost couldn't go wrong. It was like shooting fish in a barrel. I remember Dad giving Bob Pickles a lift home from a game and him saying to me, 'Right, Rob, who should we sign next?' I said they should sign a lad called Matt Diskin, who played for Dewsbury Moor. And they did. I'm sure Bob already had his eye on 'Disco', but it was just so obvious to me, even as a sixteen-year-old, that he had what it took. Sure enough, he became a Rhinos legend, just like everyone else I've mentioned.

Not that there was anything inevitable about what tran-spired over the next two decades. The academy had been strong for a while before my arrival, but the club hadn't been able to translate that into consistent success in senior rugby. Also, the longer it went without us winning a league title, the more the pressure mounted. But there was a feeling around the place that this time things might be different. The talent was just that strong and that deep.

What was it Alan Hansen said about Fergie's Manchester United, before they won their first Premier League title? 'You can't win anything with kids.' I'm sure there were lots of people who thought the same about us. I'm even more sure there was hardly anybody who thought I'd play a big part in the revolution, if it were to happen. To give you an idea of what Leeds fans thought of my chances, let me tell you a story about my academy debut at St Helens.

Richard Stockdale was there that day – he never even missed the kids play – and when he saw me run onto the pitch as a second-half replacement, he started laughing. He literally couldn't believe his eyes. The following week, Richard bumped into Bob Pickles at a reserve game, and he said to Bob, 'What were that on the bench the other day?'

'Rob Burrow?' replied Bob. 'He's probably the best of the lot.'

'Give over, Bob. Not a chance. He's going to get hurt.'

'Just you watch . . .'

Richard did as he was told. And, if my memory serves me correctly, I was pretty good that day. In fact, Richard watched every game I ever played, from my academy debut all the way through to my swansong. He says I never stopped making him laugh. Thankfully, it was usually for the right reasons.

3

BEFORE I CHAT ANY MORE ABOUT RUGBY, I IMAGINE some of you want to know a bit more about this bloody disease I've got. Don't worry, I don't find that morbid. I get it. It's human nature to want to know how and why things go wrong with other people's bodies. And that, of course, is one of the points of this book, to get awareness out there. It would be daft to avoid the elephant in the room.

I see a wonderful consultant neurologist called Dr Agam Jung, who's the director of the Leeds MND Care Centre. And you know what she told me? People are coming in and saying, 'I think I might have Rob Burrow's disease.' Over in America, MND is called ALS, for amyotrophic lateral sclerosis. But a lot of people still know it as Lou Gehrig's disease, after the New York Yankees baseball player who got it back in the 1930s. Maybe one day, they'll start calling it Rob Burrow's disease over here. Or maybe Rob Burrow's disease in England and Doddie Weir's disease in Scotland. I mean, it's not one of the classic childhood ambitions, to have a disease named after you. I'm sure it's not as common as kids wanting to become a train driver, a spaceman or a rugby player. But if you are going to get a disease, you might as well aim high.

Anyway, as they say in those shampoo adverts – and after a chat with Dr Jung, to make sure I've got my facts right – here comes the science bit. Concentrate! You, me and everyone else have sensory nerves and motor nerves (also known as neurones). Whenever you touch something, a hot cup for example, the sensation will run through your arm and into the brain via sensory nerves, before the brain registers that the cup is hot and you need to put it down. For the brain to inform the muscles in your hand to do that, it has to send signals via the spinal cord to the cells where motor nerves originate. These cells then chit-chat with the motor nerves, which in turn order the muscles to put the cup down. Clever stuff, I'm sure you'll agree. But if you've got MND, the cells where the motor nerves originate are degenerating. As the bright ones amongst you have probably worked out, that means the signals stop getting sent out, you stop using your muscles and they start wasting away.

Early signs that you might have MND vary, depending on what part of the body is affected. Your body is divided into different regions, so one person might start feeling weakness in their legs, another person might start struggling to do up their buttons, another person might start having problems swallowing. In my case, it was my speech that finally gave the game away. Some people's symptoms are so minor they don't notice them for ages. And because your GP might only see one MND patient in their entire career, the penny sometimes takes a while to drop. It can take up to a year for MND to be diagnosed, usually after all other avenues have been explored. I was lucky, because I was diagnosed three weeks after first visiting the Rhinos doctor, before being referred to Dr Jung's clinic in Leeds. She's been looking after me ever since.

Mercifully, MND is rare, with about 5,000 people living with it in the UK at any one time (Dr Jung usually has eighty to ninety patients under her care). You're more likely to get MND after turning fifty. I was quite young, at thirty-seven, but Dr Jung has seen younger patients. Some forms of MND progress more slowly (Stephen Hawking lasted for over fifty years, the tragedy being that he wasted all that precious time trying to discover the origins of the universe, when he could have been playing Nintendo or watching Leeds Rhinos on Sky), but I've got the more common rapidly progressive condition, hence being given a couple of years to live. There is no cure (not even anything that works every time, 60 per cent of the time – don't worry, Will Ferrell's not going to sue either), only a tablet called riluzole, which might extend a patient's life for a few months.

Because MND is so rare, there's not a lot of funding for research. There aren't a lot of patients, so there wasn't much racket being made about it in this country before me and Doddie turned up. They don't even know why people get it. A small percentage of MND patients have a genetic predisposition, but you can have the gene and not get the disease and not have the gene and get the disease. For years, scientists suspected physical activity was linked to MND, but couldn't prove it. However, a recent study by the University of Sheffield apparently proved that regular and strenuous exercise increases the risk of MND in people who are genetically vulnerable. That means the high numbers of athletes with MND isn't a coincidence.

All the medical professionals can offer is symptom control medication and quality of life supportive measures. But don't get me wrong, I'm grateful for that. At Dr Jung's clinic, there are about a dozen multidisciplinary professionals, including specialist MND nurses, a physiotherapist, an occupational therapist, a speech and language therapist, a dietician, a psychologist and a palliative care consultant. Dr Jung also has dedicated links with respiratory doctors, for patients requiring assisted ventilation, and gastroenterologists, for patients requiring assisted feeding. Not too long ago, many people would get diagnosed with MND, go home and wait to die. But with Dr Jung and her gang by my side, I at least feel assured that I'm getting the best possible support. And do you want to know the best thing? It's all for free on the NHS, with the MND Association supporting each care centre.

Aside from my voice, everything seemed normal for a while after my diagnosis. If you'd seen me walking down the street, you wouldn't have known there was anything wrong with me. I could eat, drink and exercise with no problems. I could drive the kids to school. And, having taken a couple of weeks off, I went back to coaching the academy kids at Leeds. I felt fine, the boys needed me and it was the right thing to do. But there were a few telltale signs.

I was playing cards with the family at Christmas and couldn't keep up with the banter. There was a slight lag between my brain and my mouth – the words were in my head, but I couldn't get them out – which was frustrating. I'd always been quick with a comeback, but now I was being left for dead, even by the old folks. My balance was slightly off. I was stumbling putting my shoes on and I almost tripped over Jackson a couple of times. My right hand was shaky. I kept pressing the wrong buttons when I was texting and having to delete things. I couldn't blame fat fingers, because I've got the hands of a lady.

Luckily, there are some very clever people around, to make things more bearable. A kind lady from a company called SpeakUnique got me to read a story aloud and went through hours of old interviews, before the words were downloaded onto my phone. When my voice finally conked out, I'd be able to type a sentence and hit play. It also meant I wouldn't have to sound like Stephen Hawking. Not that I've got anything against Stephen Hawking, but it would have sounded a bit weird, a bloke who used to have a broad Yorkshire accent suddenly speaking like an American robot. Doddie tried to persuade me to become a Scotsman, but that would have been even weirder.

By the summer of 2020, my voice was almost gone, and I was relying more and more on my speech app. I found it frustrating. If there were a few people chatting, the conversation had usually moved on by the time I'd finished typing. But I could still tell the kids off: 'Get down! Stop doing that!' The normal things a dad says, stuff that got a laugh out of them. And at least Jackson would hear my voice, maybe remember me telling him I loved him.

★

A few of the lads popped round the other day, for coffee in the garden. I can't offer much in terms of banter nowadays, but just listening to them telling all the old stories and taking the piss brings me so much joy. When I close my eyes, I can picture myself back in the dressing room. It's mostly schoolboy stuff, the sort of nonsense all rugby players love and miss desperately when they retire. Everyone making fun of the size of someone's nose, someone filling a teammate's boot with shaving foam. If I'm the butt of the joke, all the better.

Barrie pays a visit every couple of weeks and usually tries to drag someone along with him. It got to the point where when he did come on his own, he'd talk non-stop for an hour while I was just nodding or shaking my head. So every opportunity I had, I'd try to make him feel a bit less awkward.

The last time he was round, he made the mistake of leaving his phone with me, while he was off making a brew. He'd left it unlocked, so I typed out a message to his daughter: 'SEND ME A NUDE PHOTO.' Don't worry, she was twenty-one. And I wasn't going to send the message! When Barrie returned with our coffees and saw what I'd written, he fell about laughing. And whenever Baz starts laughing, I just fall to pieces. Tears were rolling down my cheeks and I couldn't help farting. That's when Baz completely lost it. Lindsey was probably looking at us thinking, 'What are those two idiots up to?' But there can't be a better way to spend an afternoon, just sitting in the garden and giggling with a mate.

★

Back in the day, Sky broadcast academy fixtures. Baz tells the story that he was watching one of our games with his parents when his mum said, 'I really like that Rob Burrow.'

And Baz replied, 'Yeah, so do I. But he's not going to make it. He's too small.' Baz's mum still reminds him of it now, and it doesn't really surprise me that she knows more about rugby league than him.

In 2000, I was part of the academy side that won the Rhinos' sixth championship in a row. Dean Bell has to take a lot of credit for that. All us kids had watched him as a player in that all-conquering Wigan side of the '80s and '90s and were in awe of him. He was strict, and I don't think any of us could quite believe that a bloke with his reputation was coaching us. And he didn't just concentrate on the on-field stuff, he was also a big advocate of personal development. Yes, Dean thought it was important for us to be good rugby players. But he thought it was even more important for us to be decent people. Given what that group of players went on to achieve, Dean should be proud.

The following year, I captained the England academy on a tour of Australia and New Zealand. That was a huge honour, not least because it was a bloody good squad. There was me, Danny McGuire and Richie Mathers from Leeds, as well as Shaun Briscoe, Gareth Hock, Sean O'Loughlin, Eorl Crabtree and Jamie Langley, who all went on to have long and illustrious careers in Super League and play for England and/or Great Britain. We beat New Zealand in both Tests, winning the second in Christchurch 72–16. And we didn't do bad against the Aussies either, losing the first Test 18–12 and the second 44–22. There was an article in an Australian newspaper, asking why English clubs kept importing ageing Aussies when there was so much young talent on their doorstep. On the evidence of that tour, they had a point.

Early in 2001, I played my first game against men, for Leeds Rhinos reserves against St Helens. Saints had Wayne McDonald in their team, and he was six foot seven, weighed nineteen stone and had already been a pro for seven years. Meanwhile, I was eighteen years old, five foot five (on tiptoes) and barely ten stone. But at some point during the game, I hit Wayne just right, lifted him up and dropped him on his back. I'm sure that raised a few eyebrows. And I'm sure Wayne was quite embarrassed.

There'd been a lot of optimism going into that season, what with the signings of four top-class Aussies: Robbie Mears, Brett Mullins, Bradley Clyde and Tonie Carroll (who had played for New Zealand and was later capped by the Kangaroos). But things didn't pan out as expected. Players kept getting injured – Mears broke his collarbone on his debut and was burgled four times while he was recovering – and we kept losing games. And after a hammering at Wigan and losing to St Helens in the semi-finals of the Challenge Cup, I was named in the squad to play Hull at Headingley, on Friday 6 April 2001.

It was quite surreal, walking into that dressing room and seeing my name on the back of a shirt. It was all I'd ever wanted, but I felt quite overawed. I was changing next to Kevin Sinfield, who was already a regular for England, and Bradley Clyde, one of the greatest Kangaroos of all time. Hull were a good side and going great guns. And, to add to my anxiety, Iestyn Harris, our most potent attacking weapon, was injured and it was pouring with rain. I wondered if it was a step too far. Had I finally hit my ceiling?

No word of a lie, while we were warming up, one of the Hull officials mistook me for a ball boy. And when Dean

Lance, the head coach, threw me on, Sky commentator Eddie Hemmings said, 'I wonder if this young lad's mum and dad know he's out of the house.' The first time I got the ball, someone dumped me on my backside, and Eddie followed up with, 'Welcome to the big time, young man.' My poor parents were watching at home, through their fingers. Mum said she was thinking, 'God, this is going to be awful.'

As it turned out, I did OK, causing Hull a few problems and setting up a try. Unfortunately, we lost by a couple of points and Dean Lance was sacked as head coach. But Daryl Powell, Dean's replacement, didn't have any choice but to stick with the kids (Matty Diskin and Mark Calderwood, my best mate from the academy, had made their debuts earlier that season and the average age of the team that played Hull was only twenty-three). As a result, I found myself in the starting line-up for the game against Warrington the following week.

We were missing something like seven regular starters, including Mullins, Carroll, Keith Senior and Baz, who was suspended (as usual). Warrington had lost their first four Super League games of the season and were bottom of the table. But they had some decent players, including the great Alfie Langer, who I was often compared to. I probably spent far too much time staring at him, wondering if he'd be good enough to sign my programme after the game. And on the night, they battered us 36–6.

I did at least score our only try. Early in the second half, Iestyn Harris told me to go on a run and I did, arcing past three or four Warrington defenders and diving over. Eddie Hemmings was raving about me now. And while I didn't exactly feel like I had my feet under the table, I did at least feel more at home. It was a pretty gloomy atmosphere in the changing room afterwards. But I remember Daryl Powell telling us that everything from that point on was going to be built on the youngsters coming through the academy.

★

Barrie McDermott, Rhinos teammate

It's true that I didn't think Rob had much hope of making it when I first saw him play. Rugby league has always been a tough, tough sport. But when Super League came along, it got even tougher. Players turned into Universal Soldiers, brick shithouses who could run all day, often very quickly. So it's only natural that when a new player appeared on the scene, you looked at him and thought, 'Will he be able to handle himself?' And when Rob turned up to train with the senior squad for the first time, there were a lot of eyebrows raised. He was tiny, and all teeth and nose, so I thought to myself, 'My God, what have they brought us here? He's not going to survive long. The opposition are going to get hold of him and throw him around like a rag doll.'

But I soon realized that getting hold of him was almost impossible. His size wasn't a weakness, it was his super-power. He was just so low to the ground, had phenomenal agility and was ridiculously quick. He was quiet when he first turned up, but he had an air of confidence. He wasn't fazed. And, most importantly, his bravery was ten out of ten. That's what clinched it.

Rob's right, I was suspended when he played his first couple of senior games (any Rhinos fans reading this won't be surprised to hear that), but I watched them on TV. Whenever he got the ball, I could see the opposition players thinking, 'How do we deal with this fella?' They just hadn't seen his like before. Rob's first try against Warrington, when he got the ball from a scrum and burned everyone with his pace, was slightly comical. Especially when a teammate grabbed him and Rob's head was buried in his chest. But I remember thinking, 'This kid is going to come in very handy, because he's just so different.' He reminded me of Jason Robinson, with his pace and ability to change direction in the blink of an eye. There's no greater compliment, because Jason was one of the best I played with and against.

In training, I always liked to align myself with whoever was the best at a particular facet of the game. If I wanted to work on my speed, I'd do extra work with the quickest, or if I wanted to work on my strength, I'd do extra work with the strongest. So before long, I was practising my one-on-one defence with Rob. We'd set up a small grid, a couple of metres by a couple of metres, he'd run at me and I'd try to tackle him. The problem was, I could never get hold of him. I'd be telling him to tone it down and stop making me look like a dickhead, and he'd be taking the piss out of me for being too fat and too slow: 'No wonder you need to practise this stuff, you're shit at it . . .'

★

That was a pretty patchy season for Leeds. One week we were beating St Helens, who had just won the Challenge Cup, 74–16, the next we were getting thumped at home by arch-rivals Bradford. Then, in the summer, it was announced that Iestyn Harris was switching codes at the end of the season. It wasn't exactly a surprise, because the

Welsh Rugby Union had been tempting Iestyn for years. But it was a big blow, because Iestyn was so influential, a brilliant goal-kicker and distributor of the ball, who had been Rhinos player of the year three years in a row between 1998 and 2000. And, of course, my hero.

A lot of players were defecting to union around that time. Jason Robinson had jumped ship in 2000, Bradford's Henry Paul signed for Gloucester at the same time as Iestyn signed for Cardiff and there were rumours that St Helens's Keiron Cunningham and Wigan's Kris Radlinski were set to follow suit. As such, there were quite a lot of newspaper articles predicting the impending death of rugby league. League officials made a lot of noise about it, but it all sounded a bit rich because loads of players had gone the other way before union went professional in 1995. And it says a lot about league's enduring strength that the bloke who would become Super League's record points-scorer (Kev Sinfield) and Super League's highest try-scorer (Danny McGuire) were already at Leeds.

Maggsy made his debut that July, in a big win over Salford, and I scored a couple of tries in another win over St Helens. But Bradford hammered us 62–18 at Odsal in the final game of the regular season (the fourth time they'd beaten us that year), before Saints took revenge in the elimination play-off. I scored a try, set another up and kicked five goals, but we were no match for Keiron Cunningham and Paul Sculthorpe that day. Bradford won the Grand Final that year, but the less said about that the better.

On the bright side, I was named Super League young player of the year at the end of the season. I'd captained an England team in New Zealand and Australia, played with my hero and scored a couple of tries against another in Alfie Langer. Eddie Hemmings and his Sky sidekick Mike 'Stevo' Stephenson were even talking me up as a possible bolter for Great Britain's Ashes squad, what with Saints scrum-half Sean Long still recovering from a knee operation.

But all the newspapers really wanted to focus on was my size. The tabloids ran with an early nickname, 'The Mouse'. And when a journalist asked Daryl Powell if he'd seen smaller rugby league players, he replied, 'Only in the Under-10s.' Looked at another way, at least they were talking about me.

★

Dave Woods, BBC rugby league correspondent

As a rugby league journalist working in the mainstream media, you're constantly having to explain the sport to the wider world, because it's not a sport the wider world knows much about. So we were tickled pink when Rob turned up. We were able to say, 'Come on everybody, have a look at this fella. He's brilliant to watch, just mesmeric, and here's the reason why . . .' Then we could explain how rugby league was a game for giants, a game for extremely tough men, and that what Rob was doing – running rings round all these huge fellas, making them look stupid at times – defied logic. Any opportunity we get to shine a light on the sport, we're going to take.

We'd seen small players down the years, but nothing like Rob. Wigan famously told Andy Gregory he was too small, let him go to Widnes and had to buy him back for a fortune a few years later. But Andy was a different type of player to

Rob, more rugged, and players were nowhere near as big in the 1980s, when Andy was at his peak. Then there was Jason Robinson, who was smaller than most, but even he was three inches taller than Rob.

There was a bit of competition among the journalists as to who could come up with the best nickname. Rob got called everything from the 'Tiny Terror' to 'Will-o'-the-Wisp' to the inevitable 'Pocket Rocket'. One week, we filmed a feature with Rob for the now-defunct *Grandstand*. It was based on the classic sketch from *The Frost Report*, the one where Ronnie Corbett, Ronnie Barker and John Cleese play three men of different classes. Rob turned up to the training ground in his little sports car and was well up for it, really chirpy, chatty and friendly. We had Rob playing the Ronnie Corbett role and the six-foot-seven-inch Wayne McDonald, who had joined Leeds from St Helens, playing the John Cleese role. And I remember Rob delivering the final line, with a big grin on his face: 'I'm a scrum-half, and I look up to nobody.'

But as a commentator, I was careful not to patronize Rob, make him sound like a novelty. Yes, Rob was joyful to watch, made the game fun and brought a lot of smiles to people's faces. But he wasn't a cartoon character. Never mind his size, he was a real bloke doing a tough job, and doing it very well. There are no cowards on a rugby league field. The game is brutal, players frequently get hurt, and anyone who crosses that whitewash must be courageous. But Rob's courage was on a whole different level to most.

★

I was a big fan of Daryl Powell, but he had a tough job on his hands. For a start, he'd only just retired from playing, and there's always a bit of weirdness when you're suddenly coaching a load of blokes who used to be your teammates. Lads he'd played with thought they could take liberties and he had strained relationships with a few of them. Daryl had also inherited a squad that simply wasn't good enough to compete for the Super League title.

As was often the case with Leeds, most of the overseas signings hadn't really worked out. Bradley Clyde and Brett Mullins spent most of that season injured, while poor old Robbie Mears had his jaw broken by St Helens's Sonny Nickle in the penultimate game of the season. Those three broke their contracts and returned to Australia, and only Tonie Carroll chose to stay. I also got the feeling that some of the English lads had got too comfortable. There was a clique in the dressing room, and those lads weren't close in a positive way. Their hearts weren't in the club. You could see that in their faces after a defeat. I might be wrong, but they didn't look like they were hurting enough.

Daryl was in the right place at the wrong time. He had huge pressure on his shoulders, to start bringing silverware to this great, underachieving club, and some brilliant young talent coming through. But that talent wasn't quite mature enough, so he had to find more experienced talent to blend it with. As well as Wayne McDonald, Daryl signed New Zealander Willie Poching from Wakefield and Aussies Adrian Vowles (who had done great things at Castleford), Matt Adamson and Ben Walker, the latter to fill Iestyn's big boots.

The first few months of the 2002 season were hit and miss. We beat Bradford in the fourth round of the Challenge Cup but got tonked by Saints in the semi-finals. We had some big wins in the league, and I scored my first try against Castleford (a pretty good one as well), but we were stuffed by Hull and suffered a shock home defeat to newly promoted Widnes. We were unbeaten in May, including seeing off Bradford and Wigan in successive games, and finished the month second in the league. But things went downhill from there. When we lost to Castleford at home (five of our players were involved in a Test against Australia in Sydney), fans were heading for the exit before the final hooter. Some of those who remained were calling for Daryl Powell's sacking.

We just managed to scrape into the play-offs courtesy of a comeback win over London, only to be smashed by Wigan in the elimination semi-final, having beaten them a couple of weeks earlier. It was a similar story to the season before. Too many senior players kept getting injured and some didn't look like they wanted to be there (I'll gloss over the fact that Baz got banned for four games after lumping Bradford's Stuart Fielden – Google 'Barrie McDermott' and 'suspended' and you'll get about 10,000 results). But in amongst the gloom, there were plenty of glimpses of what was to come. Richie Mathers and Ryan Bailey made their first-team debuts, while Maggsy turned in some brilliant displays and was already being talked about as a potential great.

I can't remember which game it was after, but at some point during that season Gary Hetherington stormed into the dressing room and read the riot act. It was something along the lines of, 'We pay you well and we're not putting up with performances like that any more. If anyone wants to leave, we won't stop you. But some of you will be leaving whether you like it or not.' I reckon that was a calculated risk by Gary. That was him saying to the clique, 'You might feel comfortable here, but I've got total faith that these kids coming through will be better.' It could have backfired, because he didn't actually know if we were good enough. But as one of those kids, I knew that outburst from Gary wasn't really aimed at me. I saw it more as a vote of confidence.

At this stage, I should make clear which of the older fellas weren't part of the clique and made me feel at home. Big Fat Barrie Mac was like a big brother from the start (maybe father figure is more accurate, because I'd been watching him sit in the sin bin since I was about two years old). Whatever the sport, it can be unsettling coming into a professional environment as a teenager. Everywhere I looked there were international players, hardened pros with bent fingers, scarred eyebrows and noses splattered across their faces. But Baz took me under his wing and put me at ease, just as he did with any youngster who graduated from the academy. At least when he wasn't banned.

I'm not sure I can say Baz looked after me from day one, because he bullied me into shaving my head on a trip to Jacksonville in 2001 (that's not a good look for a man with a big nose, which is probably why Baz made me do it). But Baz was always generous with his time and offering advice. He certainly never mentioned he'd had any doubts about me. We made for an odd couple, because Baz was a big, brutal prop forward and the team's enforcer, while I was this ten-stone scrum-half who looked about twelve. But we just clicked.

Baz gave me plenty of stick in those early days. Actually,

he never stopped. If he wasn't taking the piss out of my teeth and nose, he was making jokes about my size. On one of my first away trips, I was struggling to reach the overhead luggage rack on the coach when Baz snatched my bag off me and tossed it up there. He looked at me and said, 'Are you happy?' I replied, 'No, I'm not happy.' And he hit back with, 'Which one of the dwarves are you then?' He'd tell me I was the only man he knew who had a life-sized photo in his passport; that the next time I picked my nose I should pick a smaller one; and that I must save a fortune on my wardrobe, because you don't pay VAT on kids' clothes. Come to think of it, Baz's after-dinner speeches must be terrible.

I must be drawn to blokes whose pints you wouldn't want to spill – or maybe they're drawn to me? – because another old boy I hit it off with was Keith Senior. He thought the sun shone out of my arse. Isn't that right, Keith?

*

Keith Senior, Rhinos teammate

Everyone goes on about how great Rob was, but it's important to note that he was also a little shit. There's no other way of putting it. When he first turned up, I'd look at him, with his bleached blond hair, big nose, and those NFL shoulder pads he used to wear (I swear his mum packed them every morning) and think, 'He's still a little boy. Who does not stop talking.'

Rob was part of the fun group, so to speak. He loved the changing room banter, whether it was hiding a fish in your bag or moving your car and saying someone had nicked it.

He pushed things to the limit, which frustrated some people, to put it mildly. When we moved to the Kirkstall training facility, there were hardly any showers. You'd have to hang around for a bit, and when you did get your shower, Rob would start pissing on you. Some people took that well, some people didn't (when Paul McShane joined the club, he revived it, as if it was some magical forgotten Leeds tradition).

Rob was also quirky and had his rituals. If we were kicking off at eight o'clock, we'd have to be in the changing room by 6.30. But Rob would be in there by 5.15 at the latest. By the time everyone else had turned up, he'd already be strapped up in his chair, with two cans of Red Bull either side of him. He drank so much of that stuff he should have had shares in it. And when he wasn't drinking Red Bull, he was drinking cup after cup of coffee. That's probably what made him so sharp-witted, and such a pain in the backside.

Rob would always find an angle, a way of getting under someone's skin. But because he couldn't fight for toffee, he had to pick his targets carefully. He went for Barrie Mac a lot, because he knew Barrie wouldn't punch him. But he didn't go for me that often, because he knew I might. There were a few occasions when I had to say to him, 'Rob, get out of my face', because I'd had enough. But however irritating Rob might have been at times, you have to have people like that in the changing room. And one of the beauties of the Leeds changing room was that everyone understood and respected each other's boundaries. If I'd had enough of Rob, and Barrie was banned, he'd just move on to the next target, who probably found it hilarious.

The one thing we mocked Rob for mercilessly was his utter boringness. When it came to socials or celebrating wins, Rob was the boringest man in the world, and I don't even care if that's not a real word. Don't get me wrong, he'd always turn up. And if it was fancy dress, he'd always throw himself into it (it would be Michael Jackson, his musical hero, every single time without fail). But it would get to seven or eight o'clock and Rob would disappear.

When Rob broke into the first team, there was still a lot of partying going on. Some nights, twenty of us would head into Dewsbury or Batley and take over some grotty old pub. Things were quite loose and had a habit of getting out of hand. But Rob never joined us for a Dews Fests, as we called them. And seeing him drunk was very, very rare. Even then, he'd probably only had a can of ginger beer.

But while we took the piss out of Rob for being so sensible, we never pushed him to do anything he didn't want to do. That's just how Rob was, and we respected it. A lot of young kids in his situation would have gone with the flow, for an easy life. But Rob was very single-minded for someone so young. One thing's for sure, he was a lot smarter than most. That's why there are no stories about Rob getting himself into horrible situations but there are loads about me.

★

Thanks, Keith. Because of you, I will now be remembered as the little weirdo who liked weeing on people in the shower. For the record, it was good for team morale. I always thought some of the lads enjoyed it a bit too much . . .

Daryl had a bit of a clear-out in the off-season and didn't bring too many new players in. He clearly thought the kids were about to come good. The most significant departure, as far as I was concerned, was Ryan Sheridan, because that meant less competition for me at scrum-half. The few signings Daryl made were very shrewd. He nabbed a couple of gems from Wigan, in former Kangaroos forward Dave Furner and Great Britain back Gary Connolly, as well as Aussie stand-off Andrew Dunemann from Halifax. Australian signings didn't always come off, but Dave had already proved himself in Super League, winning a Challenge Cup and appearing in a Grand Final, while Andrew had spent four seasons at Halifax. They weren't in England to make a quick buck.

But probably the most important decision Daryl made was to appoint Kev Sinfield as captain. Kev had already played for England and Great Britain but was still only twenty-two. The bloke he replaced as captain, Franny Cummins, had been at the club for almost ten years and not missed a game for God knows how long. I don't know how that conversation between Daryl and Franny went – Franny was probably fine with it, because he was such a good bloke – but that was a clear statement of intent. From that point on, Leeds Rhinos were going to be modelled on Kev Sinfield: young, gifted and brimming with belief.

We started the 2003 season with a bang, winning our first ten games, including two in a row against reigning league champions St Helens. I didn't play in the second game, a Challenge Cup semi-final, because Andrew Dunemann started and Maggsy was named on the bench ahead of me. I'd started every game up until then, and now Daryl had axed me, so I was absolutely gutted. But as it turned out, Maggsy was sensational, scoring a last-ditch try to take the game into extra time before diving over for the winner.

The media were now talking about Maggsy as the

rightful heir to Iestyn Harris. But I'd known for years how good he was going to be. We'd been playing with and against each other since we were ten. We'd signed for Leeds within a few months of each other. We'd been half-back partners for Rhinos and England academies since we were sixteen. Mad as it sounds now, we'd train with the first team when we were thirteen or fourteen, and I saw what Maggsy was capable of against men. Maggsy was so good that I sometimes found playing with him quite daunting. But while the media were now trying to make out there was a rivalry between us, that wasn't the case. Me and Maggsy were great mates, and him being picked ahead of me for a big game wasn't going to change that.

I didn't expect to play in the final against Bradford in Cardiff, but Daryl decided to leave Maggsy out and stick me on the bench instead. As you can imagine, that raised a few eyebrows, given what Maggsy had done a couple of weeks earlier. Now Maggsy would know how I had felt, only ten times worse. There were 72,000 fans in the Millennium Stadium that day, more than four times an average crowd at Headingley, and I well remember the feeling of excitement and nerves beforehand. Unfortunately, I don't remember much about the game, because five minutes after coming on in the first half, I was knocked unconscious. I'm told we didn't really get the rub of the green, and a few dodgy decisions went against us, but all you really need to know is that we lost 22–20.

We did manage to finish second in the league table, courtesy of a ridiculous comeback against St Helens in the penultimate game of the season (we were 20–0 down but scored five tries in the last seventeen minutes to win

30–20). But Bradford blew us away in the Grand Final qualifier (the Bulls beat us all five times that season), before Wigan beat us in the final eliminator. I scored two tries, but Warriors winger Brian Carney got two of his own, including an absolute scorcher, before Maggsy limped off injured in the second half and Danny Tickle kicked the winning drop-goal with two minutes to go. That meant we were the first team to finish in the top two not to reach the final.

A season that had promised so much ended up being a big disappointment. And not just on the pitch. In July, Chev Walker and Ryan Bailey were arrested and charged after a brawl outside a nightclub in Leeds. That cast a cloud over the club for the rest of the year. What they did was wrong, but Ryan got locked up with armed robbers and murderers. Yes, they were mates of mine, but they didn't deserve that. However, in a funny sort of way, it did the team a favour. It gave management an excuse to start policing players' social habits and drinking. And it probably made them think, 'If we had a head coach who could instil iron discipline, this team could actually start winning things.'

4

TALKING OF DISCIPLINE, LINDSEY'S GOT IT IN SPADES.
Thank God. I can hear her downstairs now, making
breakfast for the kids. Once she's done that, she'll take
them to school, come straight home and start dealing
with me.

It's the same routine every day. She'll drag me out of bed
at about 9.30, before showering me, getting me dressed,
helping me down the stairs, giving me my medication and
feeding me breakfast. Then she'll start her day job, which
during the coronavirus pandemic meant doing virtual
physiotherapy consultations from home. Meanwhile, I'll be
sat on the sofa, watching something on Netflix. Now and
again, I'll ask her to make me a coffee or help me to the
toilet. I sometimes think Lindsey should quit that job and
take up juggling.

In the afternoon, Lindsey will pick the kids up from
school, get them fed, bath them, read them a story and get

them off to sleep. Then she'll give me my medication, get me fed, help me upstairs, shower and toilet me and put me in bed about 10 p.m. While I'm watching a bit of TV, I'll be able to hear her downstairs again, catching up on house-work, doing some ironing, replying to emails and making another to-do list for tomorrow. As soon as Lindsey's head hits the pillow, she's out like a light. Thankfully, I don't need a bedtime story.

Things started deteriorating fast in March 2020, just three months after my diagnosis. That's when Lindsey's role changed. Almost overnight, she went from being a wife who went out for nice dinners with her husband to having to feed him three times a day. She essentially became my full-time carer, while running a practice and raising three young children, one of them still a baby.

There are so many everyday things I can't do. I'm too weak to make myself a coffee. Just turning in bed is murder. Lindsey has always looked after me, because I was a waste of space even before MND. Couldn't put a photo up, couldn't cook. Not that I even tried. But this is something else completely.

It's difficult watching Lindsey do so much and not being able to do anything in return. It makes me feel worthless, like a passenger in a rugby team, who might as well not be there. No one should have to go through what Lindsey's going through. I actually think it's harder for her. I know she doesn't like anyone to call her Superwoman, but she is to me. I'm the luckiest man alive to have her as a wife. I love her so much, more than I could ever describe.

★

Lindsey Burrow, Rob's wife

I went to the same dance school as Rob's sisters and first met him at a presentation evening, when I was thirteen. He got my number from a mutual friend, gave me a call and we arranged to go to the pictures in Wakefield. But someone tipped my mum off, I got embarrassed and didn't turn up. This was before mobile phones, so Rob was stood there for ages kicking his heels.

We eventually got together when we were fifteen. My dad had always said, 'Make sure you marry a tall man', and Rob's probably the smallest person I could have found. But what he lacked in height he made up for in personality. I knew from the very beginning that I wanted to spend the rest of my life with him.

Rob had a heart of gold, was the most kind, generous boyfriend a girl could hope for. There were two sides to his personality – the cheeky chappy his friends saw, and the loving, romantic Rob who treated me like a princess. I know that's a cliché, but that's exactly how he was. I'd come home to find candles all over the house. He was constantly buying me little things. When I was at university in Manchester, I'd come back on the Friday evening and Rob would pick me up from the station. For the whole weekend, Rob would be at my beck and call, before dropping me back to Manchester on the Sunday evening. People used to say to me, 'Rob idolizes you.' And they were right. He could never do enough for me, worshipped the ground I walked on.

Rob always says I only married him because he was a rugby player. It's true that I grew up in a rugby town and supported Castleford, but when we first started dating, I had no idea how good Rob was. Never in my wildest dreams did I think he'd go on to achieve all he did. Even when he started playing for the Rhinos first team, he never gave the impression he was doing anything special. He always had time for people, signed autographs or stopped for a chat. Some players might let a bit of stardom go to their heads, but Rob was always just so level-headed, made it seem so ordinary.

I was the reason Rob used to slip out of drinks with his teammates early. When he came home, we'd watch something on the telly. When Rob started earning more money, he bought me a designer handbag, which I didn't really want. I'm a Primark girl, not a Gucci girl, and he never did that again. I wasn't particularly interested in material things or flashy bars, all I wanted to do was spend time with him. We were quite boring really. Just Rob and Lindsey, a couple of working-class kids who were madly in love.

I'm very organized, always planning and making lists, while he was laid-back, messy and forgetful. I'd have to ask him to do something twenty times before he'd do it. If he ever did it. He'd leave his kit bag mouldering in the house for weeks. In many ways, we were chalk and cheese. But we worked together. Rob was always the one, there was never going to be anyone else.

You'll enjoy the story of our engagement. I booked us a trip to Euro Disney and before we went, Rob said to me, 'What ring size are you?' I replied, 'I assume you mean my ring finger?', before finding a tape measure and scribbling down my measurement. Rob spent the whole of the first day walking around Euro Disney with a huge box in his pocket. It was difficult to miss. And the whole time I was thinking, 'When is he going to pop the question?' That night, we were having dinner in a packed restaurant when Rob suddenly got down on one knee. I said to him, 'What the hell are you doing? Please get up. You're embarrassing me.' Poor guy. He ended up proposing the following morning, in the hotel room. Of course I said yes.

I always used to say to Rob, 'You have it easy, you don't have to work.' But I was only joking. He worked so hard and sacrificed so much. I was always there to watch him play, but it wasn't always easy. Every game, he was so much smaller than everyone else. I'd be thinking, 'I can't wait for this to be over.' It wasn't nice seeing him get knocked out or injured. But it was an exciting journey. When he played well, I was like the cat that got the cream. But even if he didn't, I was the proudest wife in the world, because I knew he'd given 100 per cent for the team. It was always about Rob's career, never about me. That's how the partners of professional sportspeople have to be.

Other players' wives and girlfriends would tell me how upset or depressed their partners got after a defeat. But Rob almost had a split personality, his rugby side and his family side. He never brought rugby home with him, it always stayed on the pitch or the training ground. I didn't have a clue about rugby anyway, so there was no point talking to me about the finer points. Sometimes I'd congratulate him on having a good game, because he'd scored a try, and he'd patiently explain that rugby wasn't all about scoring tries, it was about how many tackles or yards a player makes for the team.

Our life was perfect. A great marriage, supportive families, three beautiful children. And then Rob was diagnosed with

MND. It's a disease not many people know much about, but I knew how terrible it was. One of the things about having a medical background is that you deal in cold, hard facts. That can make you seem a bit negative, but Rob wasn't having any of that. In those early days, he was a tower of strength. I couldn't even begin to imagine what was going through his head, but it was him putting on a brave face and telling me to pull myself together, not the other way around.

Rob made me understand that we had a stark choice: either we could waste what time he had left by dwelling on all the things he'd miss out on when he was gone, or we could make as many happy memories as possible.

I could see that Rob's health was deteriorating fast, but there was no point in focusing on that. I'm a bit of a control freak by nature, but I learned that you can't control everything. You just have to focus on the things you can have some influence over. It helped that I always had to be doing something, could never sit still. That meant I didn't have much time to think about things. On the odd occasion I did sit down and think about what was happening – 'Wow, this is my life, this is real' – it probably wasn't helpful, because I'd wonder how I was getting through the days. How I got dressed in the morning, how I found time to eat anything, how I was still standing up.

I had no choice but to get on with things and try to carry on as normal. But carrying on as normal is easier said than done. After a while, it just becomes something you say. Normal would be Rob picking the kids up from school or taking them swimming. Normal would be Rob reading Maya a bedtime story or changing Jackson's nappy. But Rob couldn't do those things any more, so I had to be Mum and Dad.

I was still working from home three days a week, doing the school run, taking the girls here, there and everywhere. Sometimes, I'd wonder if I should still be working at all, or spending all my time with Rob instead. I felt guilty and worried that I might look back with regrets. There was a stage, during the first coronavirus lockdown, when I had no outside support. I was home-schooling and the kids were hungry every two minutes. I was speaking to patients on the phone. Occasionally, I thought, 'Gosh, I've had enough.' I felt like crawling back into bed and pulling the duvet over my head. And I'm sure I grew a few grey hairs and developed a few more wrinkles. But looked at another way, all those distractions added up to a coping mechanism.

There are lots of things that come under the umbrella of 'love'. Romance, affection, doing nice things and sharing nice memories. But when I married Rob, I vowed to have and to hold him in sickness and in health. That might not sound very sexy, but when all the other constituent parts of love are stripped away, it's all that's left.

When Rob was diagnosed with MND, love was being the best carer to Rob I could possibly be, just as I knew Rob would have been for me. It's important that people reading this don't think I'm in any way special. I honestly believe that anyone in my shoes would do the same. Rob might think I'm Superwoman, but when you love and care about someone, your priority is to make them happy, whatever the circumstances. And as long as Rob and the kids are happy, then so am I.

★

Asking for help wasn't easy, because I'd always been so fit and so quick. For the first couple of months, it was a case of, 'I'm not having this, I'm not doing that, I'm not having them coming round the house. I feel absolutely fine!' It felt too much like charity. Or pity, which is even worse. The doctors told me I should have a PEG inserted (Percutaneous Endoscopic Gastrostomy), which is a feeding tube that goes directly into the stomach. I was up for having the thing fitted, until Doddie advised me to put it off for as long as possible. In Doddie's world of little victories, he viewed having a PEG inserted as a defeat, something it was impossible to come back from.

But I soon realized that you have to pick your battles with MND. Me digging in and being stubborn about every bit of assistance that's offered isn't helpful in the grand scheme of things. It's only fair to Lindsey and my family that I be honest about the process. If I'm not honest, day to day, they can't make the adjustments that will make all our lives easier. And stubbornness doesn't necessarily make you happy, or the people who want you to be happy.

I didn't want the kids to live in a hospital, so we've kept modifications to a minimum. There's a shower chair in the bathroom and a raise on the bed, but not much else. The time came when I had to start using a wheelchair, otherwise I wouldn't have been able to leave the house. Just going to the park with the kids is an operation. Suddenly, getting from the front door to the car – something that used to take me a few seconds – can take as long as ten minutes. It relates to what Lindsey was saying: yes, going to the park with the kids is normal; but taking that long to get out of the house isn't normal at all. But there's no alternative. Either I go to the park or no one goes to the park.

We could probably do with a stairlift, and if my weight hadn't dropped to eight stone, we'd probably have one. Lindsey sometimes jokes that it's a good job I wasn't a prop. Lindsey more or less carries me up the stairs. Getting to the top is becoming a major achievement, like scaling Everest while wrestling. This evening, Lindsey said to me, 'It's a good job I work with spinal surgeons, because I might need their help by the time I'm finished with you.' But she knows that unless she keeps me moving, I'll get weaker even faster.

It would be very easy to sit and watch TV all day, or stare at the walls and wonder if there will ever be a boy born who can swim faster than a shark. But as Doddie said, 'If you don't use it, you'll lose it.' That's why Lindsey's constantly cracking the whip, being the bossy wife. She told me off the other day for not communicating enough with the kids. But it isn't easy, because they're like little streaks of lightning, running all over the house. By the time I've typed 'How was your day?' and pressed play, they've disappeared into the garden or up into their bedroom. Moments to connect are constantly slipping through my grasp, because moments don't last long in children's heads.

Looked at one way, the kids are lucky: I'm a stay-at-home dad, so spend lots of time with them. Me and Jackson spend hardly any time apart. But more and more, I'm sep-arate from what's going on around me. I absorb everything that's happening, but I'm not really a part of it. For example, it's about ten metres from my perch on the sofa to the door leading onto the garden. But this afternoon, when Lindsey's brother was kicking a ball about with Jackson, it seemed like ten miles. It was like looking through the bars of a prison cell, at something I'd been robbed of without ever having the chance to experience.

★

One of the good things about getting MND is that it's given me time to try and work out what Jamie Jones-Buchanan was going on about for twenty years. Only teasing, Jonesy. But I've got to be honest, it was often hard to keep up.

He's an enigma, Jonesy: a great friend who'll do anything for you, as long as he remembers; the dumbest smart bloke I've ever met. Jonesy was like the team's philosopher, always speaking in riddles. I remember one game against Huddersfield, when we were losing at half-time. Jonesy started comparing our situation to a passage in the Bible, and I was thinking, 'This is all well and good, Jonesy, but we're getting dicked on by Huddersfield. How's the Bible relevant to this?' I soon learned that if you couldn't understand what Jonesy was going on about, it was best just to go along with it. But often what Jonesy was going on about made a lot of sense.

Listen to Jonesy describe his journey from Bramley, a district in west Leeds, to the Rhinos first team, and you'll realize that he personified what the club was all about in the late 1990s and early 2000s. There were no scholarships when Jonesy was a kid – you either got spotted by a scout or you didn't. Jonesy had plenty of interest from other Super League clubs, but he'd grown up watching Leeds at Headingley, in the famous South Stand, and only ever wanted to play for them. So he waited and waited and finally Leeds got in touch. They were the last team to come in for him, but he loved the club so much, he probably would have hung around for the call until he was fifty.

By 2003, the Rhinos' senior squad was full of players like Jonesy, lads who had been ardent fans and never wanted to play for anyone else. As well as Jonesy, there was me, Maggsy, Chev Walker, Matty Diskin, Ryan Bailey, Mark Calderwood and Richie Mathers. Kev was from Oldham and could have signed for Wigan, who were far and away the best side at the time, for double the money. But Ellery Hanley was at Leeds, so he joined them instead. If Leeds were good enough for Ellery, they were the only team good enough for Kev.

When Kev was growing up, his parents were big fans of the revolutionary Che Guevara. Apparently, there were Cuban posters all over the walls of his house. I'm not particularly political, but it makes sense that Kev, who was brought up with those kinds of socialist values, would end up as captain of that team. All those academy graduates came from similar working-class backgrounds and were bonded by a shared sense of struggle. We learned together, hurt together, and grew used to overcoming adversity together, through perseverance and sheer determination. When a group is as close as that, winning stuff becomes almost incidental. Jonesy calls it love, and he's right. It was brotherly love, an almost soldierly brand of camaraderie.

Kev had this idea that you become the average of the five people you spend most time with. And being in that environment at Leeds, where we were surrounded by strong personalities with special talent, forced all of us to up our games and be more like each other. We were like the Borg from *Star Trek*, all of us bound together to form a single hive mind. To a certain extent, it didn't really matter who the coach was or which foreign players we signed, the culture was kept alive by that nucleus of academy kids, with Kev at the very centre. I remember Jonesy saying that he strived to be like Kev and Maggsy and me, not so much because it would improve him as a player – although it did – but because not doing so meant he might be torn away from the group.

When Jonesy does his after-dinner speeches, he tells a story that ends with the line, 'Even though he's not here today, there'll always be a little bit of Kevin Sinfield inside of me.' It sounds like something David Brent would say, and it always gets a big laugh from the old fellas, but Jonesy is also making a serious point. Even as far back as 2003, we were all made up of bits of each other. We knew how each other thought, what each other would do on the pitch. Luckily for Jonesy, he probably had room to fit two of me inside of him.

★

I've always thought Daryl Powell's contribution to Leeds's golden era has been unfairly overlooked. From a purely selfish point of view, Daryl saw my potential and gave me a run in the first team, when other coaches would have been scared to (he even admitted that he was flabbergasted when he first saw me in training, because of my size). But never mind me, Daryl gave a lot of future Rhinos greats their debuts (Maggsy, Richie Mathers, Ryan Bailey). He also handed Kev Sinfield the captaincy and came up with the formula for sustained success, a blend of proud local kids and experienced pros. But you want to know the best thing about Daryl Powell? He was just a thoroughly nice bloke.

So when, midway through the 2003 season, it was announced that Daryl would be stepping aside at the end of the year, I was more than a little bit surprised. In fact, it was all a bit weird. Some fans had never really warmed to Daryl, because of his lack of prior coaching experience and a perception that he'd only got the job because he was pals with Gary Hetherington (they were at Sheffield Eagles together, Gary as coach and Daryl as captain). But we were top of the Super League table and had narrowly lost in the final of the Challenge Cup only a few months earlier. Weirdest of all was the fact that when Gary announced Daryl's successor – Huddersfield Giants' Tony Smith – Daryl was sitting next to him at the press conference.

The plan, which had been hatched a few months earlier, was for Daryl to spend the next two years as director of rugby, brushing up on his coaching skills before taking over again in 2006. I remember Daryl's quote at the time: 'I'm not saying I'm not good enough. But I'm not as good as I want to be.' You can't get more honest than that. Gary had been keeping his reshuffle secret until a suitable head coach became available. When he heard that Tony had turned down a new contract from Huddersfield and was all set to join Union Treiziste Catalane (who would become Catalans Dragons on joining Super League a couple of years later), Gary pounced. Apparently, Gary and Daryl interviewed Tony together and offered him the job a couple of days later.

Of course, Daryl didn't become head coach again in 2006. In fact, he hasn't been back since leaving the club in 2005. Not because Daryl didn't become a better coach, but because the bloke who was supposed to be a caretaker turned out to be a bloody marvel.

Tony had a decent career as a player in Australia before finishing his playing days with Workington (him and his wife lived above a fish-and-chip shop and had to burn all their clothes before returning to Australia, because they stank of fat and vinegar). In 2001, Tony became head coach of Huddersfield. He lost his first thirteen games in charge and the Giants were relegated from Super League, before bringing them straight back up again and managing to keep them there the following season.

Some fans and journalists didn't think Tony was a good fit for Leeds. We were supposed to be this glamour club, all about playing the game with style, and there was a feeling that Tony's Huddersfield had been mainly about stopping the opposition, instead of playing themselves. But as soon as Tony turned up, I could tell he was the right man for the job. He was obsessed with the fundamentals, like no coach I'd had before. He literally spent the first couple of weeks teaching us how to catch and pass. Once he was satisfied we'd grasped the basics, he then started tuning our skills, as individuals and as a team. He taught us tactics and technical details I didn't even know existed.

Tony was also big on work ethic and fitness. Even when we could barely stand in training, we weren't allowed to look tired. And he was a strict disciplinarian, almost like a schoolmaster. He shook hands with everyone in the morning. In one of our first training sessions, he said to Chev Walker, 'Don't look at your boots when I'm talking, look straight at me.' He had no problem reintegrating Chev and

Ryan Bailey – that was all in the past as far as Tony was concerned (he even went to visit both of them in prison before he took over). But he wasn't going to allow something like that to happen again.

Tony wanted to create a winning culture at Leeds, and he didn't think drinking could possibly be part of it. That meant no more Dews Fests for Keith and the lads. He banned players from going to nightclubs and even introduced a curfew, which meant players had to tell him where they were going and ask his permission to stay out after midnight, even after a game. That didn't go down well with some of the players, who felt like they were being treated like schoolkids. It does sound a bit daft, but it was Tony's way or the highway.

★

Tony Smith, Rhinos head coach

I timed my arrival just right. I suited Leeds and Leeds suited me. The club already had a lot of good things in place, so it was mainly a case of adding little bits and doing some tweaking. They had a pretty good team, a nice balance of young and experienced players, but I felt the players needed toughening up. I also needed to instil some confidence, because I'm not sure they realized exactly how tough they could be or how talented they were.

One of the first things we did was get them to change their body language in training. When things got difficult, they weren't allowed to put their hands on their hips or heads. There was to be no slouching. We discouraged 'porno' faces, the grimacing and gurning you normally see when players are suffering. We didn't want them to look like they were feeling sorry for themselves, even during the most vicious of sessions, when they were rattled and ragged and wanted the ground to swallow them up. Instead, we wanted them to stick their chests out and keep swinging their arms. It was psychological stuff, all about getting them to fool themselves.

The boys will all remember running up the hills at Round-hay Park – and it won't bring smiles to their faces. They'd do anything between ten and fifteen hills, it would be absolutely torturous. But after a few of those sessions, I noticed them acting as if they weren't hurting, and telling each other not to put their hands on their hips or double up in pain. That's when I knew they were already taking things on board and buying into the culture.

My coaching philosophy is about making players self-sufficient, helping them make the right decisions during a game. And every successful team I've coached has had good leadership on the field. But when I arrived at Leeds, they were largely led by experienced players who weren't necessarily good leaders. So I needed to encourage the youngsters who were good leaders – players like Kev Sinfield, Danny McGuire, Jamie Jones-Buchanan, Chev Walker and Rob – to step up, have more say and take ownership.

My brother Brian is thirteen years older than me and was coaching from when I was young, so I understood what it entailed long before I retired as a player. And it meant that I was brought up to be someone who wanted to help other people improve. And in Rob Burrow, I had someone who desperately wanted to do that.

I admired Rob when I was at Huddersfield because he

scared the hell out of my team. And I wasn't shocked that he could play because I'd grown up with Alfie Langer. When Alfie first turned up in Australia, people were amazed at his size and wondered if he'd make it. But he showed it was possible for such a small bloke to excel at the highest level. Like with Alfie, I had to put people on notice around Rob, because I knew he could tear us apart. We sent a lot of traffic his way, not only because of his size, but also to take some of the speed out of his legs. But he'd always front up to it.

When I started coaching Rob, I admired him even more. He didn't say a lot in team meetings, because he hadn't grown into a leadership role yet. He was a little bit shy, but a good listener, a sponge when it came to learning about rugby. He wouldn't just nod when people spoke, you could tell he was taking things on board, from me and his team-mates. But while he was reserved and respectful around me and the rest of the coaching staff, he was a live wire around the boys. He'd pick on the big, boisterous lads, run rings around them mentally, just as he ran rings around them on the training ground. And that's what you look for in a half-back, plenty of cheekiness.

But the best thing about Rob was that he just loved coming to work. Whatever we did, he threw himself into it at 100 mph. Coaching someone like that, who is just so happy to be there, is an absolute pleasure.

It wasn't long before that hard work started paying dividends. He'd always had electrifying speed, but he started to learn more about the finer points of rugby league. He developed his kicking game and organizational skills. He became a half-back who was prepared to bark at his teammates, lead them around the park, tell them where to be and what to do. And over time, he started to come out of his shell in team meetings. Watching his confidence bloom, on and off the field, was the most rewarding part of coaching him. I just knew he was going to be a big part of that team for a long, long time.

★

Even before Tony's arrival, there was a feeling among the younger lads that something special was about to happen. There was a whole bunch of players still in their early twenties who were already seasoned pros. Kev had been playing for the first team for six years, Jonesy and Chev Walker for four. Me, Maggsy, Matty Diskin, Ryan Bailey, Mark Calderwood and Richie Mathers had two or three seasons under our belts. We were no longer rookies.

We'd all been part of a winning culture in the academy and expected that to continue. We weren't like previous generations of Leeds players, who were used to and maybe too accepting of underachieving. And the fact that Tony only signed one player before the 2004 season, Papua New Guinea winger Marcus Bai, spoke volumes: clearly Tony believed that, for the first time in decades, everyone already at the club had pride in the shirt.

But Tony wasn't afraid to make unpopular decisions. He dropped Franny Cummins for the first game of the season, breaking his unbroken run of 182 appearances. Franny was part of the furniture at Leeds, a club legend who had just had his testimonial. But Tony had brought Marcus Bai to the club and thought he was a better bet on the wing than Franny, simple as that.

It must have been a big disappointment for Franny, but

it says a lot about him – and that Leeds side – that instead of spitting his dummy out, he said to Tony, 'Don't worry, I'll work my way back into the team.' As it turned out, Marcus scored a hat-trick on his debut, against London Broncos, while Franny scored a couple in the next game, a one-sided Challenge Cup victory over Workington, and remained an integral part of the squad that season.

Me and Maggsy were the half-back pairing for the first three games, until St Helens did a number on us in the Challenge Cup. I was on the bench for the next six games, before Tony picked me to play hooker against Saints in the league. We got thrashed 56–10 that day, with Saints scoring nine tries, which was a bit of a shock to the system. A few journalists had been tipping us to win the title after our fast start to the season, but they were now having second thoughts. Afterwards, Saints fans were singing, 'Top of the league, you're having a laugh!' But there was an awful lot of rugby still to be played.

In May 2004, second-row Ali Lauiti'iti joined from the New Zealand Warriors and fitted right in, scoring five tries in his first five games, which included a second win of the season over Bradford. Even a narrow defeat at Wigan, only our second in the league, wasn't enough to knock us off the top of the table. Then came a 70–0 drubbing of St Helens, who had won the Challenge Cup since stuffing us at Knowsley Road. We ran in twelve tries, with Maggsy bagging a hat-trick, and that was the first time Saints had been white-washed in Super League. Now it was our fans singing, 'Top of the league, we're having a laugh!' The following game, against Wakefield, Maggsy scored two more tries to break

Dad, a big Leeds fan, met Mum at the Burberry factory in Castleford. They had a few rows about rugby but got on well enough to marry and have three kids – Joanne, Claire and me.

Claire (left) and Joanne teased me something rotten when we were kids. They soon worked out that the worst thing I could possibly imagine was to be kissed by them. As a result, I spent a lot of time on the run.

Dad obviously loved my sisters to bits but was chuffed when I turned up. Almost as soon as I was out of nappies, we were playing rugby all over the house, with me scoring the tries and Dad providing the commentary.

Dad played a bit of rugby in his youth but was more suited to mucking about in a swimming pool. No one can really pinpoint where my sporting talent and determination came from.

When I was seven, I started playing for Travellers Saints (later known as Featherstone Lions). I was tiny but very difficult to catch, like a bar of soap on legs – not only was I quick, I had a wicked swerve and sidestep.

In the early days, my coach Bob Woodhead would only put me on when the team was well ahead. But having shown I loved tackling as much as I loved running, Bob thought I was destined to make it.

Robert is star of the show

SCRUM-half Robert Burrow starred for Travellers Saints under-11's in a 22-4 win over Half Acres in a Castleford Cup match which was a curtain-raiser to Friday evening's Featherstone-St Helens game at Post Office Road.

Burrow won the Saints man of the match award after scoring two second-half tries, while skipper William Jordan crowned an impressive display with two tries and three goals.

Half Acres put up an excellent performance. Shaun Douglas scored a first-half try and Tommy Saxton, Wayne Sutcliffe and Philip Rodgers were also outstanding for the Castleford team who gave all 23 players in their squad a run out.

Leading only 6-4 at half-time, Saints took command in the second-half with hard-working forwards Stephen Jones and Mark Spurr leading the way.

William Jordan switched to loose-forward, enabling Natalie Towning to make an impressive debut at stand-off after her transfer from Smawthorne.

Gareth Beard gave another strong display on the wing and centre David Backhouse caused problems every time he had the ball.

William Jordan scored four tries as Travellers chalked up their second win in less than 24 hours by beating Hunslet Boys Club 32-11 in a Yorkshire Junior League match on Saturday.

Man of the match Stephen Jones gave his best-ever performance for Saints, making a big impact in attack and also topping the tackle count.

Burrow and impressive loose-forward Thomas Traylor were the other try scorers for Travellers who were also well served by centre Darren Jordan, full-back Chris Mann, winger Chris Butterworth, second-rower Stewart Woodhead and lively hooker Richard Walker.

As a kid growing up in Castleford, my garden and the surrounding streets were my main training grounds. Fellow pros Michael Shenton, Ben Crooks and James Clare also honed their skills on our cul-de-sac.

By the age of eleven, I was starring for Travellers Saints most weeks and playing representative rugby for Yorkshire. And every time I took the field, Granddad Bob would be clapping and cheering on the touchline.

You can tell which one I am in these team photos – because you almost can't see me! While I was talented, scored a lot of tries and won a lot of man-of-the-match awards, most people thought I had no chance of making it because of my size.

When Leeds scout Bob Pickles told head coach Dean Bell (left) and his assistant Hugh McGahan that they should sign me, they thought he was pulling their legs. But after a lot of agonizing, they eventually signed me up when I was thirteen.

While others were quick to write me off, Granddad Bob always thought I'd make it. He thought the world of me and the feeling was mutual; he often used to say, 'I think the sun shines out of your backside!'

Me and Lindsey were meant to go on a date when we were thirteen, but she got cold feet and stood me up. We finally got together two years later and were inseparable from that point on – she was the only girl for me.

Me and Lindsey got married in 2006. It was just about the perfect day, probably because Lindsey arranged absolutely everything and all I had to do was turn up on time.

There were Leeds teammates everywhere you looked on our wedding day, which just goes to show how close we were. Here's me and Lindsey with (from left) Keith Senior, Barrie McDermott, Gareth Ellis, Danny McGuire and Kev Sinfield.

Our honeymoon was in the beautiful Maldives, although I took my training gear. A couple of weeks later, I was slogging up hills in Leeds's Roundhay Park; family life was important to me, but being a professional sportsperson was relentless.

When Jackson followed Macy and Maya into the world in 2018, our family was complete and everything seemed perfect. But two months after this happy holiday in Florida, I was diagnosed with MND and our lives changed forever.

the record for most in a Super League season (that made it thirty in twenty-one games).

Our third game of the season, against Bradford, was slightly odd, because Iestyn Harris was playing for them. When Iestyn left for rugby union, it was apparently agreed that if he ever decided to return to league, he'd rejoin Leeds. But, for whatever reason, he ended up at the Bulls instead. Gary Hetherington wasn't over the moon about that and sued Iestyn for breach of contract. It didn't go down well with our fans, either.

But to the players, Iestyn was still a mate. When he was at Leeds, he'd travel to training from Oldham every day with Baz and Kev, and they'd stayed in touch with him. So before the game, Baz did a newspaper interview, in which he pleaded with our fans to go easy on Iestyn. They didn't listen, as Iestyn was booed every time he got the ball. Even worse for Iestyn, we ran out 40–12 winners, with Maggsy scoring two more tries.

The following week, we beat Castleford 64–12 to win our first League Leaders' Shield since 1972, before finishing the regular season nine points clear of Bradford. We'd lost only two of our twenty-eight games, which was something to be proud of, but nobody really remembers who finishes top of the table, it's all about winning the Grand Final. When we lost to the Bulls in the qualifying semi, suddenly the media were calling us chokers. Iestyn was great that day, as was Robbie Paul, who had been written off as past it by some in the media. And while the Bulls could now put their feet up for a couple of weeks before the Grand Final, we had to play Wigan in the final eliminator six days later.

Andrew Dunemann was injured, so Tony decided to

have a reshuffle, moving Kev to stand-off and Maggsy to scrum-half, with me on the bench. And we absolutely spanked them. Marcus Bai scored a hat-trick in a 40–12 win and the feeling was that losing to the Bulls had maybe done us a favour. It had got rid of any complacency, kept us sharp and battle-ready and turned us into underdogs for the Grand Final, which relieved some of the pressure. But I still felt uneasy in the lead-up to that game. The Bulls were used to playing in Grand Finals, but we weren't. And it didn't seem right to me, walking the league by nine points but now having to beat the Bulls at Old Trafford to prove we were the best team. It made me nervous, as if an injustice was inevitable.

Before the game, Dave Furner, who was making his final appearance for the club, slipped in the dressing room and hurt his knee. Dave being Dave, he had it injected, strapped it up and carried on as normal, and his attitude summed up the team that day. We liked to entertain, but it wasn't that kind of game. The atmosphere was unbelievable, but it ended up being an arm-wrestle rather than the free-flowing spectacle the fans might have expected. It was tailor-made for warriors like Dave, rather than us fancy Dans in the backs.

We'd learned lessons from the qualifying defeat, and didn't panic when Lesley Vainikolo, Bradford's eighteen-stone winger, scored after just seven minutes. Instead, Kev made Vainikolo's life hell for the rest of the first half. As instructed, Kev repeatedly kicked the ball behind him, and every time he picked it up, Chev Walker and Mark Calderwood were all over him like a rash. Good job they were, because – as well as being built like a tank – Vainikolo could run the 100 metres in eleven seconds. By half-time, Vainikolo was absolutely knackered.

A try from Matty Diskin and three goals from Kev gave us a 10–4 interval lead, before Shontayne Hape scored a bit of a soft try for Bradford. The result was up in the air until five minutes from the end, when Robbie Paul inexplicably dropped the ball on his own twenty-metre line. From the resulting scrum, Keith got held up just short of the try-line but managed to offload to Maggsy, who burrowed over to seal the deal. That's about the only thing I remember about that game; the rest of it is a blur. But everyone remembers what they saw when the final hooter went: Franny Cummins storming onto the pitch in his suit, fists pumping, jumping up and down like a lunatic. Franny had had a few injuries and didn't make the squad, but he was as thrilled as the rest of us. That showed what kind of team we'd become.

To witness those delirious Rhinos fans, who had been starved of success for thirty-two years, was just beautiful. I think most of them were in a state of shock. And very relieved. Relief was my overriding emotion as well. When you play for a club that is expected to win things but never does, the monkey on your back is more of a gorilla. As for the Bradford fans, they weren't singing 'What a waste of money!' any more. Not least because half our team cost nothing.

One of the beauties of rugby league is that the blokes on the pitch aren't much different to the fans in the stands. They hail from the same towns and cities. They go to the same schools. In many cases, they know the players personally. Their dads know our dads, their mums know our mums, their kids know our kids. That means that when we win things, it's that much more personal than if we were from all four corners of the globe, like in football. Some of those fans would have been watching us busting a gut in a Leeds shirt every week since we were kids. I can only imagine how sweet it was for them.

I savoured those great moments. Kev lifting the trophy. Singing along to Green Day's 'Time of Your Life' on the coach back to Leeds. The hugs, the smiles, the joyous conversations, the shared realization that all those savage training sessions, all that yomping in Roundhay Park, all that shared pain and sacrifice had been worth it. I wish they hadn't flashed by so quickly, but at least I've got them banked. Because while MND can do its worst to my body, it can never rob me of those memories. They sometimes seem like fragments of another person's life. But they are concrete evidence of the lucky life I've lived.

5

I WISH SOME DAYS WOULD NEVER END. TODAY IS ONE
of those days. Sat on the clifftop, listening to the sound of
the sea and the gulls and the girls laughing. Big blue sky,
sun shining, Jackson toddling around in his Leeds shirt (no,
it's not one of mine), his face covered in ice cream. Lindsey
looking as pretty as she's ever looked. If I could freeze this
moment and live it forever, I would.

I try to avoid too much bad news, but I know coronavirus has been a nightmare for so many people. For me, it's
been both a blessing and a curse. When the first lockdown
kicked in, I was stuck indoors for weeks. People couldn't
visit because we were worried they might kill me. I loved
spending so much time with Lindsey and the kids, but
I think lockdown accelerated my decline. Just like a lot of
people, I found it too easy to sit on the sofa doing nothing.

Lindsey had so much on her plate, what with me, the
kids and her job, so I was desperate for us to get away for
a holiday. We made plans to visit Gran Canaria or our villa

in Florida, but they fell through. In the end, I gave up hope of hopping on a plane and settled on making memories in the garden. Being water-bombed by Macy and Maya is just as fun in Yorkshire as it is in Spain.

When the rules loosened up, and I didn't have to shield as tightly, we packed our bags and headed to the caravan park in Primrose Valley, where Mum and Dad used to take us when we were kids. There's something magical about seeing your children do the things you did when you were their age, probably because you know exactly how much fun they're having. When I watch Jackson charging around the fields, happy as Larry, I can see myself. It's two for the price of one, creating new memories while reliving my childhood.

The other day, someone said to me, 'Is it on your mind that this might be the last family holiday you ever have?' To be completely honest, I hadn't given it a moment's thought. There might not be much treatment for MND, but when I watch my kids running around the place with big smiles on their faces, giggling and screaming and hollering, it feels like I've been cured.

★

Even after I started playing for the Rhinos first team, we'd still go on caravanning holidays. We'd often go with one of my teammates Carl Ablett and his family. We'd spark up a fire (or, more accurately, Carl would send me off to gather sticks before he sparked up a fire) and sit around it chewing the fat until the wee small hours. If anyone saw us and knew who we were, they probably wondered what a couple of professional rugby league players were doing holidaying on the Yorkshire coast. And they might have felt sorry for our wives. But I was always a low-key sort of bloke, never one for the bright lights.

Every day after training, I'd go round Granddad Bob's for dinner. I'd been doing that since I was at school, when he lived just around the corner from Airedale. When I started playing for Leeds, and he started getting on a bit, he'd serve me up a Marks and Spencer steak and pasta. It would be all laid out for me when I walked through his front door, regular as clockwork. I'm pretty sure he didn't cook my sisters' steak, but it was only the best for me.

As far as I was concerned, I was just a bloke who was lucky enough to play rugby for a living. When I first asked Lindsey out, I didn't say, 'I don't know how to put this, but I'm kind of a big deal. People know me. I'm very important.' I probably said, '*I Know What You Did Last Summer* is on at the pictures, fancy watching it with me? I'll buy you a bucket of popcorn.' It would kill me if I found out that anyone thought I was a big-head or an idiot, because I'd feel like I'd betrayed the values my mum and dad instilled in me.

One time, I was in the Freeport shopping centre in Castleford when I fancied a Subway. When I walked in, my mate was sitting on his own in the corner, so I crept up behind him and whacked him in the side of the head. But when he turned around, it wasn't my mate at all, but some complete random. I couldn't apologize enough, and I then had to hang around while my sandwich was made. I was absolutely mortified and, for ages afterwards, I kept thinking, 'That bloke has probably told everyone in Castleford that I'm a dickhead.'

I'd shake anyone's hand and chat with anyone who

fancied chatting. And I never turned down someone who wanted an autograph, even when they asked me to stand back-to-back with their five-year-old kid, to see who was taller. I never had many leather-bound books, my apartment never smelled of rich mahogany and I never wore Sex Panther. About the only flash things I ever did were to buy Lindsey that designer handbag she hated, and a Toyota MR2 when I was eighteen. One night, I flipped it and hit a tree, and some teammates had to come and lift it back onto its wheels. Luckily, the only injury I got was a smashed nose. The lads liked to joke that the swelling never went down.

When I wasn't training with Leeds, I was coaching York-shire League side Ackworth Jaguars. I played with quite a few of the Ackworth lads when I was at Featherstone Lions and loved hooking up with them again. I'm not sure you'd find many Premier League footballers coaching non-league teams in their spare time, but it was quite common in rugby league. And it's not like I was preparing for a career in coaching after I retired from playing; it was just a hobby, as well as a way of giving something back to the community. What else was I going to do with my spare time, apart from watch *The Office* on loop?

★

Widnes wanted to sign me before the 2005 season, but I didn't want to be playing for anyone apart from Leeds. And I certainly wasn't going to move from Ponte Carlo, as some of us locals call Pontefract (actually, that's probably just me). Unsurprisingly, no one else wanted to leave either, meaning the squad was pretty much the same as the season before, apart from the departure of the old warhorse Dave Furner, who'd hung up his boots and returned to Australia, and the addition of Wakefield skipper Gareth Ellis.

Before Super League got underway, we played Canterbury Bulldogs in the World Club Challenge. Aussies can be a bit dismissive of British rugby league. That's fair enough, I suppose, because we haven't beaten them in an Ashes series since 1970. But it is slightly irritating when the Australian media makes out that the World Club Challenge is nothing more than a pre-season friendly and bangs on about their team's lack of preparation, jet lag and having to play in the cold. But we weren't bothered about any of that. Leeds had never won the competition before, which was a major motivation. And we wanted to show that there is a bit of talent up north, which I think we managed to do.

The result was never really in doubt. Maggsy scored a scorcher in the first half, we led 26–6 at the break and, despite a late surge by the Bulldogs, we ended up beating them 39–32. Apart from us winning (and beating any Australian side is always a beautiful feeling), my main memory of that day is of Sonny Bill Williams, Canterbury's nineteen-year-old second-row. Almost every time we tackled him, he managed to offload the ball. And he hit harder than almost anyone I'd seen. One shoulder-charge on Marcus Bai must have loosened Marcus's fillings. It was absolutely monstrous.

There was some newspaper talk about us signing Sonny Bill, but that was never going to happen, because of the Super League salary cap. I'm not sure what happened to Sonny Bill after that game. I vaguely remember someone telling me that he started playing rugby union and won a few things with a team called the 'All Blacks'. What a tragic waste of talent.

There had been a bit of a fuss in the off-season, after Keith Senior and Ryan Bailey got done for taking banned substances. They both said they didn't think they'd done anything wrong, and I've got no reason to doubt them. But some people, especially Bradford fans, wanted to believe we'd won the Grand Final because we were all off our tits on drugs. That was a bit of extra motivation, not that we needed any. We made a blistering start to the Super League season, winning our first seven games, including comfortable wins over St Helens and Bradford. And because Maggsy was out after groin surgery, I got an extended run in the starting line-up, partnering Kev at half-back.

We played some eye-catching rugby during that period, exhibition stuff at times – the word 'rampant' kept popping up in newspaper reports – and looked nailed on to retain our title. But a shock defeat by Wakefield, which stopped us from equalling Bradford's Super League record of twenty-one games undefeated, proved that nothing is ever inevitable in professional sport.

We won thirteen of our next fourteen, including sticking seventy points on Wakefield and Wigan in successive games. And with Maggsy now out with a hand injury, I was starting every week. That summer, I signed a new five-year deal, keeping me at Leeds until 2010. That length of deal was quite unusual in Super League, and made me feel even more at home. We were halfway through the season, I was scoring stacks of tries and we were top of the table. What could go wrong?

We lost a strange game against London in France

(Griffin Park wasn't available, so the Broncos experimented with a 'home' fixture in Perpignan, home of Catalans Dragons, who were joining Super League the following season), which led to a few too many drinks being had on the beach the following day. Chris McKenna, our Aussie centre/second-row, then had a barney with Tony Smith at the airport, which didn't look great. I know Keith Senior was a bit upset about that weekend, because he was skipper in the absence of Kev, who missed the game with an injury. However, other than that, everything seemed fine. We won our next five games, including beating Toulouse in the semi-finals of the Challenge Cup, hammering Leigh 74–0 and gaining revenge over London. But that was when we started to come undone.

Not only did we get spanked by Bradford at Headingley, but Keith Senior also got stretchered off with an ankle injury and Maggsy hurt his shoulder. The following week, we were playing Hull in the final of the Challenge Cup at Cardiff's Millennium Stadium. Hull had upset St Helens in their semi-final, but we were red-hot favourites (the bookies had us 7–2 on). We hadn't lost two matches in a row since Tony had taken over, and we had beaten Hull twice already in the league that season. On top of that, Hull hadn't won the Challenge Cup since 1982, or even reached a final for twenty years. Some journalists were predicting we'd romp it. Most of our fans probably agreed.

Keith somehow managed to get himself fit enough to start and I was picked ahead of Maggsy, who had to make do with a spot on the bench. Beforehand, I just hoped I'd be able to remember what transpired, having been knocked out in the final two years earlier. Afterwards, I wished

I could have forgotten the whole thing, because it was an absolute heart-breaker.

We just couldn't get going in the first half, in the face of some rugged defence by Hull, and the score was 6–6 at the interval. Keith didn't reappear for the second half, which began with Marcus Bai making a bad mistake behind his own goal line and Richard Whiting scoring an opportunistic try. Hull looked in control at 19–12 up, before tries from Mark Calderwood and Marcus Bai edged us ahead. But with three minutes to go, Paul Cooke scored under the posts to level the scores, before Danny Brough kicked the conversion to make it 25–24 to Hull. Kev had a last-ditch drop-goal charged down and that was the end of another bad day for Leeds on the biggest stage.

We then lost successive games to Wigan and Warrington (who had Andrew Johns, the great Aussie scrum-half, playing for them), making it four defeats in a row. Luckily, we'd already secured second place in the table, so we were able to make the final regular game of the season at Headingley a bit of a celebration for our departing players. Mark Calderwood, Chris McKenna, Andrew Dunemann, Marcus Bai, Franny Cummins and Baz McDermott were all off at the end of the season, either joining other clubs or retiring. The suits even let Baz off a suspension, so that he and Franny could lead us out. Thankfully, we beat Wakefield 34–26, breaking our dismal run and giving us a bit of a lift before the Grand Final qualifier against league leaders St Helens.

Saints had lost only one game since May, their Challenge Cup semi-final against Hull, which made us slight underdogs. But we went 19–0 ahead in terrible conditions at Knowsley Road, with Ali Lauiti'iti scoring a mad length-of-the-field try, and managed to hang on, despite three Saints tries in the final eleven minutes. Saints then lost to Bradford in the final eliminator, meaning it was us against the Bulls in the Grand Final, just like the season before.

No team had ever won the Grand Final after finishing outside the top two in the league, but Bradford's storming run-in, combined with our patchy recent form, meant the bookies were unable to separate us. This time, I started alongside Maggsy in the half-backs, while the Bulls had a couple of former Leeds favourites in their squad, in Iestyn Harris and Adrian Morley, who was on loan from the Sydney Roosters. And on the night, we simply weren't good enough. A Maggsy try midway through the first half gave us the lead, before Bulls winger Leon Pryce, who had a brilliant game, touched down to give them a narrow lead at the interval. In the second half, we just couldn't put a dent in them. And when Lesley Vainikolo barged over, that was pretty much that.

That was Bradford's third Grand Final win in five seasons. If someone had said back then that they'd never appear in one again, you'd have laughed in their face. But that's how things have turned out. As for us, we were left wondering how a season that had promised so much had delivered so little.

We scored 1,152 points in the regular season, which is still a Super League record. That included 209 tries, which worked out at more than seven a game. We hardly kicked any penalties, preferring to run it from all over the pitch. Tony loved to see us chucking the ball around, drawing and passing and offloading in the tackle. The consensus among the fans was that they'd never seen a Leeds side serve up such entertaining rugby. But in professional sport, fanciness and flamboyance often gets trumped by hard-nosed pragmatism.

On a personal level, the season had been a big success. I had been getting a little bit fed up with sitting on the bench, so to start so many games, score so many tries (twenty-seven in all competitions, behind only Mark Calderwood and Keith for the Rhinos) and cement a half-back partnership with Maggsy was very pleasing. I was also named the best scrum-half in Super League and called up by Great Britain for the 2005 Tri-Nations, which was another dream come true.

I'd already played a few games for England, in the 2003 and 2004 European Nations Cups, but Russia and France weren't in the same league as the Aussies and the Kiwis. As an aside, I played against Baz in the 2004 European Nations Cup Final, because he was playing for Ireland. I was hooker that day and he gave our poor prop, a former Rhinos teammate called Ewan Dowes, a proper going-over. Every time there was a scrum, Baz would stick the nut on him, and I remember Baz looking at me as if to say, 'Don't worry, Rob, my argument isn't with you, it's with the big fella.' Nevertheless, I made sure to stay well out of Baz's way for the rest of the game. I was worried that if I made him look stupid, like I usually did in our one-on-one training drills at Leeds, he'd change his mind and give me one of his trademark Scottish kisses.

Brian Noble, the head coach of Bradford and Great Britain, picked me on the bench for the tournament opener against New Zealand in London, which we lost 42–26.

I made it onto the pitch but had to come off with a nasty head injury – and that was my only contribution to the tournament. When journalists were calling for my selection and we were down to just one scrum-half, after Bradford's Paul Deacon suffered a terrible facial injury against the Kiwis, I didn't even make the bench for the must-win game against Australia. Maybe Brian didn't really know what to make of me, or worried that my size would make me a defensive liability against the Aussies and Kiwis. He wasn't the only one, because my international career would be a pretty stop-start affair.

★

Leeds's biggest signing for the 2006 season was Bradford's Jamie Peacock, who had won three Grand Finals with the Bulls, including one against us in 2005. The news that JP was joining Bradford's arch-rivals hadn't exactly gone down well with the Odsal faithful. When he made his 200th Bulls appearance, at Headingley of all places, he was cheered by our fans and given the silent treatment by his own (Bradford hammered us 42–10 and JP played a blinder – as usual). When he played against Hull, Bulls fans waved placards showing JP with a noose around his neck. I mean, it's nice that rugby league fans are a passionate bunch, but that's weird behaviour by anyone's standards.

JP was born and bred in Leeds, just around the corner from Jonesy, but I know the decision to join the Rhinos was a difficult one. JP had been at the Bulls since he was a kid and was adored by their fans. But as far as Gary Hetherington and Tony were concerned, it was a no-brainer. JP wasn't the most talented, but he was an animal on the pitch and

made of granite. There couldn't have been a more determined and competitive player on the planet, which is why
he'd also been made captain of his country. JP is probably
the best signing Leeds have ever made, and I'm sure he now
thinks joining the Rhinos was the best thing he ever did, at
least in terms of his rugby career.

JP was handed Barrie Mac's old number ten shirt
(thankfully, they'd made it a few sizes smaller, otherwise
it would have looked like JP was wearing a dress). And
as well as JP, Tony brought in a few experienced Aussies,
including second-row Mark O'Neill, who had just won an
NRL Grand Final with Wests Tigers, and Manly winger
Scott Donald, to replace Mark Calderwood.

As was usually the case, some imports worked out, some
didn't. Poor old Mark knackered his shoulder in the traditional Boxing Day friendly and barely played a game all
season, while Scott, who was like shit off a shovel, scored a
hatful of tries and was a truly great player for Leeds for the
next few years. Knowing you've got an out-and-out finisher
on the wing, someone who frightens the life out of defenders every time he gets the ball in space, does wonders for
the confidence of those inside him. We knew that if we
took risks by being creative, Scott would be there to make
the risk-taking worthwhile.

After the highs of the previous two seasons, 2006 turned
out to be a year of uncertainty. We were travelling pretty
well until the summer, with a 30–0 victory over the Bulls
at Odsal the obvious highlight (I scored one of my best tries
to break the deadlock, picking up the ball on the halfway
line, stepping past one defender, swerving past another
and touching down in the corner). But we kept picking up

injuries to key players, while others kept announcing they were leaving. As a result, there was a sense around the place that this special thing we'd created was beginning to come apart.

Richie Mathers suffered a season-ending knee injury against Hull, before news broke that he was joining Australian club Gold Coast Titans. In June, Chev Walker announced he was switching to rugby union at the end of the season, before Tony was admitted to hospital with severe gastroenteritis. And after Tony had recovered and got back to work, our assistant coach Brian McDermott immediately announced that he was taking over as head coach at Harlequins, as London Broncos had been rebranded.

After Brian's departure, the wheels fell off our season. We lost our next five games, including to Huddersfield in the semi-finals of the Challenge Cup, and slipped to third in the Super League table. Unsurprisingly, people started asking whether Brian had been the brains of his partnership with Tony and the main reason for our rise. Brian was an excellent coach, and I know some of the lads thought he was a better man-manager than Tony (Tony was notoriously sarcastic and blunt, which rubbed some players up the wrong way). But the truth was that we sustained too many injuries to key players (Maggsy missed most of our run-in through injury) and didn't have enough strength in depth. By September, a lot of our most experienced heads were running on fumes.

After St Helens spanked us 54–18 in the penultimate game of the regular season, Garry Schofield wrote a newspaper column saying it was one of the worst performances he'd ever seen from a Leeds side. Garry was scathing and not afraid to name names (although he was quite nice about me – thanks Garry!). He had a pop at Keith and reckoned JP didn't look like he was enjoying himself. There were also rumours swirling that JP and Tony had fallen out, which wasn't the case at all. Yes, they'd had one or two frank discussions, but they were both understandably frustrated at how the season was panning out. JP had played in five Grand Finals in a row, winning three of them, so the thought of missing out must have been a shock to the system.

We finished third in the table, behind Saints and Hull, which meant we'd play Warrington in the elimination play-off. We'd beaten the Wolves 54–16 only three weeks earlier, and had home advantage again, but this time they pipped us at the post. I scored an early try and we were six points up at half-time. But Warrington drew level after the break, before Maggsy limped off with an injured ankle and Lee Briers kicked the winning one-pointer with a minute to go. That was pretty much the story of our season: we'd been in winning positions in most of our games, but had not been able to close them out. We thought we'd cracked it, but it turned out we hadn't. Time to think again.

★

I was in the Great Britain squad for the Tri-Nations series down under, but might as well not have been. The Aussie media was fascinated by me, as if I was a freak in a travelling circus. And Brian Noble made all the right noises, told the Aussie journalists how brave I was and that I'd be a big threat despite my size. But I never really got a look-in.

I scored a try in the warm-up against Newcastle Knights but didn't play a single minute of the actual tournament.

I could understand why I wasn't in the squad for our first two games against New Zealand and Australia, because St Helens's Sean Long started at scrum-half. And he was brilliant in Sydney, inspiring us to our first victory over the Kangaroos down under since 1992. Before the game, Leon Pryce had uttered the immortal line, 'I'd rather be in Blackpool than Bondi', which caused quite a big stir. The way the Aussie media reacted, you'd have thought Leon had dropped his trousers and curled one out in the middle of the Sydney Opera House. The Australian players didn't seem too thrilled about it either.

About a minute into the game, Willie Mason punched Stuart Fielden and broke his nose, before engaging in a brawl with JP. I'm not sure how Mason stayed on the pitch, but in the second half he elbowed Longy in the head, opening up a big gash. Longy might have been bloodied but he was completely unfazed (as was Adrian Morley, who put in a monstrous performance that night). But having shown the Aussies just how good he could be, Longy didn't stick around for much longer. That was the thing about Longy – he was a massive talent, but he made some pretty strange decisions.

New Zealand beat us 34–4 in Wellington, after which it was decided we'd stay off the beers (the boys had probably celebrated a bit too hard in Sydney). Naturally, a few of the players had a few lagers anyway, which is when things really started going wrong. Longy was a bit loud on the plane back to Australia and had to be moved, because the people in front of him were kicking up a fuss. And after landing,

Brian gave Longy a bit of a telling off. I thought that would be the end of it – some of the lads had gone a bit overboard and a few harsh words had been exchanged, the sort of thing that happens on most rugby tours. But the following day, we were told that Longy was flying home.

As far as I know, it was Longy's decision to jump ship. I think Brian found him difficult to handle, but he knew his team was better with Longy in it. JP, who was skipper on that tour, has since said that he and Brian tried to talk Longy out of it, but Longy, stubborn as he was, wasn't for turning.

I thought his departure might mean Brian would pick me for the must-win game against the Kangaroos in Brisbane, but he plumped for Hull's Richard Horne instead. Richard was a great player, but I was bitterly disappointed. I didn't travel down under thinking I'd play every game, because we had a lot of quality players. And being around those kinds of players for five weeks, training with and learning from them every day, was great in some ways. But it was a long way to travel without getting a chance to show what I could do.

I'm a positive bloke and I didn't get moody. I even felt up to a prank or two. Whenever a Great Britain team was staying in Manly, it was tradition for the whole squad to stroll out of the hotel and straight onto the beach wearing only their towels. They'd then drop their towels, run naked into the sea, have a bit of a swim, collect their towels and head back in. You probably know what's coming next. I started running towards the sea, did a sharp U-turn, gathered all the towels up and legged it. I must have looked like that little old man from the Benny Hill sketches. Our fellow guests were then treated to the sight of twenty-five blokes, all built like brick shithouses, running through the hotel corridors with their hands over their cocks and balls. I say that, but Keith probably just strolled straight past reception, bold as brass, arms swinging by his sides.

Maybe Brian would have given me a go had we reached the final, but the Aussies beat us 33–10, meaning the Kiwis played them instead. There's no getting away from it, I felt like a bit of a spare part on that tour. And there's a strange postscript to that tournament. After we got home, Longy gave my dad his Great Britain shirt, with number seven on the back. When my dad asked him why he was giving it away, Longy replied, 'Rob should have had it in the first place.' Instead of giving it to me, my dad gave it away as a raffle prize.

★

Jamie Peacock, Great Britain captain

I've got no idea why Brian didn't give Rob a chance. We'd lost our key pivot, needed a scrum-half, and Rob was coming off a great season for Leeds, so it was a little bit strange, as were some of the other selections. And it must have been incredibly frustrating for Rob. Can you imagine being on tour that long and not being able to do what you want to do? It's the equivalent of being on a lads' holiday and not being able to drink. But it says a lot about the man that he didn't moan once. He was always positive, always chipper, always supportive, exactly the sort of bloke that every changing room needs. It was all about the team for Rob, rather than his own disappointments.

Rob had a severe caffeine addiction – I'd never seen

anything like it – and never shut up. By that point, he'd probably moved on from *The Office* to *Anchorman*, which he could quote word for word. And did most days. He was constantly taking the piss out of people, pulling pranks. He knew his place, but mostly it didn't matter who they were, he'd say and do what he wanted to them. And because he was a funny fucker, with great wit and timing, he got away with it. As captain, and someone who had recently moved from Bradford to Leeds, I was desperate to create a bond between different players from different teams. And Rob made that job a lot easier.

Actually, I did hear a whimper from Rob, just the once. We'd been on tour for about a month, Rob hadn't played a minute and knew he wasn't going to feature in the do-or-die match against the Aussies. But he was still being flogged in training every day, along with the rest of us. One day, the conditioner had us doing this fitness test he'd nicked from the Canberra Raiders. Rob being as fit as he was, which was probably the fittest in the team, he hit the required levels. But while he was recovering, flat on his back and gasping for air, the conditioner looked up from his clipboard and said, 'Hang on a minute, I got those levels wrong. You need to get one higher . . .' Rob looked across at me and said, 'JP, this bastard's making stuff up . . .'

6

I RECEIVED ANOTHER GANG OF VISITORS TODAY – Barrie Mac, Maggsy, Keith and Mitch Garbutt, a top Aussie lad I played with in my final few seasons at Leeds. Sometimes I think it must be strange for those boys. I spent years taking the piss out of them, picking them up on everything they did, and now they're probably looking at me and thinking, 'I wonder what Rob would have said, if he could still speak.' The banter will be flying and my eyes will be as wide as saucers, because I've just thought of a wicked one-liner (probably about Baz's weight). Unfortunately, it will never leave my head. But it could be worse. At least I'm still well enough to think it. And at least I've still got my mates.

★

Keith Senior, Rhinos teammate

As a group of mates, we can't understand what Rob's going through. We can try, but it's pointless. And he doesn't want us to sit around with long faces, watching what we say, just because he's ill. He just wants us to be normal, to carry on treating him like we always have. Because if we're not normal, and not treating him like we always have, that would suggest we're trying to be sympathetic. And the last thing Rob wants is our sympathy.

It's hard at times, when we're all reminiscing and Rob can't join in. But we try to make sure he's involved as much as possible, shifting the conversation so that Rob can chime in with yes or no answers. But most of the time we just take the piss out of him, just like the old days. He doesn't get spared because he's got MND, he gets it in the neck like everybody else. It's beautiful to see his reaction. He's constantly grinning, and occasionally he'll dissolve into floods of laughter, with tears rolling down his face. One time, Rob was laughing so much he started choking, which is probably not ideal. And when he goes, we all go. It probably does us all the world of good.

We know there's nothing we can do to make Rob better, but as a group of friends we can take him to another place for a couple of hours. Just by telling old stories, just by being as natural as possible. And it's great for us to know that whatever it is he's going through, he hasn't lost his positivity and wicked sense of humour. Despite it all, he's still the same Rob inside.

★

Keith's right. Empathy is fine, sympathy not so much. And nothing should be off limits, because it certainly wasn't at the Rhinos. Some of the chat we have on WhatsApp can get pretty dark. The other day, the lads were talking about a racehorse they'd all bought shares in, called Burrow Seven, to raise money for the fight against MND. One of the investors – whose name I won't divulge, because he'd be mortified – is tight as anything, so I popped out and started digging him out about it. And he fired back with, 'Are you still alive?'

Reading that, you might be wincing. You might think it was out of order. But you have to understand how close we are. I immediately hit back with, 'As long as you're spending money, I'll make sure I'm still breathing.' I love stuff like that, the more inappropriate the better. I imagined the lads all giggling in their living rooms and having to lie to their partners about what they found so funny.

As far as I'm concerned, if you can't have a laugh and a joke, however desperate things might seem, life's not worth living. For that reason, since being diagnosed, I've created an atmosphere where I'm friend first, former rugby player second, probably entertainer third (see footnote, p.24).

★

Me and Lindsey got married on 30 December 2006, followed by our honeymoon in the Maldives. And yes, I did take my training kit with me. Our wedding was just about the perfect day, probably because Lindsey planned absolutely everything. As with most things outside of rugby, she told me what to do and I just made sure I turned up on time. The reception was in a place called Oulton Hall, a big old country house just outside Leeds. It needed to be big, because Lindsey's nana had thirteen brothers and sisters (no TV in those days) and almost everyone I'd ever played with was invited to the evening do.

There was a chocolate fountain (Big Fat Barrie Mac was like Augustus Gloop from *Charlie and the Chocolate Factory*, virtually on his knees, ladling it into his mouth with his hands), a casino (right up Granddad Bob's street) and the first dance was 'Time of My Life', from *Dirty Dancing*. That didn't go quite to plan, because the DJ played a different version of the song than we'd been practising to. You can hear me in the video, counting the steps and telling Lindsey what to do, while my sisters – competitive dancers, remember – are flinging themselves all over the place, like a couple of Jennifer Greys.

But besides that fairy-tale day, when Lindsey became Mrs Burrow, there wasn't much laughing and joking before the 2007 Super League season kicked off. Going two seasons without a trophy hadn't been part of Gary Hetherington's grand plan. Meanwhile, fans were wondering if talk of a Leeds Rhinos dynasty had been a pipe dream and Tony Smith was a busted flush. But when Tony announced he was leaving Leeds at the end of the season to become full-time Great Britain head coach, I was shocked and disappointed.

I completely understood why the RFL wanted him and why he went for the job. He'd been head coach of Leeds for four seasons, led them to their first title for thirty-two years, and wanted a new challenge. There was a World Cup coming up in 2008, and Tony probably looked at some of the talent he'd have at his disposal and thought, 'You know what? We could actually give the Aussies and Kiwis a run for their money.' But Tony was the best coach I'd ever had, by a long shot. Him becoming GB head coach might be good for my international aspirations, but I hated the thought of not working with him day in, day out.

Tony wasn't one of those coaches who simply worked with what he had; he was all about improving players. That's what the best coaches do. That Leeds project was perfect for him. He had a load of young players to work with, none of whom had achieved anything and all of whom were desperate to learn. At the start of every season, he'd have a look at a player, size up his deficiencies and go about polishing him up. Tony's attention to detail was second to none, and no one was so good that they couldn't be made better.

But Tony didn't just improve players, he created a culture. When he first arrived at Leeds, he knew exactly what he wanted the club to be like. He got rid of players who didn't fit his system and brought in players who did. You might have been the best player in the world, but if you were a dickhead, Leeds wasn't the place for you. Tony was blunt but honest. If you played well, he'd tell you. If you didn't, he'd have no problem telling you that as well. But under Tony, I felt confident every time I walked onto the pitch. I loved every minute of working under Tony, and he made me the player I ended up being.

During our pre-season training camp in Dublin, I had a distinct feeling that something was different from the year before, that everyone seemed more focused and determined. And the announcement of Tony's impending departure affected the younger players, those academy graduates whose careers he'd shaped, particularly. We desperately wanted to give him the send-off we thought his efforts deserved, namely another Grand Final victory.

Tony's only two pre-season signings seemed to increase that possibility. New Zealand full-back Brent Webb had been brilliant in the recent Tri-Nations, scoring three tries against us in two games. Less was known about Samoan prop Kylie Leuluai, and there were the inevitable gags about his name in the newspapers. But after witnessing a couple of his gym sessions, I could safely say that he didn't just bench-press more than any female Australian pop stars I knew, he could probably bench-press Australia. And on the field, he was one of the hardest hitters I'd ever seen. That's why fans of Manly Sea Eagles, who we signed him from, had soon stopped calling him 'Minogue' and started calling him 'The Hulk' instead.

Kylie's reputation as a hard man embarrassed him a little bit. He was actually very religious, very easy-going and very hard to wind up, which is why he became my new changing room target. He was basically a straight replacement for Barrie Mac. I teased poor old Kylie relentlessly; every day I'd try to get under his skin. And the best thing about Kylie was that he couldn't resist getting sucked into a bit of tit-for-tat – and wasn't very good at it.

One day, to get him back for something he'd done to me, I nicked Kylie's car keys, borrowed a hole punch from the office and poured all the little paper circles into his air conditioning fan. When Kylie got in his car after training, he turned his fan on full whack and all these paper circles came blasting out. He must have sensed I was watching – of course I was, from behind a curtain – and managed to keep his temper in check, but I could tell he was absolutely fuming.

I also hid prawns all over the inside of Kylie's car and

sprayed his hubcaps pink. Amazingly, Kylie only lost his temper with me once. I'd gone the whole hog and stolen that poor car, and when I finally brought it back, he started strangling me, like Homer Simpson with Bart. If JP hadn't stepped in, Kylie might have killed me.

★

Danny McGuire, Rhinos teammate

Rob seemed to have a thing about props, he was always picking on them. The bigger the better. Maybe it was because he knew they couldn't catch him, or maybe it was because he knew that if they did catch him, they'd be too embarrassed to do anything – apart from that one time with Kylie, when he almost put Rob to sleep. Not that I blamed the big man, because that must have been about the twentieth time Rob had played a serious prank on him.

I was one of the quieter members of the team, liked to just go about my business. But I loved having someone like Rob in the changing room. Whatever you do for a job, you want it to be an enjoyable environment. And Rob was one of those people I looked forward to seeing every day. You get so many different characters in any team – serious people, laid-back people, miserable people, happy people – and Rob was the bloke who'd get everyone laughing. Even after a bad defeat, he'd usually manage to make you smile.

Me and Rob had a pact – an unspoken agreement – that we'd look after each other. We exchanged lots of nods and winks, usually when he was about to pull off another one of his pranks. And while he was wading into Jamie Jones-Buchanan for five minutes, doing Bo' Selecta! impressions

115

and calling him a 'proper bell-end', I'd be keeping my head down and giggling. But he did get me a couple of times, inevitably. He just couldn't help himself.

Before one top-of-the-table clash against St Helens, me and Rob turned up early, as we always did. After a bit of a chat – quite a sombre one, because it was such a big game – I wandered off for my usual massage. And when I came back, my white Calvin Klein pants, which were hanging on my peg, had a big brown stain down the backside. I grabbed them as quick as I could and turned them inside out, but all the lads had already seen them and were rolling about on the floor, laughing their heads off.

Those pants were fresh on that morning – honest! – and it turned out that Rob had licked a Jaffa Cake and smeared chocolate on them. That was classic Rob. Everyone was trying to be serious but he couldn't help messing around. He was the littlest bloke in the team, with the biggest sense of humour.

★

In the interests of historical accuracy, I must admit that teammates did occasionally get the better of me. Every week, the players would be given these sheets of blue paper, detailing our various promotional and community responsibilities: appearing at sponsors' dinners, cutting ribbons at fetes, coaching kids, that kind of thing. Anyway, JP got hold of the template for these sheets, printed one off and wrote on it, 'Judging gnome contest, Harrogate garden show', before giving it to one of the coaches to pass on to me.

The next time I bumped into JP, I sidled up to him and said, 'JP, they're taking the piss out of me now.'

'Why's that?' JP replied.

'They're sending me to Harrogate garden show.'

'Harrogate's not far. What's wrong with you?'

'They've got me judging a gnome contest.'

'Really? Out of order. I can't think why . . .'

I soon twigged it was a wind-up, unlike some of the other lads JP had targeted. Kylie seemed over the moon that he was being sent to judge a dog show, while Lee Smith and Jamie Thackray were less pleased that they were being sent to judge a chav fancy-dress contest at Beeston Working Men's Club. When Jamie asked why they'd got the gig, I replied, 'Because you both look like one.'

Then there was the time we all attended a dinner in Leeds. When we got out, it was absolutely freezing, so Keith took the opportunity to wee in a bottle and pour it all over the locks and windscreen of my car. It took me about fifteen minutes to open the door, and I then had to sit there for half an hour, shivering and staring at Keith's frozen urine. Try explaining that to your wife: 'Sorry I'm late home, honey, had to wait for Keith's piss to defrost . . .'

Brent and Kylie showed exactly what they were all about in our Super League opener against Salford, the former scoring two tries and the latter putting in some bone-crunching hits in a narrow win. It wasn't long before fans in the South Stand were chanting, 'Brent Webb is Super-man!', while Kylie would also be massive for us that season, a lovely bloke off the pitch but bristling with bad intentions on it.

But after two defeats in three games, against Catalans and newly promoted Hull KR (my 200th senior game), one or two journalists started questioning our title credentials and there was even a bit of disquiet among the fans. But what some people hadn't realized was that Super League had simply become more competitive, which was surely a good thing. We weren't the only so-called big side on the wrong end of surprise results in those early rounds: defending champions St Helens lost two of their first three games against Harlequins and Wakefield, while Wigan lost at home to Hull KR. There were no easy games any more, with hammerings few and far between.

The doubters were out in force again following a last-gasp defeat by Wigan at Headingley. But we then reeled off three big wins in a row, beating Warrington 52–10, St Helens 38–19 and Catalans 54–8. That victory over Saints was particularly pleasing because the media had been banging on about how great they were all season, or at least since their stuttering start.

Our game against Bradford in Cardiff, as part of the inaugural Millennium Magic Bank Holiday weekend, was about as strange as they come. The game was a heavyweight slugfest, two sworn enemies trading almighty blows, but also very controversial. With a few minutes to go, twelve tries had been scored (including my fifth in five games and Brent Webb's second hat-trick in a row) but we were trailing 38–36. The Bulls then had two tries disallowed by the video referee (both decisions could easily have gone the other way), before on-field referee Steve Ganson awarded us a dodgy penalty (Matt Cook was ruled to have picked the ball up in an offside position, even though it had come off one of our players' boots). Kev's penalty came back off the crossbar, Jordan Tansey seized on the loose ball and went over for the winning try, just as the hooter sounded. We were obviously ecstatic, but replays showed that Jordan was miles in front of Kev when he kicked the ball. Why Steve Ganson didn't refer it upstairs I'll never know, and the Bulls were understandably furious.

That was a shame, because Millennium Magic, which should have been remembered as a big success, was now being called a 'farce' and a 'debacle' by the media. Bulls head coach Steve McNamara said his side had been cheated and accused Ganson of 'inventing' the penalty that led to our winning try. But things started getting a bit silly when the Bulls chairman demanded we 'do the right thing' and hand back the two points. Sometimes in sport, bad decisions go against you and you've just got to suck it up. The saga dragged on for weeks, during which time any sympathy for the Bulls evaporated.

Wigan knocked us out of the Challenge Cup in our next game, before Hull pipped us on their patch. Up until the end of May, the most wins we'd managed to string together was four. And at the end of June, we started to have our traditional summer stumble. First, Bradford got their revenge by spanking us 38–14 at Headingley, which must have tasted sweet as anything for the Bulls players and fans. And after beating St Helens, with me scoring a nice solo try on my 200th Rhinos appearance and Ryan Hall notching his first of many for the club, we lost two in a row against Wigan and Wakefield.

That left us third in the table, and suddenly some fans wanted Tony Smith sacked. I thought that was incredibly unfair. We were still in the hunt and as determined as ever, but our tuning was just a little bit off. Maybe we were just a little bit jaded because, after a two-week break, we found our stride again. We were trailing Harlequins 16–6 at half-time, in baking heat in London, before everything suddenly clicked. We won the second half 48–4, running in eight tries, and I had a feeling that we were bubbling up at just the right time. Even Brent Webb's three-match ban for two high tackles during that game was a blessing in disguise. Brent had played a lot of rugby and was starting to creak, so the break did him the world of good.

Losing against Hull meant we couldn't finish above St Helens at the top of the table, but we secured second place by beating Wakefield 46–4 on the final day of the regular season. The nature of that win, razor sharp in attack and robust in defence, suggested we were peaking at just the right time.

I was one of four Rhinos to make the Super League Dream Team, along with JP (for a sixth time), Gareth Ellis and Scott Donald. I was also named Rhinos player of the season, while some people thought I should have been Super League Man of Steel, or at least in the running. Looking back, I probably reached my peak in 2007. I started every game I was fit for and had developed into a more complete player. I wasn't just an attacking threat, I was also a solid defender, an organizer who teammates listened to. No one was calling me a novelty any more. My size had almost been forgotten. Almost.

It was nice getting those personal accolades, but I would have swapped them all for another appearance in a Grand Final. And I really thought we'd get there. We were training like demons and I'd find myself looking around the dressing room, at people like JP and Kev, and thinking, 'I like how these lads look. I like how they're talking. They're not going to put up with anything but winning.' Then there was the Tony Smith factor, this feeling among the younger guys that we needed to come through as a farewell present to him.

Our first play-off game was away against St Helens, who had finished one point ahead of us in the league table. We'd beaten them twice already that season and were one of only two teams to turn them over at Knowsley Road. The media were mostly backing Saints to win their second straight title and the bookies had installed them as odds-on favourites. But I didn't think we were the second-best team in the country, despite what the league table said.

That was a grim game of rugby. Some of the big lads will tell you it was up there with the most brutal they ever played. There weren't even ten seconds on the clock when JP clattered his opposition prop Nick Fozzard, hitting him high, which set the tone for the rest of the game. To be fair, there was a bit of class on display. Lee Smith gave us the lead with a length-of-the-field try, before Saints stand-off Leon Pryce pulled off a nifty bit of footwork and scored next to our posts. But most of the rest of it was a savage war of attrition.

Saints deservedly led 8–6 at half-time, but we battered them after the interval. Kylie Leuluai was like a wrecking ball, repeatedly crashing into their defensive line, while JP was a man possessed, as ferocious as I'd ever seen him on a rugby field. How St Helens stopped us from scoring I'll never know.

Their refusal to yield was best summed up by the sight of Aussie centre Matt Gidley, his face all bloodied and bandaged up, chasing down Brent Webb and pulling off a try-saving tackle. In fact, that moment was the game in miniature. It was two groups of blokes unwilling to accept that they could possibly lose. As it was, they pipped us 10–8. But we wasted a few chances to win it, and there was a feeling after the game that we'd softened them up, taken them to their limit, and that if we met again in the Grand Final, they'd break.

But before we could think about getting revenge over Saints, there was the not-so-small matter of playing Wigan in the final eliminator. The Warriors were coming like a train at just the right time, winning six and drawing one of their previous seven games, including two sudden-death play-off victories over Bradford and Hull. They'd also beaten us three times that season, twice at Headingley. Every campaign, there are teams you can't quite work out, and Wigan were that team for us in 2007. But when it came to the big one, it wasn't even close.

We barely made a mistake in the first half before cutting loose after the interval. I grabbed a couple of tries, as did Brent Webb, JP was immense once again and Kev couldn't miss with the boot. He even popped over a couple of late drop-goals, as practice for the Grand Final. That was Kev all over: we'd put the game to bed, and were entitled to ease off a little, but he was already planning ahead. And winning 36–6 sent our confidence through the roof.

Amazingly, Leeds hadn't played St Helens in a major showpiece since the 1978 Challenge Cup Final, when Leeds came from behind to win at Wembley. St Helens's current side was a very good one, with class throughout. They had a world-class half-back pairing in Sean Long and Leon Pryce, a brilliant full-back in Paul Wellens and a couple of world-class centres in Australian Matt Gidley and

Kiwi Willie Talau, who were just about the perfect combination. They also had an inspirational skipper in Keiron Cunningham, while James Roby and Maurie Fa'asavalu were proper handfuls off the bench.

Saints were also gunning for a back-to-back treble, having swept the board in 2006 and already won the Challenge Cup and League Leaders' Shield in 2007. Oh, and they were unbeaten in their four previous Grand Final appearances. But despite all that, we were confident we were more than a match for them.

It was becoming apparent that getting knocked out of the Challenge Cup so early had been a blessing in disguise, because it meant we were able to recover properly during the blank weeks, while Wigan and Saints were doing battle. Wigan eventually lost in the semi-finals, while Saints went all the way to Wembley, where they beat Catalans. That might explain why they looked close to folding at the end of our play-off game. They were like a heavyweight boxer who had built up an early lead but was now backed onto the ropes, blowing out of his arse, just trying to survive the championship rounds. And while Saints players were up on bricks, smoke pouring from their bonnets, we were still on the road, keeping sharp and grooved. We lost some juice in the eliminator against Wigan, but it meant we were revving coming into the final.

The night before the big game at Old Trafford, Tony gathered the squad together for a meeting. That was an emotional couple of hours. I remember looking around the room and thinking, 'There's no way we're losing.' I saw the belief in my teammates' eyes, and belief is catching.

There was Kev, our dear, dependable leader, exuding

calm; Maggsy, a playmaker capable of conjuring rabbits from hats; Kylie, the nastiest nice bloke I'd ever met; Scott Donald, electric on the wing; Brent Webb, a world-class full-back who could create and finish; Matty Diskin, a good old-fashioned hooker who controlled the ruck area and defended like a demon every week; Jonesy, who Kev once said 'would fight you for fresh air'; Gareth Ellis, a top-class back-rower respected all over the world; Lee Smith, the best young winger in the country; Clinton Toopi, our Kiwi centre who skittled defenders like ninepins; Keith, who had been doing it for club and country for a decade; Ali Lauiti'iti, who could do things with a ball other players could only dream of; Ryan Bailey, another Leeds lad who intimidated opponents and was the last person they wanted to see coming off the bench; Carl Ablett, who had sustained a potentially career-ending knee injury, stayed mentally strong and come back stronger. Ian Kirke, quiet as a mouse but who never stopped grinding.

Most of that team had won and lost Grand Finals, so we discussed the bitter experience of losing and the sheer joy of winning, and how wonderful it would be to feel that way again. Keith talked about wanting to win it for his daughter. Kev (who had just signed a new four-year deal, which spoke volumes about his love for the club) talked about wanting to win it for his son. When it came to JP's turn, I thought he was going to break down. He had won so much with Bradford that I think he was quite emotional – and relieved – about finally having the chance to win something with Leeds, as had been his plan.

JP echoed Jonesy's thoughts, as outlined earlier, the idea that he'd taken on the spirits of his teammates, and that they'd be with him throughout the eighty minutes to come. I've never known anyone as passionate or proud as JP, for club and country. He emptied the tank every game he played, and his form in the final few weeks of that 2007 season, when it really mattered, was simply awe-inspiring. The fact that a towering figure like JP seemed so confident, and so at one with his teammates, was very comforting.

I honestly can't remember what I said. Looking back, I had a hundred reasons for wanting to beat St Helens. I wanted to do it for my family, I wanted to do it for my teammates, I wanted to do it for Tony, I wanted to do it for the fans and the city of Leeds. But you can overthink these things. When all is said and done, sport is simply about winning. I suppose I just wanted to do it for me.

I always had nerves before a game of that magnitude, but never so it was a problem. I'd spent all week thinking what it would be like, walking out at Old Trafford again, and when I did, it was even better than I'd imagined. Nerves translated into positive energy, and I was desperate to get stuck into St Helens.

There were over 70,000 people in Old Trafford on the night and the weather was unusually balmy for October. But one thing you can normally rely on is Sean Long running a show, which he did for the first ten minutes. However, when Longy missed a straightforward penalty and Kev popped one over a few minutes later (making him the first Leeds player to appear and score in every game of a season), that changed the momentum. We'd won the first skirmish within the war, and we took a lot of confidence from that.

Brent Webb went over for the first try of the game, after some beautiful interplay between Kev, Keith and Scott

Donald, and a try of that quality always gives a team a major boost and takes the wind out of the opposition. James Roby did reduce the deficit, after a great break by Longy, but we were all over them in the closing stages of the half. Twice they had to drop out from under their own sticks, and Scott Donald went agonizingly close to scoring, after some silky footballing skills from Maggsy. And when the half-time hooter went, there was a feeling among our team that if we cranked it up just a couple of notches, Saints would finally sag on the ropes and stop punching back.

Sure enough, two quick tries early in the second half finally broke the Saints' spirit. The first was from the barn-storming Ali Lauiti'iti, who beat Matt Gidley on the outside before holding off three tacklers to score in the corner. We knew that was a huge moment, which is why we celebrated so wildly. The second was one of the greatest ever seen in a Grand Final, Keith releasing Scott Donald and our trusty Aussie flyer leaving Paul Wellens for dead with a savage swerve. That made it 18–6 with just over half an hour to play, and the ear-splitting noise of our fans suggested the game was pretty much up.

When I knocked over a drop-goal, it meant St Helens had to score at least three times to have any chance of winning. That didn't happen. Instead, Lee Smith, yet another academy graduate, scored a brilliant try, leaping like Michael Jordan to retrieve a cross-kick from Maggsy and touching down next to the posts, before Jonesy blasted over in the dying seconds to make it 33–6. No one loved Leeds like Jonesy loved Leeds. He was the ultimate unsung hero, a bloke who gladly ran through walls every week for too little recognition. For all the individual brilliance on display that night, Jonesy's try was the most symbolic.

I knew we'd won long before the end, but it's only when the hooter goes that it all starts to sink in. It's impossible to describe the feeling of elation, ecstasy almost, when you're running around the pitch like a headless chicken, celebrating with your mates. Only six weeks earlier, some of our own fans had given up on us. But now we'd pulled out one of the greatest team performances in a major final. And winning in style is what Leeds were always meant to be about. On top of that, by winning our second Grand Final in four years, we'd got rid of the tag of bottlers and under-achievers once and for all. If we could win two in four years, what was stopping that side from winning a few more?

Sadly, the great Leeds scrum-half Jeff Stevenson died on the morning of the game. Like me, Jeff was only five foot five. And while I'd never seen any footage of him, I'm told he played a bit like me, too – quick off the mark and a terrier in defence. I don't know if they awarded me the Harry Sunderland Trophy as a nod to Jeff (he won the Lance Todd Trophy in 1957, when Leeds beat Barrow in the Challenge Cup Final), but it only made the day more special. If Jeff was looking down on us, I'm sure he would have been chuffed by the tribute the team served up.

When I finally got back to the changing room, after my man-of-the-match interviews, it was pandemonium. It was a load of blokes who had been through hell and high water together, who had looked down and out but somehow dredged up their finest performance of the season when it mattered most. That's character, and no wonder they'd completely lost control of their emotions. As far as I was concerned, any one of those blokes could have been man of the match, whether it was a back who had led Saints a merry dance or a forward who had smashed Saints to bits. That's how good we were that day.

We were certainly a better side than when we won the Grand Final in 2004, although the basic recipe remained the same. Tony still regarded that group of players who had come through the academy together – me, Kev, Maggsy, Jonesy, Matty Diskin – as the team's backbone.

On a basic level, he thought we were decent blokes, which was a big part of his coaching philosophy. We respected each other, worked hard for each other, made sacrifices for each other. And he believed that as long as we were there, any signings he made would soon get sucked into our way of thinking, converted to our cause. And if they didn't, Tony knew they couldn't possibly be decent enough blokes and therefore weren't proper Rhinos players.

Tony was brilliant at what he did, but most coaches don't have the luxury of walking into a club and finding a backbone, as well as a heart and soul, already in place. They have to try and build it all themselves, conjure some chemistry from nothing, which is a lot harder to do. It also helped that his backbone included the playmaking combination of me, Kev and Maggsy.

Me and Maggsy had been playing with each other for so long it was like we were connected by a piece of invisible string. I knew what he was going to do and where he was going to be, and vice versa. When I went on a break, he was there next to me. When he needed someone to pass to, I was right behind him. Sometimes, me and Maggsy would be running side by side and the rest of the team would be

nowhere in sight. It was really quite spooky, almost tele-
pathic. To be fair, Keith was also in on the witchcraft. He
was the perfect, big-striding centre, always punching holes
in the opposition defences. And whenever he looked to
offload, I'd be on his shoulder. Sometimes he didn't even
look, just lobbed it over his head. That's how much we
trusted each other.

Having said all that, that core group wouldn't have won
anything if it weren't for Tony's additions and refinements.
Tony changed the ethos, instilled a winning mentality. If
he'd gone out on a loss, it would have been a travesty. But
winning meant the fans would remember him as the great
coach he most certainly was.

Tony knew we weren't the finished article after winning the Grand Final in 2004 and that consistent success
would take time and patience. So, each year, he made
players better, added new ones and removed others, as if
he was trying to create a perfect machine. That wasn't
easy, because not every top-quality player was right for the
group. If a player was too selfish or too negative or didn't
work hard enough, Tony wasn't interested. Even the overseas players were never full of themselves. People like Kylie
Leuluai and Ali Lauiti'iti were world-class, but they were
down-to-earth grafters. And they had that trait of any great
Rhino – desperate determination. Come to think of it, JP
should have 'Desperately Determined' written on his grave-
stone.

Everyone in that side could play rugby, was fast, strong
and skilful. But they were just the basics. On top of that,
everyone came to know his teammates' strengths and
weaknesses inside out, so that he could complement and

compensate. No one wanted to let anyone else down – even when we were getting battered, we stayed proud and never stopped trying. And everyone was ravenously hungry. Whether it was Keith Senior, Jamie Peacock, Jamie Jones-Buchanan or Kylie Leuluai, they loved the club – and each other – so much that they'd do anything to win, short of scratching someone's eyes out. None of us was ever satisfied. Greedy bastards, that's what we were. Once we'd tasted success, we wanted more and more of it. That in turn made us want to work even harder, so that we'd get better and win more. It was a virtuous circle.

★

Tony Smith, Rhinos head coach

To be honest, I didn't think I had a dynasty on my hands at Leeds. I'm not sure anyone thought that. It was probably Gary Hetherington's grand plan, as I'm sure it would be any team owner's grand plan, but I don't think even he thought the success would continue for another ten or so years.

As a coach, you can't just presume it's going to continue, because every year is a new campaign, with different challenges. The moment a player leaves or a new player joins, it's a different team and you have to start again. You just hope things are going to be better than the year before. What made it easier was that when I did make changes, everyone bought into it. That's what made that team special, and why those changes appeared seamless. And it made no difference whether we'd won the Grand Final the season before or not, we always wanted to improve, as individuals and as a team.

I was just delighted to be working with such a talented bunch of blokes. But more than that, I was incredibly grateful to be working with and learning from some great human beings. Even the best people have their idiosyncrasies and faults, and it's not as if players and staff were turning up at Headingley every morning with bouquets of flowers. But those Leeds players were good people. Respectful, hard-working, put the team before themselves and were determined to solve problems whenever they arose. The way they went about their business is how every team should operate.

Every time someone asks me about coaching the Rhinos, I'm reminded how fortunate I was and of the lasting friendships I made, which mean so much more than any material things in life. And one of the guys I was most honoured to call a friend was Rob. I admired him for his bravery, his humility, his loyalty and his incredible commitment to improvement.

Too often in life, we wait until tragedy has struck before we pay tribute to people we respect and think most of, which can make those tributes sound insincere. There's a lesson there for all of us. And it's important to note that people like me aren't saying all these nice things about Rob just because of his illness. It's not out of sympathy; we're saying these things because they're an accurate reflection of the great player he was and the great man he still is.

As a coach, you don't always know what kind of impact you have on players. But a few years ago, when Rob was working with the Rhinos academy, he phoned me out of the blue. He said how much he respected me as a coach and asked if I'd do some mentoring for him. That was one of the biggest compliments I'd ever been given. For the next year or so, we'd meet up every few months. I'd give him advice and things to work on before the next meeting, or we'd just sit and chat about different aspects of coaching.

During one meeting, Rob suddenly started reciting something I'd said to him way back in 2004. I couldn't remember saying it, but he remembered it word for word. He went on to explain the impact those words had on him and how every time someone opens their mouth, they can affect the person they're speaking to. That had a huge impact on me. If one of your players is going to recite something you say fifteen years later, whether it makes them feel good or bad, then you have a big responsibility to say the right things.

Since then, I've spent a lot more time thinking about how I speak to people. And that story tells you so much about Rob and why he was a coach's dream. The best players are like sponges, take everything in. And they never stop teaching you things, even long after you've stopped coaching them.

7

My dad's a union man and still does a bit of work for the GMB trade union. When he was doing it full-time, he'd work with rugby players, get them to think about what they might do with their lives after they'd hung up their boots. One year, he came up with the idea of a cookery course, an NVQ in international cuisine, and a load of players from Leeds and Wakefield signed up for it. If I remember rightly, Lee Smith, Scott Donald and Brent Webb got involved. None of them made a career of it, although Scott was pretty handy and Brent still posts dishes on social media. I'd be surprised if Lee can cook a Pot Noodle.

I mention it because it shows that Dad has always been about getting people justice and helping them find a way forward. And since my diagnosis, he's been determined to get me fixed. He's head of Burrow MND Research Inc., always Googling and watching YouTube videos. He follows different MND groups on Facebook and Twitter and tells me about all the exciting stuff that's going on, in terms of possible treatments. It gives me hope but can also be frustrating, because there seems to be a lot of stuff going on in America that isn't going on in the UK. And you've got to have a healthy dose of scepticism, because YouTube is full of Americans who claim to have been miraculously cured of all sorts of diseases. People who couldn't walk or speak and suddenly can.

Dad's also mates with a guy called Neil Verner, a physicist and inventor with MND who lives down the road in Wakefield. Neil was diagnosed in 2016 and given eighteen months to live, but came up with his own treatment, based on electronic signals in the brain, and is still hanging in there. Neil played rugby himself and could empathize with what I was going through better than most.

When I first met Neil, he said to me, 'Do you get fed up with people fussing around you? All I want to talk about is rugby and boobs, but all anyone else wants to talk about is my illness, very earnestly.' Neil also said he was going to cure the both of us. I don't think Dad actually thinks Neil, or anyone else, is going to cure me. But he's like me, a man on a mission to find a cure in the future. Like Dad says, wherever there is hope, there's potential, and what sounds like science fiction one day is humdrum the next.

I spend a couple of days a week at Mum and Dad's, when Lindsey's working. I don't like to talk about the ins and outs of MND and they respect that. It's simply about spending precious time together, ploughing through tea and biscuits, chatting about nothing and having a few laughs, exactly the things we'd do if I didn't have MND.

Lindsey will drop me off and Mum and Dad will help

me into the house, one on either side of me. I find accepting their help difficult, because it's what I thought I'd do for them, when they got old and frail. I'll keep telling them I'm fine – it's become my catchphrase – when I know full well I'd topple over if they weren't there to support me.

Mum is always upbeat, chuckles away the whole time I'm there. I'll point to my head and she'll start scratching it, because she'll think I've got an itch. What I'm actually saying is, 'Can you give me my phone?' We'll stick *Impractical Jokers* on the telly, or some Will Ferrell, and giggle away. If the sun's out, we'll sit in the garden. If I want to go for a wee, I'll go in the bushes. It's a bit trickier if I need a poo, because they haven't got a downstairs toilet and I draw the line at dropping my trousers and doing it on the lawn.

The other day I was desperate, so Mum and Dad had to help me up the stairs. We only managed a few steps before someone lost their footing (probably Dad, because he's clumsy as anything) and we all fell backwards and ended up in a heap on the floor. Dad thought I was crying, but I was actually in hysterics. Mum found it funny as well, but Dad was a bit upset. He thought he'd let me down. For days, he kept asking me if I was OK, and I'd just start giggling again. Meanwhile, the story had become more and more exaggerated. By the time my sisters got to hear about it, we'd fallen from top to bottom.

Dad tried to feed me the other day and I flashed him a look of pure fear. To be fair, he has a habit of missing my mouth and hitting me on the nose with the spoon. Eventually he said, 'Do you want your mam to feed you instead?', and I summoned the strength to say, 'Yes!' Dad looked at me surprised, as if to say, 'Blimey, he must be terrified, that's the first thing he's said in ages.'

Mum says I seem more worried about Dad than myself, and she's probably right. Actually, I worry about the both of them. For Mum and Dad, it must seem like only yesterday that I was that tiny little kid with bundles of energy, running riot at Primrose Valley. And it *was* almost yesterday that they were watching me run riot for Leeds. Now they're helping me walk, pushing me around in a wheelchair, feeding and falling down the stairs with me. I can't even say thank you. But I am grateful. And I hope they know I'd do it for them.

★

Geoff and Irene Burrow, Rob's Mum and Dad

Irene: When Rob phoned us from the clinic to tell us he'd been diagnosed with MND, we were on our knees. Literally. I'd had a bad feeling for a while – call it mother's intuition – but the moment we had it confirmed, our whole world collapsed. Poor Lindsey was in such a state, she fell to the floor when she walked through the door. But the first thing she said to us was, 'I'll look after him. I'll make sure he gets all the love in the world.'

Lindsey is unbelievable. We call her Superwoman, because she never looks any different or seems to be down. The kids don't miss out on anything and watching her with Rob is amazing. When she's helping him get about, she'll get behind him, put her arms underneath his and say, 'Look, I'm hardly touching him and he's doing fine.' But when Rob sees me and Geoff coming, I'll see the fear in his eyes. I'll have one arm, Geoff will have the other, and we'll be wobbling all over the place. He must feel like he's in a scrum again.

They've always had this thing that everyone has to carry on as normal, with no moaning or crying, and we know we have to be positive for Rob. But sometimes that's easier said than done. On Jackson's second birthday, I felt so sorry for Rob. Jackson is a proper little lad, loves rough and tumble, and if Rob had been well, he'd have been throwing him all over the place. But Rob couldn't even sit Jackson on his knee without the fear of dropping him. And because Jackson has seen us feeding his daddy, he'll toddle up to him and put his cup to his mouth. That's very sweet, but it also makes me feel sad.

We have good and bad days. Sometimes, we're able to talk about Rob's illness. It even helps. Other times, we shy away from it. Geoff can be terrible, and I can tell when he's struggling. He'll admit that Rob and Lindsey are coping with it better than him. But it's to be expected in a situation like this.

Geoff: When Rob was diagnosed with MND, I did wonder if it was our fault for letting him play rugby. The first thing Irene said to Rob was, 'Do you think it's because of all the head knocks you got?' She blamed the sport, couldn't even watch it for a while. But it's difficult to stop someone doing something they enjoy. And if he hadn't played, we wouldn't have all those happy memories. Obviously, I'd swap all those memories for Rob having his health back. But we don't want to be knocking rugby, and Rob wouldn't want us knocking rugby. It's been so good to him, and it's probably just bad luck.

Irene: When Rob was a boy, I'd be worried watching him play. I remember Chev Walker, who was a really big lad, enormous for his age, chasing Rob and me thinking, 'My God, Rob! Run! Run! Don't let him catch you!' Eventually, Chev did catch him and I thought Rob would never get up.

When he started playing men's rugby, I'd get uptight a couple of days before a game and be right on edge until the final hooter. I'd watch the teams walking onto the field and say to Geoff, 'Look at him, he's a big 'un. Rob will have to stay out of his way.' But we weren't the only ones. Most of the other parents were nervous, because it's such a physical sport. Thank goodness Rob was able to dodge out of harm's way, most of the time. And when he did get injured, which wasn't often, he dusted himself down and carried on.

Geoff: When I was a kid, I played for Leeds in my dreams and scored in every game. I watched all the greats, back when Leeds used to win things – Lewis Jones, the Welsh wizard who captained Leeds to their first Championship in 1961; Bev Risman, who kicked four goals in the 1968 Challenge Cup Final, most famous for Don Fox's missed conversion in the final minute; John Atkinson, who scored the winning try against Castleford in the 1969 Championship Final; Syd Hynes, who, along with Atkinson, won the Ashes with Great Britain in 1970; John Holmes, who played 625 games for Leeds and had the dubious honour of playing one game with me. So to sit in the stands at Headingley and watch my son follow in the footsteps of all those heroes was surreal. It felt like all my dreams had come true. Maybe I should take some credit for Rob's successes? Actually, no. I can safely say that Rob got none of his sporting talent or fighting spirit from me.

It was a proud day when Rob signed for Leeds. We've still got the photograph of him with Dean Bell and Bob Pickles. It didn't really bother me when people kept saying he was too small, I was just happy he'd found something he enjoyed doing. I must admit, I thought Rob might have a short career in rugby, even when he was doing well in the academy. I almost hoped he would. I could remember when rugby league was a far more violent game in some respects, when fisticuffs were par for the course. But when I first started watching, a player like Billy Boston, the great Wigan winger, was considered a giant, and he was maybe fifteen stone. If Billy was playing now, he'd be told to bulk up, because players are so much bigger. So when Rob made his debut, I thought, 'Right, he's done it. He's proven his point. I don't want him to keep getting battered. And why would he want to keep putting his body through all that punishment week after week?'

When Rob kept showing that he could handle all the battering, I started thinking, 'Keep going, son. Keep proving them wrong.' But even then, I sometimes imagined him looking at himself in the changing room mirror, admiring his muscles, before Jamie Peacock and Jamie Jones-Buchanan sidled up beside him. Those two make Billy Boston look small, while I've never been convinced Rob's even the tallest in our family. And I'm five foot four.

When we watched him play, all we were worried about was him having a good game and getting through it safely. Fans and parents were always saying to us, 'How does he do it, being his size?' And if he did get through a game unscathed, we'd watch it again when we got home. That's when we got to appreciate his bravery. It would completely blow us away.

When Rob started winning trophies, my pride went through the roof. After the 2011 Grand Final, when Rob scored an incredible try and was named man of the match again, me and Irene got the parents' coach back to Leeds. Part of me wanted to jump on the roof and tap dance all the way home. Instead, I spent most of the journey staring out of the window, with nothing more than a small smile on my face. Irene said to me, 'What's up with you? You should be pleased.' I was pleased. I was over the moon. But it didn't seem right to show off. Rob had been magic, but it had been a team effort.

I sometimes think the same way now, when Rob's getting all this attention and other people with MND are sat at home with none. I was on Facebook one day and someone had written, 'I'm sick of hearing about Rob Burrow.' I was obviously upset, but I could understand it in a weird way. I even said to the BBC, when they were making all these programmes about him, 'What about all the people with MND who haven't got the fame that Rob's got? They just get told they've got it, go home and suffer in silence.'

But I soon realized that Rob wasn't doing it for himself, he was doing it for everyone living with MND – just as he didn't play rugby for himself, he played it for his team. If he can use his profile to raise awareness and money, and inspire some clever people to find a cure, that can only be a good thing.

But Rob doesn't just do stuff in the public eye. He gets loads of people sending him direct messages on Twitter, people living with MND or whose partners or children have been diagnosed, and he responds to as many as he can. I'll type the messages out for him, but I won't send them until he's given me the all-clear. He tells them to stay positive, that a cure is getting closer. Some of them are just amazed he replied; all of them are thankful. It might seem like a small thing for Rob to do, but it's a big thing to other people.

Irene: Apart from the odd person on Facebook, there's been so much love for Rob, which makes us incredibly proud to be his parents. Not many players are loved by fans of all teams, but Rob is one of them. People in Castleford have always thought the world of him, even though he played for Leeds. People love an underdog, and Rob being the size he was, he always seemed like an underdog playing rugby league, the land of the giants.

I was in town with Rob and one of my daughters when he took his Covid face mask off and people started flocking around him. My daughter was calling him Brad Pitt. They were asking to have their photo taken with him, even putting money in his pocket, bless them. Rob was embarrassed by that. Even when he was a player, he never really enjoyed the attention. He was never rude to anyone, but found people slapping him on the back and telling him how great he was uncomfortable. But on this occasion, we had to say to him, 'They're doing it because they love and admire you.'

One positive to take from this situation is that it's given us a better opinion of humanity. I can't believe how kind and generous people are, especially given the tough times the country is going through. Whether it's the person raising money for Rob in Castleford town centre, the person putting money in his pocket or the person giving him a thumbs up and wishing him good luck, they've proved that there are more nice people in this world than bad.

Geoff: I know this book will probably make you sad in parts, but Rob would also want it to inspire you. He certainly inspires me. I knew he was strong, but I didn't know how strong until he got this terrible disease. He's never shown any self-pity, asked 'why me?'. That's an amazing trait to have, and I can completely understand why other people don't think the same way. I certainly wouldn't.

Rob would also want this book to give you hope. They are making progress and we know they're miles ahead of the game in America, because we've spoken to some of their top specialists. There's going to be a cure one day, and we pray it's going to come sooner rather than later.

Last, but not least, Rob would want this book to make you smile. We certainly still manage to have a laugh. When Rob's sister Joanne did the Three Peaks Challenge, to raise money for MND, she was literally crawling at times. Joanne has many strengths, but is a bit of a wimp when it comes to that sort of thing. It was as if she was on a battlefield, all a bit dramatic – 'Take the dog and go on without me!' Nevertheless, after she'd completed the first peak, everyone was telling her how inspirational she was, as you're meant to do. All apart from Rob. He took one look at her and said, 'Pathetic.'

Then there was the time, just before Christmas, that Rob started a new treatment, which had been making waves in America. When they gave him the medication, they said, 'You must take precautions, because your partner must not get pregnant while you're on this.' I looked at Rob and said,

'I'm popping into the chemist later, for my blood pressure tablets. Do you want me to pick anything up for you while I'm in there?' I'm not sure the nurse was too impressed, but I gave Rob a wink and he started giggling. Despite it all, he's never really stopped. If that's not inspiring, then I don't know what is.

★

Mum and Dad were always proud when I was picked to play for my country, as any parents would be. They could remember when Great Britain were a match for Australia and last beat them in the Ashes, way back in 1970. They had a lot of faith in me, but I'm not sure even they thought I'd be able to change our fortunes. However, with Tony Smith now in charge and Sean Long retiring from international duty, at least I'd be given a go. And I appeared to be a shoo-in for the three-Test series against New Zealand in autumn 2007.

After the Grand Final, Tony had called me 'the general the Great Britain team has been looking for', which was nice of him. And there was no doubt I'd play, because I was the only number seven in the squad. That was some turn-around after the frustrations of the 2006 Tri-Nations down under, when I didn't play a single minute.

Tony picked five Rhinos for the first Test in Huddersfield – me, Keith, Kev, JP and Gareth Ellis – and I don't think anyone could have accused him of favouritism (it might have been six, but Maggsy had been injured in the Grand Final). Tony also picked Bradford's eighteen-year-old prop Sam Burgess and St Helens's Maurie Fa'asavalu, who had played twenty-odd rugby union Tests for Samoa. Maurie's selection caused a bit of a stir, but most of his GB team-mates didn't give a monkey's. His passport said he was British, and we knew he'd be a handful for the Kiwis, and that was good enough for us.

Despite making his international debut in 2000, Kev had never been able to nail down a starting spot in the England or Great Britain teams. He had a lot of competition at loose-forward, particularly from Wigan's Andy Farrell and St Helens's Paul Sculthorpe, and was reduced to a bit-part player. That was summed up by his Great Britain debut against Australia, when he was named at hooker and wore the number nine shirt but played at scrum-half for the first twenty minutes. He'd never played hooker or scrum-half in his life before that game. For whatever reason, Tony's predecessor Brian Noble just didn't seem to fancy Kev, as he didn't seem to fancy me, which was difficult to understand.

If you could put up just one statue of a Rhinos player outside Headingley, it would have to be of Kev. My whole time at the academy, I wanted to be like Kev. I think because he was a couple of years older than most of the rest of Leeds's so-called golden generation, he saw it as his responsibility to shepherd us, show us the right way. He became a great friend, but I never stopped looking up to him. If you wanted good advice, Kev was the bloke you asked. You'd walk away from the conversation thinking, 'No one else would have told me that, but it makes perfect sense. Thanks for that, Kev.'

On the pitch, he was the perfect skipper. Even when JP joined from Bradford, having just led them to victory in a Grand Final, there was never any question that Kev would give up the captaincy. Kev wasn't a ranter and a raver; you wouldn't find him bashing his head against a wall before a big game. He was reserved – cool, calm and collected. He had to be, because he was the bloke we counted on to knock over difficult goals to win matches. Instead, Kev was one of those captains who led by example.

You wouldn't describe Kev as spectacular, which is maybe why some people didn't recognize his value. But he had every skill in the book, was equally effective as a back or a forward and a world-class goal-kicker – opponents never expected him to miss. Kev was the ultimate professional, and his Leeds teammates understood exactly how special he was. He could handle anything, on and off the pitch, and was the perfect ambassador for the sport.

Unfortunately for Kev, he got sick on the morning of the first Test against the Kiwis and had to pull out. JP found him chucking his guts up in a gutter during the morning stroll. That meant more responsibility for me, in terms of kicking duties. The Kiwis had just been hammered 58–0 by Australia, but we didn't expect them to be a soft touch. And they actually led 10–8 at half-time, despite a try by Maurie Fa'asavalu. But we managed to turn things around after the interval, Gareth Raynor touching down after I'd kicked through and Sam Burgess also scoring on his debut. The Kiwis staged a bit of a comeback, but we held for a 20–14 win and I was named man of the match.

Kev was back for the second Test in Hull, and he picked a good time to stop shitting through the eye of a needle. We were all over New Zealand from the start, with JP blasting through five tacklers and touching down after just two minutes, before the Kiwis had even touched the ball. Me and my half-back partner – Leon Pryce – might have looked like the odd couple, what with him being almost a foot taller than me, but we fitted together perfectly in the first half, during which we scored another two tries. And with Maggsy now in the mix, we cut loose after the break, with me finishing off a brilliant passing move and Leon's late long-range try making it eight in all and the final score 44–0.

That was the best performance by any England or Great Britain team I played in, by a long chalk. After the game, New Zealand's coach Gary Kemble made a few excuses about missing players, but we weren't going to let that take the gloss off Great Britain's first series win for fourteen years. To 'nil' any team in rugby league is an achievement, but far more exciting was the free-flowing brand of rugby we played. Super League teams, particularly Leeds and St Helens, had been playing that kind of stuff for years, but it had rarely translated to the national team. Now, journalists were talking England up as contenders for the 2008 World Cup (the GB team, which was pretty much the England team, was broken up into separate home nations after that series).

At the time, that didn't seem far-fetched. We had a formidable forward pack, with JP, Adrian Morley and the young Sam Burgess a match for most; flair and imagination at half-back, in the form of me, Leon and Maggsy; and some excellent backs. But perhaps most important of all, we had a coach, in Tony Smith, who wanted us to take risks and excite the long-suffering fans. As Tony put it himself, he wasn't about 'completion rates and pumping out sets'.

We weren't as convincing in the third Test in Wigan, but still good enough to complete the whitewash. In fact, winning in a different way – coming from behind in wind and hail, having gone 12–0 down after just eleven minutes – was almost as satisfying as our one-sided win in Hull.

By the interval, we were 14–12 ahead, before I touched down early in the second half. That was my fourth try in four Tests in 2007, having also scored a couple against France in the summer. And after holding on for a 28–22 win, I was named man of the series. I thought it would be onwards and upwards from there, in terms of my international career. It didn't really turn out like that. As a matter of fact, I might as well tell you how the 2008 World Cup panned out now. It's not as if it's a glorious tale in need of a long, tantalizing build-up.

Tony picked eight Rhinos for the tournament down under, including Keith, who had reversed his decision to retire from international rugby. Sam Burgess was injured, but most of the players who were involved in the 3–0 series win over the Kiwis made the plane. Our squad was full of players the Aussie and Kiwi players respected, and not just Adrian Morley, who played six seasons for the Sydney Roosters (Roosters fans loved Moz, who had a reputation as an old-school enforcer). Even the Aussie journalists, who usually think British rugby league is a bit of a joke, were writing nice things about us.

Because the 2000 tournament had produced so many one-sided results (which was one of the reasons there was no tournament in 2004), the format was a bit weird. We were in a 'super group' with Australia, New Zealand and Papua New Guinea, with the top three going through to the semi-finals. Meanwhile, all the other teams were scrapping for the fourth spot. This meant that if we won our opener against Papua New Guinea, we'd pretty much be one win away from the final, whatever else happened in the group stage.

It took one game for the Aussie journalists to stop writing nice things about us. That wasn't entirely fair, because Papua New Guinea were actually a decent team, full of committed players who hit hard and loved to throw the ball around. We knew all about their stand-off Stanley Gene, because he'd been playing in Super League since the 1990s (he claimed to be thirty-four, but some people reckoned he was nearer forty). But for some of their players, who played semi-professionally in Australia or Papua New Guinea, the game was effectively a trial, a chance to catch the eye of an NRL or Super League club.

We were 16–12 down at half-time, but managed to grind them down after the interval, with JP putting in an enormous shift – as usual – and Lee Smith scoring a hat-trick on debut. But as far as most journalists and pundits were concerned, us winning 32–22 represented a scare. We didn't see it that way. We hadn't played any competitive rugby for a few weeks and were bound to be rusty, while Papua New Guinea had given us plenty of things to work on before our second game against the Aussies. And if anything was going to focus the mind, it was the thought of playing the Kangaroos in their own backyard.

When I was a kid, top of my list of ambitions was to play against Australia. And beat them. It's the ultimate goal of any rugby league player in Britain, and it doesn't happen often. Not only had Great Britain not won an Ashes series since 1970, but the last time they (or England) had won a World Cup was 1972, with Australia winning all six since then. Judging by their first game, a 30–6 victory over New Zealand, the Kangaroos' 2008 vintage was as impressive as ever. The Aussie media was already calling the tournament a one-horse race. It wouldn't be, but that would have nothing to do with us.

We were awful in Melbourne, there's no getting away from it. As a result, Australia mullered us 52–4. We were so bad it was difficult to get our heads around it. Some of our attacking play, particularly in the second half, was bordering on comical, while Melbourne Storm duo Billy Slater and Greg Inglis tore our defence to shreds, bagging a hat-trick each. Only a couple of our forwards emerged from the carnage with their reputations intact, and I never got another crack at them. That was my one and only Test against the Aussies.

Tony made all the right noises, about it being a tournament and his team still having time to get up to speed. But the overriding emotion in the squad was shock. We genuinely thought we were good enough to run the Aussies close and yet they had blown us to smithereens. The following day's headline in the *Sydney Morning Herald* just about summed it up: 'Too big, too fast, too good.'

Meanwhile, British journalists and pundits seemed to relish putting the boot in. Cliff Watson, who was part of Great Britain's Ashes-winning team in 1970, called our performance 'disgusting' and suggested we should pack our bags and go home. Tony's predecessor Brian Noble called us embarrassing. *The Times* called us shambolic, the *Sun* called the result English rugby league's lowest point for decades and the *Telegraph* described the game as 'like Lewis Hamilton's McLaren lining up against Chitty Chitty Bang

Bang'. In case anyone was wondering, my mum thought I'd played well.

If anything, the loss to New Zealand six days later was even harder to take. And it all started so well. We ran in four tries in the first twenty-seven minutes, including two for me, and it looked as if we were going to do to the Kiwis what the Aussies had done to us. But having led 24–8 at half-time, our defence disintegrated after the interval and they ended up winning 36–24, with winger Manu 'The Beast' Vatuvei scoring four tries, three of them virtually unopposed.

Tony was furious after the game, but probably not as furious as our 6,000 travelling fans. As for the media, they ramped up their criticism to eleven. Poor Paul Sykes, who was given a torrid time by Vatuvei after being shifted to the wing, was savaged. The *Sunday Times* claimed the game would 'haunt the memories of every Englishman who had the misfortune to be there.' The *Guardian* and the *Mirror* called us a laughing stock, as did Garry Schofield.

It was never nice to hear old heroes talking like that, and it was difficult for some of the lads to deal with. When you're at home and things are going wrong, it's easier to escape the flak, because you can close the door behind you, surround yourself with loved ones and pretend it's not happening. But when you're on tour and losing big games by big margins, everything is magnified. There's nowhere to escape to; you're spending all your time with people under the same scrutiny as you. You feel their pressure, they feel yours, and there's no release. Pressure can bring a team together, but more often than not it creates cracks that soon turn into canyons. That's why it's so common for a touring team to have a couple of bad results and fall apart.

It wasn't a particularly enjoyable situation to be in, but we just had to suck it up. Let's face it, Garry and the rest of them were right, we were a laughing stock. But we still had a chance to put things right in the semi-finals, against the same opponents (unsurprisingly, Papua New Guinea didn't get the upset they needed against Australia, meaning the hosts played Fiji). One journalist said we'd advanced to the last four 'with all the style of a mangy dog'. But we'd whitewashed the Kiwis the previous autumn and outplayed them in the first half in Newcastle, so remained confident of reaching the final.

That confidence had ebbed to almost nothing after just sixteen minutes of the game in Brisbane, three individual errors having led to Kiwi tries. Tries from JP and Maggsy made it 16–10 at half-time, but we misplaced too many passes, dropped too many balls and missed too many tackles after the interval. And, I must admit, I was outplayed by my opposite number Nathan Fien.

Three times we fought back to within a converted try, but we kept blowing chances and the Kiwis held on to win 32–22. There ended a calamitous tournament, and our fans must have wondered what on earth they'd been watching. How could blokes who regularly performed so well for Leeds, St Helens, Wigan and whoever else have become so incompetent, almost overnight?

After the game, Maggsy gave a very forthright interview, in which he called us 'crap' and lacking in skill and passion. I couldn't argue with that. We'd let ourselves and our fans down badly. But why we were so crap was a bit of a mystery. I could accept that Australia were better than us – it's a bigger sport over there and attracts more of their best athletes – but I couldn't accept that they were fifty points better than us, or that we were worse than the Kiwis.

That said, it was clear that the NRL had taken a giant leap in terms of athleticism since we last played the Aussies in 2006, with Manly and Melbourne to the fore. They were applying all the latest sports science, like GPS and heart-rate data, and tailoring diets to individual players. It was all stuff we'd soon be doing at Leeds, but which was alien to us at the time.

It probably didn't help that we were playing by a different set of rules to the Aussies and Kiwis. In Super League, there was a lot less wrestling at the ruck, with tackled players expected to be released as early as possible. In the NRL, which dictated international rules, wrestling at the ruck was a big part of the game, a dark art. So during the build-up, we had to spend a lot of time watching videos, learning the technicalities of wrestling. It was virtually all-consuming. And when it came to the actual games, we were constantly trying to remember what we'd only recently learned, while it was second nature to the Aussies and Kiwis. Super League rules made the game more free-flowing – some thought more entertaining – and meant a lot more damage was done in the middle of the field, rather than out wide. But that was irrelevant when it came to playing internationals, when all that mattered was winning.

As for media rumours of a rift between Leeds and St Helens players, they were wildly exaggerated. It's true that the rivalry between the two clubs was at its peak, with us having just beaten them for a second Grand Final in a row.

And while we didn't feel any animosity towards them, I did feel that some of their players struggled to deal with it. But we weren't like two rival gangs at school, or the warring news teams in *Anchorman* (although I'd have liked to have seen that). We weren't refusing to speak to each other, slagging each other off and tripping each other up in corridors. And as far as I know, JP and Keith never ambushed James Graham and stuck his head down a toilet.

However, it is true that we lacked a sense of togetherness and never gelled as a team. In a funny sort of way, England rugby league tours are more like British and Irish Lions tours in rugby union. It's a load of blokes who don't play with each other that often, who don't know each other very well and might be suspicious of each other, so you really have to work at team bonding. In hindsight, Tony should have forced Leeds and Saints players to share rooms, instead of allowing us to choose. As it was, Leeds boys hung out together and Saints boys did the same. That's not great for team spirit.

I didn't play for England again until 2012, when I made three appearances off the bench in the Autumn International Series. I can only assume that Tony's successor Steve McNamara wanted more of a footballer than a runner at scrum-half, although he did pick me for the 2013 World Cup.

Most of the pre-tournament talk was about the inclusion of three of the four Burgess brothers, most notably 'Slammin' Sam', who had become a superstar in Australia playing for South Sydney, and the non-inclusion of Huddersfield half-back Danny Brough, that season's Man of Steel. There was also the usual newspaper hype about us having the players to win it. But when we lost a warm-up match against Italy, who most people didn't even know had a rugby league team, we reverted to being the punchline to a bad joke again.

To be fair, it was pissing down in Salford (when isn't it?), there were unlimited substitutions and most of Italy's team were Aussies, including former Kangaroos Anthony Minichiello and Anthony Laffranchi. But as far as most casual sports fans in England were concerned, we might as well have been beaten by a bunch of random blokes dragged off the streets of Naples.

Things got even worse when Gareth Hock was thrown out of the squad for disciplinary reasons and James Graham, another big NRL star and one of the best props in the world, was dropped for our opening game against Australia for breaking a drinking ban. When Steve McNamara walked out of the pre-match press conference, we looked a lot like a team in disarray.

I wasn't even on the bench against the Aussies in Cardiff, but we played pretty well, especially in the first half, only losing 28–22. I scored a try off the bench in the win against Fiji (not that I remember much about that game, because I got another whack on the head) and was in the match-day squad for the semi-final against defending champions New Zealand.

The big news before that game was Steve McNamara's decision to drop Auckland-born Rangi Chase and partner Kev Sinfield with Gareth Widdop in the half-backs. I could see why the media and fans thought that was an odd decision. Steve had kept faith in Rangi since first picking him a couple of years earlier (controversially, I should add, because

Rangi was born and raised in New Zealand and had only been in England a couple of years, playing for Castleford), while ignoring the claims of Danny Brough and Maggsy. And now he'd jettisoned him for the biggest game of his reign and instead picked a bloke who had barely played any rugby since dislocating his hip five months earlier, and who had never started a Test at half-back. Gareth was a great player who had won an NRL Grand Final with Melbourne Storm, but it was still a gamble.

How we didn't win that game, I'll never know. But at least we bowed out with our heads held high. Sam Burgess was unbelievable that night, snuffing out Sonny Bill Williams, scoring what looked like the winning try and putting in one of the greatest performances by an Englishman in a Test match. Kev was almost as good. And it ended up being decided by a couple of inches here and there. That's how close it was.

If Kev hadn't tugged an early conversion just left of the posts; if George Burgess had hit Sonny Bill Williams a little lower and not given away the penalty from which the Kiwis scored; if Ryan Hall had held on to an attempted interception in the closing stages, with the Wembley pitch opened up before him. But had they lost, no doubt the Kiwis would have been singing the same tune. And in the immortal words of David Brent, if only my auntie had bollocks, she'd be my uncle. That's professional sport: it gives you the highest highs and the lowest lows, and often there's almost nothing between them.

After that game, I never played for England again. There were a lot of quality half-backs around at the time: Warrington's Richie Myler, Wigan's Sam Tomkins, St Helens's Kyle

Eastmond. I was always a big fan of Huddersfield's Luke Robinson, yet he only played a few games for England. But I can understand why Leeds fans might think it odd that while me and Maggsy won so much together at club level, we were never much trusted on the international stage.

However, there's no point dwelling on these things too much. And while my international career could be viewed as a disappointment, I'll always be proud of playing for my country. I did OK for a Pommy squirt.

8

You CAN SPEND ALL DAY WATCHING THE NEWS AND arguing on social media, but that's not likely to make you very happy. In fact, it's likely to make you sad and angry. So why do it, when goodness is everywhere?

I'm not sure being diagnosed with a terminal disease made me realize that, but it certainly hammered the point home. Every morning you wake up, you've got a choice: you can spend your day soaking up everything that's bad about the world, while bitching and moaning, or you can block all that out and do stuff that makes you content. You haven't got long in this world, so why waste time having a row with someone you don't even know on Twitter?

People seem to think that the world is going to hell in a handcart. Maybe it is, but you don't have to let all the nastiness rule your life. There are still so many lovely people wanting to do nice things. I know this because I've been wallowing in the niceness of others since telling the world about my MND. Believe it or not, some of the nicest people

157

I know are journalists. Strange, right? Because everyone seems to think they're bastards. Well, not the ones I've met, at least since I took Doddie's advice and started telling my story.

Me and Lindsey never had a proper sit-down chat about whether we should open ourselves up to the media and invite the public in, it just kind of happened. And it all started with a meeting between me, Doddie and the former footballer Stephen Darby, which was broadcast by *BBC Breakfast*.

Stephen, who started out at Liverpool and played almost 200 games for Bradford City (which I don't hold against him), was diagnosed with MND while he was still at Notts County. He was only twenty-nine, but his positivity is astonishing. And apart from Doddie's trousers, that was a beautiful little film. It was only ten minutes long but packed a lot in. In fact, the BBC should have called it 'Everything You Always Wanted to Know About MND But Were Afraid to Ask'. It was like a very cosy public health advert: three pretty average blokes – a Yorkshireman, a Scouser and a mad Scottish giraffe – shedding light on a horrible disease that was previously a mystery to most people.

Our interviewer, the lovely Sally Nugent, did a great job of teasing everything out of us. As she said at the start, men aren't usually great at talking about illness or feelings. But it was all on show that day. We discussed the devastation of being diagnosed and how difficult it was to tell our families (Stephen had only just got married when he was diagnosed, while Doddie had a wife and three teenage sons). And because Doddie was a few years further down the line, he was able to fill us in on what was to come, the mundane nuts and bolts of living with MND, as well as the challenges and the indignities.

There was a bit of anger, about the lack of answers. And when Doddie told us he'd just signed a 'do not resuscitate' document, which means he doesn't want any medical help when his heart stops beating, there were a few tears. But there were far more smiles. And I hope people watching were more inspired than saddened, full of positivity rather than pity. And I hope they saw three normal fellas who just happen to be ill. Or, as Stephen put it, three proud members of Team MND, accepting the diagnosis but fighting the prognosis.

Sally and her producer, the equally lovely Claire Ryan, then persuaded us to take part in a documentary, which ended up as *Rob Burrow: My Year With MND*. We didn't have any misgivings, because we knew we could trust them. We could see they weren't in it for the personal praise; they genuinely cared about us and wanted to raise as much awareness as possible.

Journalists have a lot of power, not always used in the right way. But Sally and Claire were clearly good people. Down to earth, great with the kids, they soon became friends. They never applied pressure and always ran things by us, making it clear that we were in control and had the option of saying no.

While Macy and Maya enjoyed having the cameras around (they love their drama classes and being centre of attention), Lindsey didn't find it as easy. I'm used to dealing with the media, because of my rugby career, but Lindsey was dreading doing her interview for the documentary, worrying about saying the wrong thing or breaking down in tears. But Sally was very sensitive and reassuring, and turned it into an informal chat in the garden, like two old friends having a nice cup of coffee.

Lindsey did have a little cry, as did my dad when he was interviewed, but that was no bad thing. It showed the rawness of the situation, the gritty reality. I thought that film was beautiful and represented my situation perfectly. It focused on the positive things, such as the relative normality of my life – without too much sentimentality, which isn't really me – while making sure not to ignore the fact that MND is very far from being a walk in the park.

If that documentary, which was broadcast in October 2020, had helped just one person, it would have been worthwhile. But the response went way beyond anything we'd imagined. I don't have words to describe what that outpouring of love and support meant to me and Lindsey. We got so many beautiful messages, via social media, text and email (our phones didn't stop pinging for days), and even received good old-fashioned letters, from people wanting to offer us advice and comfort. They made me cry and they made me smile. Best of all, they made me realize that we were getting the message out there and giving people without my platform a voice. Thanks to that film, millions of viewers learned about this horrible disease called MND. They discovered that MND patients could live fulfilling lives – they weren't just hanging around, waiting to die – but also that we could really do with a cure.

Sally and Claire have become great friends of ours. Claire even sent some Christmas presents for the kids, and Lindsey and Claire are planning to meet up after lockdown, just to catch up. Because of Sally and Claire, I'm never off the telly for long. I sometimes worry that the public are sick of the sight of me. And Lindsey finds the whole situation quite surreal at times. There she was, a down-to-earth, unassuming girl from Castleford, minding her own business, and suddenly millions of people were watching her cry on TV. But she sees the bigger picture, which is just one of the things that makes her such a diamond.

Me, Doddie and Stephen had another get-together in the summer, only this time we had to do it over Zoom, because of coronavirus. It was inspiring to hear that they were both still swinging punches, despite it all. And it was great to see them both still smiling, even if it was on a screen. I'd love to see them both again in person, give them a big teammate hug, compare notes and have that beer that Doddie promised me. There can be no greater motivation to stay alive than a Scotsman offering to buy you a drink the next time you meet.

★

Tony Smith's replacement was former New Zealand coach Brian 'Bluey' McClennan, who some considered to be a left-field appointment. Bluey had led New Zealand to victory in the 2005 Tri-Nations, his team beating Australia 24–0 in the final at Elland Road, and almost repeated the trick the following year, the Kangaroos winning the final in Sydney on a golden point. His New Zealand teams played with speed and adventure, which was the Leeds way and why Gary Hetherington had appointed him. But Bluey had never played rugby league at a decent level or coached in either the Super League or the NRL, so we had no idea how he'd cope with the day-to-day rigours of elite club rugby.

Bluey was a different kettle of fish to Tony, that much was obvious from the moment he arrived at Headingley at the end of 2007. While Tony was a stickler for discipline, very strict at times, Bluey was laid-back and didn't take anything too seriously. And while Tony was a master tactician, Bluey was all about man-management and motivation, getting the team up for big games.

Bluey loved an inspirational video, believed that success would follow if he created a happy environment in which everyone felt good about themselves and got on. Some players liked Bluey's methods, others found all the motivational stuff a bit naff (like the time he presented us all with medallions, which supposedly represented team unity) and thought he neglected the technical side of things. Personally, I loved Bluey as a bloke. While he was there, the team felt like one big family. And there's no arguing with the record books, they show his methods worked, at least for a couple of years.

Our first game of 2008 was against the South Sydney Rabbitohs in, of all places, Jacksonville, Florida. Some of our lads were a bit put out that all the media attention was on the Rabbitohs, but it was to be expected. They were co-owned by Hollywood star Russell Crowe, and if he hadn't spent weeks promoting the game, on TV and radio chat shows, we'd have been lucky to get twelve people through the gate, instead of the 12,000 who turned up.

I'm sure most of the spectators had no idea what was going on, but there were plenty of big hits, a couple of blokes carried off injured and a punch-up. What wasn't there to like? We steamrollered the Rabbitohs in the first half, they came back at us in the second and we ended up winning 26–24.

When the final whistle went, I half expected Russell to storm onto the pitch and start shouting, 'Are you not entertained?!' After the game, he presented us with leather jackets and we all had our photos taken with him. He said to me, 'I suppose you get bored of hearing fans shouting, "Get the midget"?' I didn't really know what to say to that. But when you're Russell Crowe, and most people in the stadium are there because of you, you can say what you like.

Bluey didn't make any new signings before the start of the Super League season, which was a tribute to the sterling work of his predecessor. And we kicked off the year with four straight wins, before hosting Melbourne Storm in the World Club Challenge. As usual, Melbourne got their excuses in early, making sure everyone knew about their lack of preparation and how much the trip from Australia had taken out of them. To be fair, British Airways did lose their luggage. And they were also missing six of their Grand Final-winning team. But when you've got blokes like Billy Slater, Israel Folau and Cooper Cronk in your side, three of the best rugby players of all time, and most of the rest are either Aussie or Kiwi internationals, excuses seem a bit unnecessary.

That was a brutal evening at Elland Road, in diabolical conditions. There were quite a few flare-ups and Maggsy had to go off with an injured collarbone, following a late tackle that went unpunished. And there wasn't much in the way of expansive rugby, with only two tries scored, both in the first half. The second half was more like trench warfare, but that only made our eventual 11–4 victory more special.

Bluey was over the moon. He already knew we could beat teams with speed and skill, but to beat a team of Melbourne's calibre in a good old-fashioned arm-wrestle proved that we'd matured into a proper hard outfit, with plenty of gravel swilling in our guts.

Naturally, the media, both in the UK and Australia, started wondering if the gap between northern and southern hemisphere rugby league was narrowing and England might be able to do some damage at the World Cup later that year. As I've already explained, that didn't happen, which made it easy for Aussie journalists and fans to continue writing the World Club Challenge off as a pointless friendly. But as far as I'm concerned, those two World Club Challenge victories are among my most precious rugby memories.

We got spanked by Castleford in our next game, which was Bluey's first loss. But we beat Harlequins 48–0 next up, with me scoring my 100th try for Leeds, before thumping wins over Bradford, who were a shadow of their former selves, and Hull. We scored 122 points in those three games and conceded only one try. Some fans think my second try against the Bulls, when I beat five or six defenders, was the best I ever scored. When we beat Saints 14–10 at Knowsley Road, the newspapers were talking as if the title race was over, forgetting that they crown Super League champions in October, not March.

Predictably, at least in hindsight, we were beaten by Wigan in our next game, despite them being without their talismanic Aussie stand-off Trent Barrett. However, we then won nine games in a row, scoring fifty-seven tries in the process. That run included two more big wins over Bradford, a 58–12 hammering of Wakefield, and a victory over Wigan

in the quarter-finals of the Challenge Cup. Then, as sure as
night follows day, we had yet another summer slump, with
three tight defeats in four games – against Harlequins, St
Helens and Wigan – meaning we were suddenly second
in the table behind Saints (I missed a last-minute penalty
against the Warriors, which would have won it). A couple
of weeks later, Saints dumped us out of the Challenge Cup,
our bogey competition, at the semi-final stage. Having won
it so many times in my kitchen as a kid, I was beginning to
wonder if I'd ever win it in real life.

Even worse, our injury list was getting longer and longer.
Jonesy and Ryan Bailey had already missed a chunk of the
season, and now Ryan Hall had broken his foot and Clinton
Toopi had knackered his knee, putting both of them out
for the rest of the campaign. When Warrington beat us
on their patch, the papers were suddenly referring to us as
'Sorry Leeds' in headlines.

Then, just like that, we clicked back into gear. First,
we made it four wins out of four against the Bulls, before
cutting loose against Castleford and Wigan, our supposed
bogey team, putting fifty points on both. We finished the
regular season one point behind St Helens, which meant
we'd have to play them in a qualifying semi-final for the
second season in a row. But while Saints just squeaked past
us in 2007, they walloped us in 2008, scoring seven tries to
two and beating us 38–10. As the scoreline suggests, they
completely outplayed us – even embarrassed us at times –
with their skipper Keiron Cunningham inspirational up
front and Leon Pryce running the show from stand-off.

Losing to Saints meant another eliminator against Wigan
at Headingley. But it was a far more torrid game than the

season before. Keith was sent to the sin bin early, for a spot of handbags (although 'suitcases' might better describe one of Keith's punches), but we led 6–2 at the interval, thanks to a try from Lee Smith. We were all over them early in the second half but couldn't get the ball down. My old mate Mark Calderwood, now a Warrior, was a man on a mission, pulling off try-saving tackles all over the pitch. And when JP was adjudged to have been held up over the line – by Richie Mathers, another former teammate – I started to think we might get mugged. But Wigan did eventually crack, Keith squeezing over in the corner for a try before Lee added another. The Warriors got a late try back, but we ended up winning 18–14.

You would have struggled to find a neutral backing Leeds to win the Grand Final. While we'd hobbled into the final straight, St Helens hadn't lost since April, winning twenty-three and drawing one of those games, plus beating Hull in the Challenge Cup Final. The Grand Final was their head coach Daniel Anderson's final game, while the injured Paul Sculthorpe, one of Saints' greatest ever players, had announced his retirement. Newspaper editors were probably saving a big space for a photo of Daniel, Scully and skipper Keiron Cunningham holding the trophy aloft, with us on our knees in the background.

But we had our own reasons for wanting to win it, other than the obvious. It was to be Gaz Ellis's last game in blue and amber, before joining Wests Tigers in the NRL, while Nick Scruton, one of the biggest characters in the team – who invariably led the singing after a big win – was off to Bradford. We were looking to become the first Leeds side to retain the title, and eight of us were hoping to become the first Leeds players to win three Championships.

We lost Brent Webb the day before the final, a back injury bringing Superman down to earth with a bump. Poor old Webby had been instrumental in getting us to Old Trafford and was understandably devastated. His absence meant Lee Smith, who had almost joined Wigan after losing his place earlier in the season, switched to full-back and Ryan Hall, who was still only twenty and had played just one reserve game since breaking his foot in July, started on the wing. It also meant our odds with the bookies became slightly longer.

It was a filthy night in Manchester, with rain coming down like stair-rods. That meant we were unlikely to repeat the scoreline of the previous year, but also that Saints were unlikely to rout us like they did in the qualifier. It was going to be a ding-dong, no doubt about it.

Saints' James Graham, that season's Man of Steel, scored the first try, and who knows how things might have turned out if Matty Diskin and Scott Donald hadn't bundled Matt Gidley into touch shortly afterwards, inches short of our try-line. But we managed to ride out that early storm, hitting back with tries from Lee Smith and Ryan Hall, our two supposed weak links. Ryan's try, after a hack through and chase, raised a few smiles – I don't think anyone had ever seen him kick a ball before.

Saints retook the lead early in the second half, Matt Gidley latching on to a high kick from Sean Long and scoring in the corner, before Kev grubbered through and Maggsy touched down under the posts. Unfortunately, Saints weren't quite done, almost scoring a few times before

Ade Gardner reduced the deficit. But when their winger Francis Meli dropped a high bomb from Kev, who had been peppering him all night, Maggsy picked up the loose ball and somehow wriggled over for his fourth try in as many Grand Finals.

That was pretty much that. Some iffy refereeing decisions gave St Helens field position late on, but our defence never really looked like breaking. And when the final hooter went, it was 24–16 to us and we'd upset the odds again. Oh, and guess who won the Harry Sunderland Trophy for man of the match? Lee Smith, who played like Superman that night. I did enjoy Maggsy's quote about Lee in the paper the next day: 'He's a great lad – just a bit daft.'

That win tasted even sweeter than the year before. It's lovely winning a Grand Final at a canter, especially when you're underdogs. But the feeling you get from winning a war of attrition – especially when you were almost down and out a couple of weeks earlier – is on a different level. It's a metaphor for life, I suppose. It's nice when it's all running smoothly, but you only really find out how big your balls are, and how much you can rely on your mates, when you're knee deep in mud in the trenches, fighting tooth and nail to stay alive.

★

Our only big signing for the 2009 season was hooker Danny Buderus, the former Kangaroo who had also played twenty-odd games for New South Wales in State of Origin. That didn't mean the squad was going stale, because there was another good crop of kids filtering through from the academy, players like centre Kallum Watkins, who had made his debut as a sixteen-year-old the previous season, hooker/ scrum-half Paul McShane and winger Ben Jones-Bishop. Suddenly, the likes of me, Maggsy and Matty Diskin were looking over our shoulders, just as old-timers must have done when we were coming through.

Meanwhile, me, Maggsy and JP had signed new long-term contracts that would probably keep us at the club until the end of our careers. In case you were wondering, all of us could have earned a lot more elsewhere. As Kev used to say, 'Leeds have the best players, but they're not the best payers.' That's why people accused Kev of being a fool every time he signed a new deal. And it wasn't just other rugby league teams who were after him, he could have switched to union pretty much whenever he wanted (they'd been sniffing around him since the early 2000s). But Kev never lost that socialist ethos.

As far as Kev was concerned – and most of the rest of us – Leeds had developed him into the player he'd become and they'd remained loyal. While you can be forgiven for thinking professional sport is all about money, that Rhinos team proved it isn't. Why would you leave a club that was winning things almost every season, ditch your mates and uproot your family, just because another club offered you a few more quid? Why would you value money over winning trophies with your pals? Call me naïve or a daft romantic, but it makes no sense to me. When I was that little kid who signed for Leeds, money was the last thing on my mind. It was all about making memories.

★

Jamie Jones-Buchanan, Rhinos teammate

What's life really about? Is it about lining your pockets with as much money as possible? Is it about always chasing more, so that you can drive a better model of car or buy a bigger house, when the one you've already got does the job just fine? Or is it about relationships? Going on amazing journeys with amazing people? Grafting together, learning together, growing together? I've got eight Grand Final rings under my bed and each one tells a story. But even those rings are a tiny part of the bigger picture.

The whole time I was at Leeds, I never discussed money with the lads. Nowadays, the media are always talking about how much players get paid and whether their ability and performances reflect that. But I had no idea what anyone else was getting paid. I didn't even know what I could get paid playing for another top-four club, because I never once thought about leaving Leeds. Leeds Rhinos were my club, in the city I grew up in, and I loved them. Why would I want to go and play anywhere else, to get my face smashed in every week for a club and a set of fans I had no connection with, just because they were willing to offer me thirty or forty grand more a year?

Whatever they were offering in monetary terms didn't come anywhere close to what we had at Leeds. Different things motivate different people, but having an identity is a huge thing for me. That's why I only ever played for Leeds. That's why Rob and Kev only ever played for Leeds. And that's why, when Maggsy joined Hull KR at the end of his career and tore Leeds apart at Headingley, our fans stood up and clapped him. They did that because they loved him for everything he'd done for the club; for staying loyal when he could have left for more money years earlier; for leaving a lasting legacy.

When you've been retired for years and you meet up with your old teammates, you're not going to discuss how much money you earned while you were playing or what cars you drove. Instead, it's that legacy you'll talk about. All the great things you did together, all the great things you achieved. But not just the triumphs, the hardships and the low points. Those horrible training sessions, yomping up hills at Roundhay Park in the freezing cold. The long lay-offs with injuries. The agony of missing out on big games.

This might surprise you, but I only visited Rob's house once in all the years we played together, and that was just to drop something off. The same with Maggsy; while I've never been to Kev's house in the six years he's lived there. I knew that Rob, or anyone else in that side, would do anything for me, if I asked for their help, but our private lives were separate. It was out on the training field, in the changing room and during games that we gelled into this tight-knit band of brothers. When I had my hands on the plough and was grinding forwards, I knew that Rob, and everyone else, would be there beside me. That was how tight the bonds were, formed over the course of twenty years.

You'll go on YouTube and there'll be videos that wrap up all Rob's highlights in a few minutes. If you made a video of everything great that Rob did on a rugby pitch, it would last for a day. You could say the same for a lot of lads in that team. But it still wouldn't capture their greatness in its entirety.

We all have a finite amount of time on earth and it's all

about how you fill that time between being born and dying. I'm so fortunate that I played with so many heroes, people I shared great achievements with, and took me to so many wonderful places. That's what life is all about, being as good as you can, so that you enrich the lives of other people, as well as yourself.

★

Bluey's big theme for the 2009 season was 'three-peat', which is a term they use in basketball for teams who win three NBA championships on the spin. No team had managed the feat in the Super League era, and no wonder: the salary cap had made the sport so much more competitive, and professionalism had gone through the roof, making it far more attritional.

Having played in thirty-four of Leeds's thirty-five games in 2008, I missed the first three league games in 2009, after knackering my back during our pre-season training camp in Florida. That meant my first game of the season would be the World Club Challenge, against NRL champions Manly Sea Eagles. Manly had beaten Melbourne 40–0 in the NRL Grand Final, so it was less a case of dipping my toe back into the water than diving headfirst into a raging sea.

There were a few verbals flying about before the game, with Manly's chief executive calling Super League a 'second-tier' competition, where old Aussies go to earn some easy money before retiring. Some people thought that was an odd thing to say, given that English teams had won the previous five World Club Challenges. But England's poor showing in the 2008 World Cup made his comments more difficult to refute. And as long as Australia kept beating

England on the international stage, they could keep dis-
missing the World Club Challenge as a quirky irrelevance,
a meaningless anomaly.

However, I'm here to tell you that Manly's players didn't
travel to England for a bit of a giggle. Because, after only
sixteen minutes, JP threw me one of the worst passes in the
history of rugby – in either code – and Manly second-row
Anthony Watmough almost took my head off. Whenever
I remind JP of 'the Watmough pass', which I do as often as
possible, he smiles sheepishly. To be fair to Watmough, I'm
not sure his intent was malicious.

Whenever someone hit me high, the referee had to take
my shortness into account. That's why Watmough wasn't
shown a yellow card and there were no protests from my
teammates. But malicious or not, my concussions were
starting to pile up. I'd experimented with a scrum cap, but
found it gave me a false sense of security. And because
I was operating at a different height to everyone else, head
shots – whether in the form of swinging arms or flying
shoulders – were just something I had to put up with. Two
weeks after being sparked out against Manly, I got another
concussion at Knowsley Road. But that was nobody's fault
but mine, because I got my tackle technique wrong and
copped a knee to the temple.

A few minutes after I had been led from the field, wobbling like a drunk at kicking-out time, JP got involved in a
punch-up with his opposition prop Josh Perry and was sent
to the sin-bin (and when I say 'punch-up', I mean actual
right-handers landing on chins, rather than the pushing and
shoving that passes for a fight nowadays). From that point
on, we were never really in it. We scored three late tries to

make it respectable, but the 28–20 scoreline was a little bit flattering. Truth be told, Manly completely outplayed us, with Watmough scoring two tries and winning the man-of-the-match award.

Having surrendered our world title, we didn't have to wait until summer for the wheels to come loose on the home front, losing five games in seven in March and April (including twice to St Helens, once in the league and once in the Challenge Cup). We were booed off the field after losing 21–4 to Harlequins at Headingley (only my last-minute try stopped us from being scoreless for the first time since 1998), and the papers were suddenly calling us a club in crisis.

Those journalists were looking a bit daft after we won nine of our next ten. And having blown the chance to go top with a loss at Wigan, we finally found top gear at exactly the right time. Ryan Hall scored five tries in a 76–12 win over Castleford before Brent Webb scored four in a 68–0 win over Celtic Crusaders, a result that took us to the top of the table. And victories over Saints and Salford meant we won the League Leaders' Shield for only the second time in Super League.

We then spanked Hull KR in our first play-off game, before choosing to play Catalans in our semi (under the controversial new 'club call' system that had been introduced, which almost everyone thought was barmy). Catalans were well up for it but three tries in five minutes before the break extinguished their fire and we ended up winning 27–20.

Two days later, a few of us attended the funeral of the great John Holmes, who had died of cancer at the age of fifty-seven. In the second of John's Championship-winning finals, in 1972, Leeds beat St Helens 9–5. Fittingly, Saints were to be our opponents at Old Trafford for the third year in a row, after they'd just managed to see off Wigan in their qualifying semi-final. Funny how these things work out. At the funeral, John's brother gave a speech, in which he told how being described as 'a great fella' or a 'smashing bloke' meant more to John than any praise he got for his rugby. I could relate to that.

Having been underdogs the previous two years, we went into that final as favourites, having finished the regular season like a train. There was a lot of intrigue in the build-up, most of it focused on what the *Guardian* called the 'mutual loathing' between the teams. As I've already explained, we didn't actually loathe each other, we were just deadly enemies on the field and quite suspicious of each other away from it.

That's just the way professional sport is, whether it's Manchester United and Arsenal in the Ferguson-Wenger era or the Chicago Bulls and the Detroit Pistons in the early Michael Jordan era. When they're old and grey, opposing players look back on those rivalries with great fondness. At the time, all they want to do is grind each other into dust.

Not only had we beaten Saints in the last two Grand Finals, but we'd also beaten them in a fiery game a few weeks earlier, with Keith getting a one-match ban for whacking Jon Wilkin off the ball and Jonesy getting away with a dodgy tackle on James Graham. As well as that, some Saints players were apparently irritated by JP's recent autobiography, which they thought came across as a bit cocky, while Jon Wilkin had accused us of celebrating too wildly after our most recent Grand Final victory. If he'd just knocked on our changing room door and told us to keep it down, I'm sure the lads would have obliged . . . Or maybe not. I'm laughing now, just imagining the look on Keith's face.

Rightly or wrongly, Saints had got themselves a reputation as moaners (Leeds fans even nicknamed James Graham the 'Ginger Whinger'), while we were meant to be the class swots, getting away with things we shouldn't because Gary Hetherington went along with governing body initiatives (even the aforementioned 'club call', which he probably thought was ridiculous). To add to that, Bluey never said anything even vaguely controversial, and Kev was the second coming of Bobby Moore, the perfect captain and ambassador for his sport, on and off the pitch. Throw Sean Long's recently serialized autobiography into the mix, which was full of scandal and must have been a painful read for rugby league purists and RFL blazers, and it added up to a lot of media attention.

With football continuing to stomp over every other sport, and rugby league constantly having to fight for column inches, that could only be a good thing. Instead of fining Longy for the things he said in his book, the RFL should have insisted on him being named man of the match before the game kicked off.

Despite all the hype, the game itself didn't really produce many fireworks. There were no punch-ups or outrageous tackles, and there wasn't much in the way of attacking flair. In fact, it was the sort of encounter that journalists refer to as 'absorbing', which is code for 'a bit dull if you're not into rugby league'.

Saints dominated the early exchanges and were 8–0

up after a Kyle Eastmond try, conversion and penalty. Normally, that wouldn't feel like an unassailable lead, but because it was cagey and their defence was right at it, it did feel a bit daunting. Thankfully, Saints started making mistakes. Matty Diskin having burrowed over for our first try, Francis Meli then deflected a Maggsy kick into the path of Lee Smith, who touched down to level the scores.

Kev knocked over a drop-goal just after the restart, before I was pinged for a high tackle on Longy and Eastmond kicked the penalty to make it 10–9 with twenty minutes to play. Kev nudged us ahead with another penalty, before pulling off a magnificent try-saving tackle on Eastmond. The final ten minutes were almost unbearably tense and it seemed almost inevitable that the game would be decided by something controversial. And that's how it turned out.

With seven minutes on the clock, Maggsy stabbed a kick through with his left peg and Lee Smith scooped the ball up and scored under the posts. The problem was, Lee appeared to be marginally offside. None of the lads in the commentary box thought it should have been given and VAR probably would have ruled it out (by a toenail, or a scab on Lee's elbow). But after running through all the different camera angles, the video referee awarded the try. Kev made the conversion, before I added a drop-goal to make the final score 18–10.

In case you were wondering, winning Grand Finals never got any less sweet. That's the beauty of sport: it's not like being a stage actor or playing in a band, when you're performing the same lines or the same songs every night. Every second of every season is different. Every trophy you win tells a different story, just like Jonesy says. Apart from my drop-goal, I was barely mentioned in the reports. But that's not what team sport is about, or at least it shouldn't be. And that's why it was so fitting that Kev won the Harry Sunderland Trophy for man of the match. His comments afterwards certainly rang true with me: 'Every one of our players could earn more somewhere else. But they choose to sacrifice a few quid to be part of nights like this. You can't put a price on the memories we've had. In many ways, we're a team of billionaires.'

Did I feel sorry for St Helens, having lost to us for a third year in a row? Not really. Actually, not at all. We didn't hate them like the media made out, but professional sport is dog eat dog, kill or be killed. It's not actually war, but it's the closest thing you can get to it without guns.

There are times during every season when you think things can't get any worse. You'll turn up for training on a Monday morning, after a bad defeat at the weekend, and wonder if there's anything you can do to turn things around. And then, a couple of months later, you'll be lifting a trophy. And if you're not singing, dancing and spraying champagne in your changing room afterwards, the other team will be, while you're sitting there with your head between your knees, listening to people weeping. Why would you want that? And there's always the next game. One thing was certain, Saints weren't going anywhere, even if Longy was . . .

★

Sean Long, St Helens scrum-half

I must admit, losing to Leeds in Grand Finals did become a bit tiresome. Those first two losses especially were shocks to the system. After beating them in the eliminator in 2007, we were all thinking, 'We've beaten them once, so we should be all right if we play them again in the final.' But they raised their game and absolutely smoked us. Their big pack got stuck into us and that combination of Sinfield, McGuire and Burrow did what they did best. They just had so much energy, suddenly seemed a lot fitter than us.

When I first started playing professionally, in the mid-1990s, Leeds were nowhere and it was all about Wigan, my home-town team, and St Helens. But when all those kids came through it changed everything. The spine of that Leeds side was so strong, and they managed to keep it in place for so long. Their overseas contingent was very handy, but they were all very good players, even those on the fringes. They had the horribleness of Peacock, Senior, Leuluai, Jones-Buchanan and Diskin, none of whom ever took a backward step, combined with the flair of Burrow, McGuire, Sinfield, Donald and Webb. They were the perfect blend and a nightmare to play against.

But without Rob, I don't think they would have won as many Grand Finals as they did. He always came up with a special play at the right time. You'd be on their line, building pressure and thinking, 'We've got 'em here, they're bound to crack in a minute', and suddenly Rob would pick the ball up and go on one of his mazy runs, duck under a few people and cause chaos. In the blink of an eye, he'd have turned the game on its head, which had a very deflating effect. That Leeds side had a few players who were able to come up with magic moments at key points, but Rob did it more than anyone else.

I still remember the first time I set eyes on him. I was

playing for St Helens against Leeds and our academy sides were playing in a curtain-raiser. I saw this little fella carving it up, ripping our lot to shreds, and said to whoever was beside me, 'Who the hell's that number seven?' A couple of years later, he was part of a young Leeds side that came to Knowsley Road and I was worried he'd show me up. I'd been playing for quite a few years by then and was in the England team, but he was just so dangerous.

He had lightning feet and could beat anyone one-on-one, so we had to double-team him. And if he still got through, he had the gas to go the full length of the pitch without anyone catching him. I always felt I had to be at my best when I played against Rob. I certainly wasn't thinking about how small he was.

All the St Helens lads hated playing against Rob, especially if they were six foot three and eighteen stone. He put the fear of God into big lads. They'd sooner have been tackling people their size, like Jamie Jones-Buchanan or Ryan Bailey, who ran straight at them. Rob would do a bit of footwork and leave them clutching at thin air, completely show them up. And the worst thing that can happen to a professional sportsperson is to be embarrassed.

But Rob wasn't all about speed and fancy footwork, he was a seriously tough competitor. He never gave me any verbals, but he gave off lots of positive vibes and was big on rallying his teammates. And he could be dirty when he needed to be. In the 2009 Grand Final, there was one point between us with twenty minutes to go when I came out the back of a play and thought I was through. I went for the line and Rob appeared out of nowhere and hit me round the chops with his forearm, almost taking my head off. If he hadn't done that, I think I would have gone over for a try and the result might have been different. But I never had any beef with him, that was just his nature. I'm sure he always has to win when he's playing Monopoly against his kids.

But what impressed me most about Rob was his bravery. When I used to take the line on, I'd sometimes be a little bit worried, and I'm five inches taller than Rob. I'd see a couple of big men in my peripheral vision and think, 'I'm gonna get clobbered here.' That was especially true before there were cameras everywhere, when players were always getting clipped and punched off the ball. But it never seemed to faze Rob. If Rob had the ball and there was a twenty-stone prop in his way, he'd run right at him, before leaving him for dead. And if a twenty-stone prop ran at Rob, he'd take him down.

In rugby league, a spot player is a lad you run at to get quick play of the ball. A weak link, in other words. But Rob was never a spot player for us, because he was such a good defender. He always made his tackles, chopping players down by the legs instead of going high, like a lot of other lads would. Instead, we'd pick on bigger lads, players we knew would fatigue quicker.

Apart from size, Rob had everything. He was quick, elusive, tough, consistent and incredibly fit (on our first Great Britain tour together, the 2006 Tri-Nations down under, I couldn't believe how hard he trained – and he never played a minute!). But it's his courage that stood out most. He was ridiculous, really, defied the laws of rugby league. He caused me a lot of hurt and I was sick of the sight of him after those three Grand Finals.

I never got the chance for revenge, because that 2009 final was my last game for Saints. But it was impossible to hate Rob. He was a fierce rival, one of the best I played against. But he was just such a nice bloke who became a good mate.

9

WHEN YOU GET DIAGNOSED WITH MND, YOU END UP having some pretty heavy conversations with your doctors. Gone are the days when your doc is some peripheral character you visit once in a blue moon and barely know, who gives you quick once-overs and hastily writes out prescriptions for antibiotics. Suddenly, you're having deep and meaningfuls about dying. What the journey towards death will look like, what it will feel like when the end finally comes.

Dr Jung tells me that some patients want to know everything, while others prefer to know as little as possible. But every patient asks how long they've got left. When I asked, Dr Jung drew a diagram of a body, inserted my symptoms and talked me through the science. That's the best way, because science is the truth. And if she'd started making wild claims about me possibly going on for as long as Stephen Hawking, I'd have known she was fibbing.

Dr Jung said it was a case of waiting and watching. I might last longer than two years, I might not. There were too many unknowns. But one thing I did know was that I was in good hands. As you can imagine, when you've just been diagnosed with a terminal disease, you feel quite vulnerable. But Dr Jung seemed like a good woman. A woman I could confide in without embarrassment, a woman who cared.

I already had a rough idea of what the end would consist of, but Dr Jung filled me in on the details, to put my mind at rest. A lot of MND patients imagine they'll end up thrashing around and gasping for breath, like a fish out of water. But Dr Jung explained that because my lungs will no longer be able to squeeze anything out, the carbon dioxide levels will build up, I'll start to feel drowsy and maybe get a bit of a headache, before slipping into a coma. Dr Jung made it sound almost peaceful, a nice way to go.

★

Dr Agam Jung, consultant neurologist

It's not easy telling someone they have MND. If a doctor gives a diagnosis of cancer, they can often go on to talk about radiotherapy, chemotherapy, surgery. They can give hope. But there's no cure for MND, so I can only talk about symptom control, our team and participation in drug trials or other research. Hopefully, that makes them feel supported, that they're not making the journey on their own.

I need to get that first meeting right, because that's when relationships are established. If that meeting doesn't go well, it can be an uphill struggle. When I first took over the service in 2011, I had half an hour to break the bad news. Now, I have an hour instead. You can't rush something like that. You need to take your time, give them all the information they need, manage the patient's emotions, as well as the emotions of their loved ones. And at the end of it, I need five minutes to gather my thoughts, because it takes its toll on me too.

But as difficult as it can sometimes be, I view my job as a privilege. I'm suddenly dropped into a person's life when they're at their most vulnerable. I start out as a stranger to the patient, but I soon get to know the real person, their inner soul. I get to know their emotions, their fears, what drives them. It's the most emotive journey, the journey towards death. So to be part of that journey, and for Rob to tell me all the things he's told me, is an honour.

During one consultation, Rob said to me, 'Would you be telling me this if I was a family member?' I replied, 'Yes. I'd say exactly the same if you were my younger brother.' Normally, medics try to maintain an emotional distance, but it's not always possible. Not many patients had asked me that question before. It showed that I'd gone beyond being just his doctor. After that exchange, I could see Rob relax. He felt comfortable, safe and secure, because he trusted me like a brother trusts an older sister. When someone sees you in that way, it makes you realize just how important your job is.

Quite apart from the physical toll MND takes on a patient, the psychological toll can be huge. Having been diagnosed, they're suddenly having to deal with their impending death, the end of all their dreams, all the wonderful things they wanted to do and beautiful things they wanted to see, such as children growing up. But in my experience, that time between diagnosis and accepting the diagnosis is short in MND patients. It soon sinks in that they've only got a certain amount of time, so they want to make the most of it. And what MND patients want most – all people, actually – is to be surrounded by love.

A colleague once said to me, 'If your patient's not really lovely, you've probably got the diagnosis wrong.' She was right, all MND patients are lovely people. There is a neurological element to why MND patients are emotional, but I think there is also a deep psychological and spiritual element that comes with knowing they're dying. MND patients want to get rid of all their baggage, find peace in their hearts. It's like they've flicked a switch.

Our clinic is not morbid or morose. It's a happy place, a positive place. I always tell my patients, 'If I were you, I'd put my foot on the accelerator and do all the things I've ever wanted to do. Live life to the full.' I don't think positivity can slow MND's march, but it can help patients cope better.

One of the reasons Rob has coped so well is because he set goals. Rob's very spirited and single-minded. As soon as acceptance kicked in, he made up his mind that he was going to channel his energy into raising awareness. I know he was brave and courageous on the rugby field, but to open yourself up and invite people into your world when you're at your most vulnerable is courage on a different level completely.

It's obvious that he was a professional rugby player, because he's more concerned about how his MND is affecting those close to him. He worries about the team, rather than himself. The night before I was scheduled to do a live interview with the BBC, Rob sent me a text: 'I know you can't make stuff up. Just be yourself. I look forward to seeing you on TV.' Being a sports personality, who had been interviewed many times during his career, maybe he thought I'd be nervous, because I wasn't used to having a camera pointed at me. After the interview, he sent another text: 'Well done this morning!'

People like Rob, Doddie Weir and Stephen Darby are so important, because they're changing the narrative around MND. Sports fans might disagree with me, but I'd argue that everything they achieved on the rugby or football field pales into insignificance compared to all that they've done to raise awareness of MND. Rob's right, since he started his campaign, I have had patients come in and say, 'I've got Rob Burrow's disease.' One patient had seen him being interviewed by the BBC, with Doddie and Stephen. They're making a difference, helping MND get spotted earlier and changing the way it's perceived, as well as raising much-needed funds for research.

Why does somebody become a doctor? To help people during their worst times. And MND is the worst of the worst. Accompanying MND patients on that journey towards death – helping them to accept it, making sure they feel supported, comfortable, and able to live their lives as fully as possible – has changed me as a person. I look at Rob, at his attitude and how his family and friends have come together to support him, and think, 'Wow.'

Before, when I taught about MND, I'd always refer to Lou Gehrig's farewell speech. It's a beautiful speech, all about how wonderful his life in baseball has been and how lucky he is to know such great people. But I won't be using it any more, I'll be using Rob's words instead. I've learned so much from him. But more important than that, he's given so many people hope. The impact he's had is phenomenal, and I can't thank him enough for that.

★

Failure is relative. And when you've just won three Grand Finals in a row, anything other than winning a fourth is bound to seem like a disaster. On paper, our squad for the 2010 season was as strong as 2009, maybe even stronger. Lee Smith, who scored four tries in those three Grand Finals, had switched to rugby union (although that didn't last long), but we'd brought in two quality players from the NRL – Kiwi World Cup-winning prop Greg Eastwood and Aussie centre Brett Delaney – and Danny Buderus, who had missed a lot of the previous season with injury, was fit and raring to go. However, what looks good on paper doesn't always look good on the field.

Having not lost since the previous July, we won only three of our first nine league games, which left us tenth in the table at the start of April. The 24–4 defeat at Wigan and the early season form of Warrington added up to cold, hard evidence that other sides had upped their games and closed the gap on us and St Helens. We also lost to Melbourne in the World Club Challenge, in a dour, scrappy game at Elland Road. We had a few chances to win it, but apart from Maggsy's length-of-the-field try early in the second half, which was one of the few highlights of the game, we couldn't get the ball down over the line.

The referee, Richard Silverwood, was English, but for some reason he changed his approach to suit the Aussies and had us playing to NRL rules in our own backyard. That meant lots of painfully slow play-the-balls, instead of the quick, clean rucks we were used to. With the scores level and twenty minutes to play, Keith finally lost his rag and got pinged for interference, before giving the referee a piece of his mind. Silverwood marched the penalty ten metres closer to our posts, Cameron Smith popped it over and we never managed to regroup, a late Melbourne try making it 18–10. A few weeks later, Melbourne had all their Grand Final wins taken away after being exposed for breaching the NRL salary cap, so I suppose we could argue that game never happened.

Lee Smith returned in the spring, having decided union wasn't for him (he clearly wasn't as daft as Maggsy thought), and we managed to claw our way up the table, so that we were fifth in June. But something wasn't the same. As I've already said, Bluey was a great bloke, but you can only take a team so far on emotion alone, and there was a feeling in the camp that the technical and tactical side of things was being neglected.

Even some of Bluey's motivational stuff was becoming slightly farcical: his theme for 2010 was Tiger Woods, who promptly crashed his car, got accused of having lots of extra-marital affairs, got dropped by a load of sponsors and announced he was taking a break from golf. He didn't win another tournament for two years. Bluey then swapped Tiger for Crazy Horse, the nineteenth-century American Indian war leader. Crazy Horse was no doubt a brave and noble chief, but what he had to do with playing Leigh on a wet and windy Friday night was anyone's guess.

Injuries didn't help, with Greg Eastwood suffering a string of them (before announcing he was leaving at the end of the season, because of homesickness), Kallum Watkins missing most of the year after busting a knee, and me missing two months over the summer after doing something similar. Chuck in a bit of unrest among the coaching staff, with Franny Cummins and Willie Poching suddenly announcing in July that they were off at the end of the season, and it was quite obvious that the club was in a bit of a pickle.

We did go on a good run in the Challenge Cup, the one trophy that had eluded us, beating Wigan in the quarter-finals (courtesy of a last-ditch try by Lee Smith) and St Helens in the semis (courtesy of a last-ditch try by Maggsy). But missing the injured JP in the final, which was like the Lakota going into battle without Crazy Horse, we were blown away by Tony Smith's Warrington.

Almost nothing went right that day, from the moment Danny Buderus fumbled the kick-off. Wolves stand-off Lee Briers put in a brilliant display (he won the Lance Todd Trophy for man of the match by a landslide vote), and they ran in six tries to one to beat us 30–6. We were embarrassingly bad – disorganized, low on energy, lacking inspiration – and we could have been beaten by more. No team likes to be humiliated in front of 85,000 people at Wembley and that result really laid bare the structural problems in our team.

Still, we managed to win our last three league games to finish fourth in the table and set up an elimination play-off against table-toppers Wigan. That game was a stone-cold classic. We were 14–0 down at one point but managed to claw our way back into it. Kev dropped a goal with five minutes to go to make it 27–26 and Pat Richards missed a late penalty that would have won it for Wigan. The one rather large downside was Maggsy buggering his knee, which meant he'd miss the rest of the season and a big chunk of the next.

Maggsy sustained the injury in the lead-up to that late penalty miss – Richards had broken from deep and Maggsy had tugged the shirt of the supporting George Carmont, although the penalty was actually for a late tackle by Scott Donald on Richards (at least I think it was). The Wigan boys weren't exactly over the moon, because they thought Carmont would have been in under the posts had Maggsy not intervened. A couple of their lads even had a go at him while he was writhing in agony. Former Wigan player Phil Clarke then chucked fuel on the fire by suggesting in a blog that 'the rugby gods' had punished Maggsy for 'unsportsmanlike play'. That was an odd thing to say about a bloke who had been badly injured while pulling an opponent back by his shirt – it was hardly eye-gouging – and didn't go down too well in Leeds.

Two weeks later, we played Wigan again in a qualifying semi-final at Headingley, the Warriors having tonked Hull KR in their preliminary. This time, Wigan beat us comfortably, 26–6, before going on to beat St Helens in the big one at Old Trafford. That was Saints' fourth Grand Final defeat in a row and Wigan's first Super League title since 1998. It was only a matter of time before the Pie Eaters, all-conquering before the birth of summer rugby, came good again. Every season, players were getting bigger, fitter and faster, so we had to keep improving. We had a lot of work to do to get back on terms.

As my teammates often like to remind me, I did at least provide a memorable moment of slapstick during that 2010 season. It happened during our Challenge Cup fourth-round tie against Hull. We were cruising at the time, about thirty points up, when I got involved in a shoving match with Epalahame Lauaki, who was over six feet tall and weighed eighteen stone. Lauaki's comic timing was perfect. After I pushed him in the chest, a look of disbelief appeared on his face. And after a split-second pause, he cuffed me round the chops. That's when I lost it and started firing back. Well, 'firing' might be pushing things.

At the time, I thought I was giving him a decent fight. But when I watched it back on TV, I discovered my punches were missing by a few feet. I looked like Scrappy-Doo trying to fight a mummy. Keith was laughing when he came flying in to protect me, before throwing a left hook at Lauaki. Only Keith could find the prospect of fighting a six-foot, eighteen-stone Tongan funny. By the time I'd been dragged away and banished to the sin bin, almost everyone had a smile on their face. I swear even the referee was trying to stifle a giggle.

I blame Baz McDermott, just spending too much time in his presence could make you a dirty player. It was like osmosis; you couldn't help but absorb his filth. But let the record show that I had three fights in Super League and was never defeated. I didn't land a single punch, but who was counting?

My dad provided a funny little postscript to that story. A couple of years later, he was doing a careers presentation at Hull, as part of his union brief. When all the Hull lads filed in and sat down, he handed out stress balls in the shape of brains, but left Lauaki out. Then Dad opened up with, 'Does anybody not have a pen? And does anybody not have a brain?' Lauaki was a good sport about it, sheepishly raising his hand, and the other lads all fell about laughing.

★

Jamie Peacock, Rhinos teammate

I was sat on the bench watching that scrap – if you can call it that – between Rob and Lauaki and thinking, 'You've bitten off more than you can chew here, Rob . . .' But the reaction of some of our more robust players, shall we say, tells you how protective we felt of him. If anyone messed with him, me, Keith, Kylie, Ryan Bailey – what you might call the heavy artillery – would be in there in a flash, helping him out of a sticky situation. As far as we were concerned, anyone taking a liberty with Rob was simply unacceptable.

While it's easy to laugh at that disagreement with Lauaki, it highlights Rob's courage. And I'm not sure I played with anyone more courageous than Rob. It's great to have blistering pace and wonderful agility, but if you're not brave enough to use it in the right areas, it's a waste of time.

Because Rob wasn't afraid of getting hurt, he spent a lot of time running into areas of the field where he could potentially come off very badly. And he didn't do it every now and again, he played every single game like that. That's what made him such a threat and allowed him to have such a big influence on games. By playing on the very edge of safety, he was better able to hurt the opposition.

Just look at what he did against the Kiwis in 2007: they were the biggest, hardest-hitting side we played against, and he was the smallest guy on the pitch, but he won man of the series. It didn't matter how many times he got hit by big men or knocked unconscious, he'd always come again. A lot of players far bigger than Rob would shrink from the fight after coming off second best two or three times, but Rob never stopped putting his body on the line. So while the heavy artillery knew we had a responsibility to look after him whenever fists started flying in his direction, we never had to worry about him otherwise. Rob was perfectly capable of looking after himself.

★

In August 2010, it was announced that Brian McDermott would be re-joining Leeds as Bluey's assistant the following year. But when Bluey resigned after our play-off defeat by Wigan (having signed a contract extension only a few months earlier), Brian suddenly found himself in the hot seat.

I was in Dubai when Kev texted me with the news, and I was happy about it. Brian had been Tony Smith's assistant for a couple of seasons before becoming head coach of Harlequins, where he'd done a decent job. Not only was he a good coach, but I'd always got on well with him. While Tony was like a strict headmaster, Brian was his approachable sidekick. He was a former Marine and boxer, but there was nothing intimidating about him. And he was a very deep thinker, had an opinion on everything. I thought he'd be like a combination of Tony and Bluey, which had to be a good thing. Or so I thought.

We had a good pre-season, with everything feeling a bit fresher. Whenever a new coach comes in, training tends to become sharper and more intense, because everyone is trying to impress him. After a few warm-up games, Brian called me in for a meeting. It went well, and I can remember exactly what he said to me: 'I can't guarantee you'll be selected, but I'm sure you'd only want to be picked on form anyway.' That's what I wanted to hear, because no self-respecting player wants to be picked purely on reputation.

Maggsy missed the first few months of the 2011 season, and life was a bit of a slog without him. We lost five of our first ten games and our defence was leaking like a sieve. Warrington put forty points on us, while Harlequins, St Helens, Hull KR and Huddersfield all racked up thirty (remarkably, that was Huddersfield's first win at Headingley for fifty-one years). Against Wigan, we were winning 22–4 with 18 minutes remaining but ended up drawing 22–22.

Some of the rugby we played in the early days of Brian's reign was pretty embarrassing, but I don't think that was down to him. JP also missed the first chunk of the season, and Brian was trying to blend younger players, like Zak Hardaker, who we'd signed from Featherstone, and Ben Jones-Bishop into the mix. On top of that, Gary Hetherington had tasked Brian with making us play with greater freedom, so he was tweaking things here and there and things weren't quite falling into place. That can quite easily happen in elite sport. Coaches are like mechanics, trying to fine-tune Formula 1 cars. If the tuning is even slightly out, you're going to get smoked by teams that are tuned just right.

We were seventh in the table in mid-April, and it was probably no coincidence that we only started to turn things around after JP's return to the team. Then, having won six games on the spin, Brian dropped me for the game against Warrington at Headingley. I remember him telling me I was starting on the bench and me saying, 'Oh, erm, OK . . .' It was a bit of a surprise to be honest, because Maggsy had only just returned from injury and I thought I'd been playing fine. We got spanked 42–6 and I only played the last twenty-five minutes.

The following Monday, me and Brian had a big meeting. I'm not a confrontational person, I like to keep my head down and get on with things. But that meeting was pretty intense. Brian was brutally honest, told me that he didn't see me as a starter. The best I could hope for, added Brian, was a spot on the bench, however well I was playing. And if I did get on, it would be at hooker, not scrum-half, because he liked the look of Maggsy and Kev in the halves. Nothing about that meeting made sense. I'd lived to play rugby league since I was a little kid, it was all I'd ever known. And now it was being taken away from me. But because of the shock, I didn't say much. I was struck dumb.

For the first time in my rugby career, I was devastated. Completely ruined. As Lindsey has already told you, I wasn't one for taking bad results or poor form home with me, but I was extremely upset for a few days. I'd been going along quite nicely and had only recently played my 300th Super League game. But now I was worried that it might all be over – that I was washed up, finished, soiled goods, over the hill. And I was still only in my twenties. It might sound melodramatic, because it was only one man's opinion of me, but I genuinely started thinking about what I might do instead of playing rugby.

Having gathered my thoughts, I asked Brian for another meeting. This one was a lot more fiery. It was like Brian had unearthed a completely different person inside of me. It was actually quite nasty. I swore at him and he swore at me. We didn't exchange blows, but it wasn't far off (although, let's be honest, Brian would have done what Epalahame Lauaki only thought about doing and bounced me off the walls). Eventually, I stormed out. I can't even remember much of what was said. But things were never really the same after that. Brian was the boss and what he said went; I just had to suck it up.

★

Brian McDermott, Rhinos head coach

I played against Rob a few times in my final couple of seasons with Bradford. When I first saw him, I thought, 'That boy's not going to last long. I'll just pick him up and throw him out of the ground.' It was actually quite alarming how small he was compared to everyone else. I don't mean to sound condescending, but it was like watching a child play against men.

But I soon forgot about his size. Instead, I was thinking, 'I hope he doesn't run at me, because there's a chance he's going to stand me up, go round me and make me look foolish.' Rob was incredibly agile, with frightening acceleration. He didn't have gears one, two, three and four, it was straight to fifth. And unlike a lot of players, whose decision-making goes out of the window when they hit top gear, Rob was able to combine his electrifying speed with vision. Rob once admitted to me that he sometimes got the ball and had no idea what he was going to do. He wasn't apologizing, he knew that it was a big part of what made him so dangerous.

Rugby league is a brutal contact sport and the pain it inflicts is immense, so people have to understand that almost all rugby league players worry about getting hurt. I was nervous about getting injured before every game I played, sometimes to the point of feeling nauseous. And I was a prop. So I can't even begin to imagine how Rob must have felt, going up against guys who were twice the size of him.

If defenders came out of the line to try and bash him – which happened quite often, because they saw Rob as an easy target, someone to bully – it left more gaps for him to exploit. But every time he went for a gap, he knew that if he got it wrong and didn't get through, he was getting crushed. That happened a number of times, but it never stopped Rob from yelling at his teammates to give him the ball.

Rob was also a smart guy defensively, and I never felt he was out of place physically. He developed a technique, where he'd rush up on a player before they'd had time to speed up, get right underneath them, lift them up and dump them on their head. And I'm talking about sixteen-stone blokes. The weight Rob could lift in the gym was ridiculous, and a few conditioners told me that he was the strongest guy they'd ever worked with, pound for pound.

Everyone says what an upbeat, positive guy Rob was. And most of the time he was. But I saw his angry side, a bloke who was pissed off with the decisions I made. I understood why he was so distraught, because he was a Leeds icon, had been the starting number seven for years, so it must have come out of left-field. And my inexperience as a coach meant that I made a right bollocks of explaining things. I get embarrassed thinking about it.

Maybe if I'd said to him, 'Rob, you're going to be a dynamic player off the bench, a role you'll be brilliant at and that will benefit the team', things would have gone smoother. Instead,

The kindness shown to me since my MND diagnosis has been incredibly heartwarming – and when people start painting giant murals of you, it can be quite overwhelming if you're a shy bloke like me.

Less than a month after my MND diagnosis, me and the gang got together for one last time. The testimonial at Headingley was hugely emotional (and Jamie Peacock thought it was a Cup Final!)

When Kev Sinfield (front row, right) decided to run seven marathons in seven days, his target was £77,777 – but he ended up raising £2.7 million. Kev was always Captain Fantastic and has never stopped being like a big brother to me.

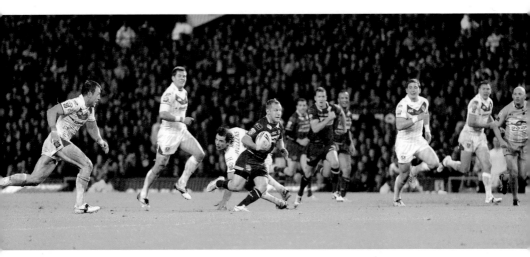

My try against St Helens in the 2011 Grand Final was probably the high point of my career. Leeds ended up winning 32–16 and I was unanimously voted man of the match, the only time that has happened.

In 2012, Leeds beat Australian side Manly in the World Club Challenge at Headingley. It was my third victory in the competition, but the high didn't compare to the recent birth of our first child Macy.

Leeds's 2015 Grand Final victory over Wigan was the end of an era – it was Kev Sinfield's last game for the club and also the last time Jamie Peacock and Kylie Leuluai pulled on the blue and amber in anger.

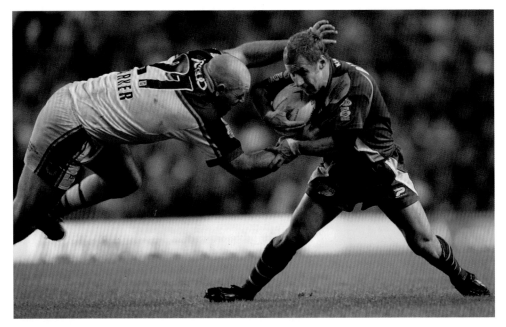

My first Grand Final appearance was against Bradford in 2004, when we beat the Bulls 16–8 for our first title in thirty-two years. We didn't know it at the time, but it was the beginning of Leeds's 'golden generation'.

Ryan Bailey, Danny McGuire, Kev Sinfield, me and Jamie Jones-Buchanan – five boys who came through the Leeds Rhinos academy – after winning our sixth Grand Final together, against Warrington in 2012.

In 2007, Tony Smith left Leeds to take over as Great Britain head coach. I was named man of the series after the 3–0 whitewash of New Zealand, but that was to be the high point of my international career.

England looked good on paper before the 2008 World Cup down under, but it turned out to be a disaster – Australia hammered us 52–4 in the group stage and we lost to New Zealand in the semi-finals.

The 2017 Grand Final was my last competitive game for Leeds. We beat my home-town club Castleford 24–6 and my daughters Macy and Maya got to see me lift the trophy for an eighth time.

Me and Danny McGuire had been playing rugby with each other since we were little kids – and had now won sixteen Grand Finals between us. When he asked me to lift the trophy with him, I was proud as punch.

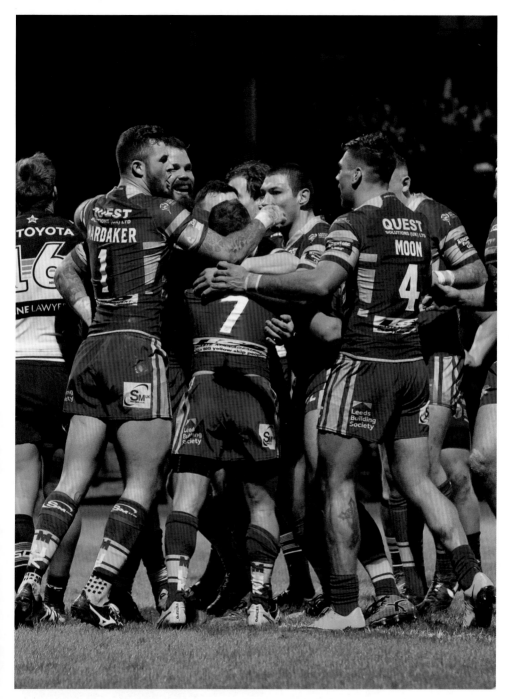

Aussies don't rate English rugby league much, so it was always great to beat a team from down under. But after three World Club Challenge wins, things went badly awry in 2016 – I scored our only try as North Queensland beat us 38-4.

In 2014, I finally managed to get my hands on the Challenge Cup after five final defeats. I started in the win over Castleford, but my relationship with head coach Brian McDermott (right) wasn't always the best.

I went into that first meeting thinking, 'Just be honest with him, even if he doesn't want to hear it.' I won't go into the technical reasons I gave him, other than to say I didn't think he possessed some of the subtleties the team needed in a scrum-half. But old dumb-fuck here made it sound as if I was attacking him. All Rob heard was, 'I don't rate you as a number seven.' Let's not polish things up, some of what he said to me wasn't great either, especially in that follow-up meeting, when there was a lot of effing and blinding. And our relationship never really recovered.

My decision completely altered his career. He never came to terms with it, the whole time I was there. As a head coach, I often didn't finalize my team until the day before a game. So I'd pull Rob to one side during the captain's run, which is essentially a light-hearted dress rehearsal, and ask for a word in the top room. He would always want me to explain my reasons again, even though I'd been through them lots of time already. I'd be thinking, 'You fucker. You must know what they are by now?' But he was just holding me accountable. And while I stood by my reasons, I appreciated how painful it was for him. Every time, Rob would say the same thing – 'I'm not happy and I don't agree with you' – before walking out in a foul mood.

But thirty seconds later, Rob would be a completely different guy in the changing room, doing what he could to lift the spirits. He never let my decision affect his attitude towards the game. Apart from our chats, he was everything you thought he was – relentlessly positive, the ultimate optimist. There are people in life who will happily put their hand up and tell you why something can't work. But Rob was the opposite, he never saw obstacles. No matter what the score was at half-time – and we found ourselves in plenty of bad situations – he'd be one of the guys trying to come up with a solution.

One time, towards the end of my first season in charge, Rob had a philosophical moment. I'd explained my reasons for putting him on the bench again and, this time, instead of telling me he wasn't happy and didn't agree with me, he said, 'You know what? If I play well off the bench on Friday night, it will just strengthen your argument?' I thought he might go out and play like shit. But instead of being that young fella on a building site, who makes you a terrible cup of tea so that you never ask him to make one again, Rob did the job I asked him to do brilliantly. After thirty minutes of all these big blokes running around, bashing the shit out of each other, tiring each other out and becoming less and less sharp, Rob went on and created havoc.

What people need to understand is that me and Rob weren't constantly at each other's throats. We even used to fire Alan Partridge quotes at each other during pre-season, before things got serious. I certainly respected Rob and I think he respected me. In a strange way, I felt privileged that I was one of the few people who saw another side of him. And I suspect Rob came to understand why I'd given him that role, because he was just so good at it. Agree with it? No. Like it? No. And I'm not sure he'd ever admit that publicly.

★

No, I didn't agree with it. No, I didn't like it. No, I'll never understand why Brian gave me that role. If I'd been showing signs of wear and tear or was out of form, I could have handled it. But, as far as I was concerned, I was as good as I'd ever been. Even now, I feel like I was unfairly done to. All I'd ever known was playing scrum-half; Leeds had won three Grand Finals with me playing scrum-half. But now, because Brian didn't rate me as a seven, I was going to have to learn to become a hooker at the age of twenty-eight.

Positions in league are more fluid than in union – it's not uncommon for league players to switch between the forwards and backs, while it never happens in union – but that doesn't mean it's easy. Sean Long once said to me, 'There's absolutely no way I could have suddenly switched to playing nine.' But by the time we played Castleford in the league in August, my new role was pretty much set in stone.

I asked for a meeting with Gary Hetherington, the first of many during Brian's time as head coach, and told him that if I wasn't going to be playing, I might have to leave. Gary was very cool and collected, told me not to overreact and to go off and have a think. I was deadly serious about it, and when other clubs started to get wind of what was going on – they could hardly not notice, because I was on the bench every week – offers started to come in.

Warrington were interested and my dad got a call from my home-town club Castleford (although talk of a swap deal involving their Kiwi half-back Rangi Chase was just newspaper nonsense). But instead of packing up my bat and ball and flouncing out, I decided to stick around, at least until the end of that season.

You might think it made things difficult with Maggsy and Kev, because they were starting in the halves every week while I was out in the cold. But I never blamed them or held a grudge. In fact, I felt a bit sorry for Maggsy, because he was now playing in my old position, which he must have found a bit awkward. But despite my frustrations, I had to be mature and rational about it. As far as my teammates were concerned, whatever went on between me and Brian was purely business.

It happens in sport all the time – a new coach comes in with different ideas which some players aren't going to like. And it's not as if I expected Maggsy to say to Brian, 'You know what? I think Kev should go back to playing loose-forward and me to stand-off, so our old mate Rob can play at scrum-half again.' In professional sport, as long as you're playing, you're happy. It's not the playground. And because they were all such good mates and we'd been through so much together, I still desperately wanted to do whatever I could for the team. Whatever had gone on between Brian and me, the club came first.

As a wise man once said: life is just a series of peaks and troughs, and you don't know whether you're in a trough until you're climbing out, or on a peak until you're coming down (see footnote, p.24). But in all seriousness, what went on between me and Brian probably made me a better person, because it meant I had to learn how to deal with adversity and adapt. That's a good lesson to take into the real world, which is often far more brutal than sport could ever be.

Sportspeople do get set in their ways, which makes them stale, so having to reinvent myself had its benefits. I did sometimes feel like a bit of a spare part in training, but I didn't let it get to me. Instead, I rolled my sleeves up, got stuck in and tried to work out ways I could still be effective as a number nine.

★

I was named on the bench for the Challenge Cup Final against Wigan. We'd only just scraped past Castleford in our semi-final, thanks to Kallum Watkins's last-gasp try and Kev's golden point penalty in extra time. And the media didn't give us much hope of beating the Warriors, who were top of the league table, five places ahead of us. Even our own fans were lukewarm, with ticket sales sluggish. They'd seen us lose five Challenge Cup Finals in a row – including the battering at the hands of Warrington the previous season – so those expensive trips down to London had started to lose some of their magic.

Not only that, but there was also a feeling in the media and among the fans that Brian had taken over an ageing team on the slide. Me and Maggsy weren't fresh-faced kids any more, we were battered and bruised veterans, with hundreds of games under our belts. JP, Kev and Jonesy were into their thirties, while Keith's career looked like it was coming to an end, the old warhorse having ruptured knee ligaments midway through the season. Keith had also criticized Brian's man-management in his recently published autobiography, which probably didn't go down too well in McDermott Towers, and suggested to the media and fans that there was a mutiny in the offing behind the scenes.

We had some talented kids coming through, but other clubs seemed to have nudged ahead of us. And not just Wigan and Saints. We hadn't beaten a top-four side all season and had been thumped by Warrington (twice),

Huddersfield and Catalans. We were truly awful against Harlequins in our last game before the Challenge Cup Final. And looking ahead to the following season, there didn't seem to be much chance of top-notch signings, because so much money was being pumped into the redevelopment of Headingley's South Stand. All in all, things were looking a little bit bleak, for me and the club.

We actually put on a decent show at Wembley, but to no avail. We looked dead and buried when Wigan went 16–0 up after twenty-seven minutes, but tries from Ryan Hall and Ben Jones-Bishop made it 16–10 at the interval. We were probably the better side in the second half and were throwing the kitchen sink at them for extended periods. And when Carl Ablett went over to cut the deficit to two points, the upset looked on. That still looked to be the case with two minutes to go, before a try from Thomas Leuluai finished us off. The commentators were raving about the game as a spectacle, but for me it was just another loss on the biggest stage, my fourth Challenge Cup Final defeat.

A few days later, me and a few of the lads were getting our kit off for a saucy calendar, to raise money for my ten-year testimonial. We were like those old ladies in the film, except with rugby balls covering our bits instead of buns and teacups. Some of the boys weren't too keen, others were champing at the bit. If Ryan Hall could wander the streets naked without getting arrested, he'd do it. The following day, we were sticking eleven tries on Wakefield at Headingley. I'm not suggesting that naked bonding session turned our season around, but there might be something in it, especially as Ryan scored a very fine hat-trick.

We finished fifth in the table, which gave us a play-off

eliminator against eighth-placed Hull. We won that game at a canter, before knocking out Huddersfield on their patch, with nineteen-year-old Zak Hardaker scoring a hat-trick. That victory set up a semi-final against Tony Smith's Warrington, who had won the League Leaders' Shield and hammered us twice already that season. The Wolves chose to play us instead of Wigan, who had beaten Catalans 44–0 in their preliminary, which gave us an added incentive. No 'chosen' team had won a semi-final before, and obviously if a team sits down and decides you're the weaker option, you're desperate to prove them wrong.

On the face of it, Warrington's choice made complete sense. Including the 2010 Challenge Cup Final, they'd outscored us 112–36 in our last three meetings. They'd also comfortably beaten Wigan twice in the league in 2011, but also been thumped by the Warriors in the Challenge Cup quarter-finals. Wigan were the reigning Super League and Challenge Cup champions and had finished the regular season only one point behind Warrington, and twelve points ahead of us. Only a madman would have chosen to play them instead of Leeds.

But more curious Wolves fans knew we were never going to be a soft touch in that semi-final. We were badly out of sorts earlier in the season, and missing key players like Maggsy and JP. But now we'd won our last four games quite comfortably, Maggsy was fully recovered and JP was back to his inspirational best. Frankly, Warrington's odds of 6–1 on were ridiculous.

The game, at their place, was a proper ding-dong, with the result up in the air until the final kick of the game. When I scored under the posts, after a brilliant run by

Brent Webb, it looked like we might have finally shaken Warrington off. But a second try from Chris Riley levelled the scores with twelve minutes to go, and it all went off after that.

Warrington's Matt King was denied a try by the video ref, their stand-off Lee Briers turned down a drop-goal opportunity, and a penalty from Kev, from inside our half, hit the post. We thought Ryan Hall had won the game with a couple of minutes left, but the video ref said I'd knocked the ball on in the build-up (I hadn't, but never mind!). However, just when we all thought we were heading for extra time, Kev had a drop-goal attempt charged down by Richie Myler, who was pinged for offside. Kev stepped up and knocked over the penalty, easy as you like, and we were off to Old Trafford for the fourth time in five seasons.

Instead of heaping praise on us, some journalists just seemed annoyed that the team that finished fifth in the table had reached the Grand Final instead of the team that finished top. Maybe they had a point, but we didn't make the rules. And the fact that Maggsy and JP both played superbly in the semi-final proved that the team that finished fifth wasn't really representative of us. Another beneficiary of the play-off system were St Helens, who finished third in the table but beat second-placed Wigan in their semi-final. That meant the 2011 Grand Final would be my fourth against Saints. But I'd be starting on the bench, of course.

A lot of the talk in the build-up was about the age of our team. And while we weren't exactly Dad's Army, most of us had a lot of miles on the clock. Aside from JP, Kev and Jonesy, Kylie, Danny Buderus and Ali Lauiti'iti were also over thirty, while Ian Kirke was knocking on the door. But all that talk was pretty irrelevant, because some of those boys had never looked better. JP's enforced break at the start of the season seemed to have done him the world of good, while Danny Buderus, who had won an NRL Grand Final with Newcastle Knights in 2001, played probably his best game for Leeds against Warrington.

The media predicted a more expansive final than normal, but Manchester's weather put paid to that. As usual, it was windy and drizzly, and the game soon settled into a typical showpiece arm-wrestle. One for the purists, as the purists often say. Kev had just made it 2–2 with a penalty when I was introduced, after about twenty-five minutes. To say I was wound up and desperate to do something special is an understatement. And a couple of minutes later, having received a pass from Danny Buderus just inside the Saints' half, I saw my chance.

Rhinos fans will know exactly what happened next; the rest of you will have to look it up on YouTube. But here's the gist of it. I noticed one of their defenders was slow in turning, creating a gap, so I decided to go for it. Maggsy was probably chirping at me, because he was supposed to get the ball from that play, but that's just the way I ran my game. I was always instinctive, off the cuff, never really knew what I might do. I stepped off my left foot, headed straight for the biggest guy, went round him, before ducking under another defender's swinging arm. I was now on autopilot. I sidestepped Saints full-back Paul Wellens, putting him on his backside, and managed to skip out of an attempted tap-tackle. But I still had three or four defenders closing in. I remember thinking, 'I'm going to have to duck again, otherwise I'm gonna get smacked.' I did get dragged down just short of the line but had enough momentum to slide over next to the posts. Next thing I knew, Maggsy had me in a sweet, loving embrace. I thought he might have turned up a little bit sooner, but he'd been chasing me all the way. What a picture. What a moment.

★

Jamie Jones-Buchanan, Rhinos teammate

You didn't need to be a fan of rugby league to know what a moment of genius that was, both in terms of speed of thought and agility. Afterwards, I asked Rob what was going through his mind when he got the ball. He replied, 'I noticed Tony Puletua was still getting back onside, which left a big hole. And in that split second, I thought, "If I take him on, one of two things is going to happen: I'm either gonna burn him or I'm gonna get knocked out."'

That might sound a bit dramatic, but Rob had been knocked out so many times before, including on big occasions. He'd been knocked out early in the 2003 Challenge Cup Final and the 2009 World Club Challenge, so he knew he was taking a massive risk in taking those big blokes on. But that's the difference between ordinary and extraordinary. Not only did Rob have the vision to see that opportunity, but he also had the courage to go for it.

That try, which has to be the best ever scored in a Grand Final, was Rob in a nutshell. And can you imagine the belief that sort of thing instils in the rest of the team? That was one of the great things about playing with Rob: every game I played, I knew that my forty or fifty tackles were going to be hard and they were going to hurt, but there was always the chance that Rob was going to reward all that graft with an unbelievable moment of magic.

★

We led 8–2 at half-time, but that all changed in five mad minutes after the interval. First, Saints winger Tommy Makinson grubbered through and reached around Brent Webb to touch the ball down, centimetres short of the dead-ball line. Then, Michael Shenton went over to give Saints the lead. When Jamie Foster kicked a penalty from halfway, St Helens were suddenly 16–8 up and my try was a distant memory. A try from Webby and a cool conversion from Kev cut their lead to two points, before our glorious leader levelled the scores with a penalty. And with ten minutes left, I thought it was time to rip up the playbook and freestyle again. It had worked once, why not a second time?

This time I was just inside our half when I got the ball. I went on a lateral run, to see if any holes might open up, before straightening and beating a tired-looking Scott Moore on the outside. I knew I had Ryan Hall in support, but decided to dummy instead of pass to him, which took Francis Meli out of the equation. When I finally got tackled, Ryan was still there, so I shovelled the ball to him and he finished brilliantly in the corner.

That try took any remaining wind out of St Helens, and Carl Ablett and Zak Hardaker both went over late on to make the final score 32–16. Having started the season like a clown's car, hobbling along on square wheels and with things falling off all over the place, we'd finished it like a Ferrari.

Were Warrington the best side overall that season? Yep.

But we were the best side when it really mattered. Brian put it best when he compared it to the Rumble in the Jungle. As he said, it's irrelevant, in the grand scheme of things, that George Foreman beat up Muhammad Ali for seven and a half rounds; all that matters is that Ali knocked him out in the eighth.

Having already won the Harry Sunderland Trophy in 2007, I now became the first player to win it unanimously, with all thirty-seven judges voting for me. I'd be a liar if I said it didn't feel like a big two fingers to Brian McDermott. But I couldn't win either way. If I'd played badly, it would have vindicated his decision to start me on the bench. But by playing so well, it did the same. But there was no point in dwelling on all that. I'd just won my fifth Grand Final with Leeds. And the taste never got any less sweet.

★

Brian McDermott, Leeds Rhinos head coach

Everyone talks about that Grand Final try, but I had the privilege of seeing Rob do something similar countless times in big games. I'd be sat there thinking, 'We're having trouble breaking this lot down and I'm not sure where the next little bit of magic is going to come from.' Sometimes I'd have got my game-plan or tactics wrong. And then Rob would get the ball and do something remarkable to turn the game on its head and save my blushes.

I've coached a lot of very talented players, but only a few of them have been able to show their best when a game was a real contest. Rob was one of those rare players who, when things were tight in a big game, would say, 'Give me the ball, because I really need to go and do something here.'

I'm sometimes asked if Rob improved me as a coach and the answer is always, 'Yes, without a doubt.' For a start, I had to dress better, because if I wore the wrong thing, he'd be on me. He'd fix me with a steely stare and cut me down with an impeccably timed one-liner. But on a more serious note, he taught me how to deliver information and to think longer and harder about any decisions I made.

You have your own theories as a coach, but when players disagree with them, it makes you examine those theories in more detail. A couple of times, I thought, 'Bloody hell, Rob, can you not just get on with it? Do we really have to go through all this again?' But by challenging me, he made me more thorough. In the end, I'd spend days preparing what I was going to say to a player, or when I would breathe or scratch my nose.

But I didn't feel like a smart-arse after that game, and the fact that Rob was the centrepiece was fine with me. It was my first Grand Final as a head coach and I was just elated that we'd won it. If Rob performed like he did to put two fingers up at me, I think that's a fair price to pay to win the trophy.

10

By the beginning of 2021, I felt like I was fading away. My fingers would no longer allow me to type words into my speech app, which finally shut me up. I almost disappeared from social media. Friends were texting and getting no reply. After five or six tries, they'd message Lindsey to ask if I was OK. She'd tell them I was fine and not to worry. But she knew full well that my world was getting smaller and smaller, and that I was becoming more and more isolated. My perch on the sofa had become a tiny island, slowly sinking into the ocean.

It doesn't matter how well your brain is working – and mine was still working fine – if you can't move or communicate, you're not much more than a shell. The girls would come home from school and I wouldn't even be able to ask them how their day had been. Lindsey would be buzzing around like a blue-arsed fly, fetching me dinner, rearranging my cushions, shifting me to make me more comfortable, and I wouldn't even be able to say thank you.

Sometimes, my mind would wander back to my playing days. I didn't have to wander far, I'd only hung 'em up a few years earlier. I'd think about what I'd been – 'The Pocket Rocket', 'The Mighty Atom', 'Little Beep Beep' – and compare it to what I was now. A burden, a passenger, a teammate not pulling his weight and destined for the exit. Not what Lindsey signed up for.

The coronavirus lockdown that kicked in after Christmas 2020 felt like a prison sentence. Pontefract in winter doesn't lend itself to coffee with your mates in the back garden and I barely left the house, not even to visit the hospital. I know I'm always preaching the power of positivity, but I'd be lying if I told you I didn't feel sorry for myself occasionally and have dark moments.

In the early days after my diagnosis, I honestly didn't give death much thought. But now I'd find myself thinking about Lindsey being alone in the house with the kids. One time, I suggested to Lindsey that we had the luckiest kids alive, and she replied, 'They're not lucky, because they're not going to have a daddy.' I'd think about life after death and whether I might be able to watch over them as a ghost. I reckoned it would be painful watching Jackson kick a ball about without me, but at least it would be something. And then I'd think, 'What if there's nothing?' The thought of that nothingness scared me.

★

Our first daughter Macy was born on 4 January 2012, which was the best day of my life, better than all my Grand Final victories rolled into one. Lindsey timed it perfectly, because I was due to leave for pre-season training in Cyprus the following day. And it's impossible to describe how I felt, laying eyes on my own creation for the first time.

Becoming a dad just felt so natural to me and I loved everything about it. I'd never been a wild man, like some of the other lads, so I didn't have to knock the big nights on the head. And I didn't mind changing nappies or being woken up in the middle of the night, because I was helping someone I loved more than anything else in the world.

★

Lindsey Burrow, Rob's wife

In 2011, I had a miscarriage, just before my twelve-week scan. That was a difficult time. The pain was worse than labour, maybe because I knew there wasn't going to be a baby at the end of it. And we did ask ourselves why, because Rob and I had always kept ourselves fit and healthy. But after speaking to family members and friends, we realized how common miscarriages were. It was just Mother Nature, one of those things, so we didn't dwell on it too much. Rob was upset, but he's just so positive in everything he does. We started trying again after a couple of months, I soon became pregnant for a second time and Macy was born the following year.

I was so ready to be a mum and Rob was so ready to be a dad. I was twenty-eight, Rob was twenty-nine, and we'd done most of the nice things couples without kids want to do – holidays to faraway places, meals in posh restaurants – so our whole focus was on Macy. Then, just over three years later, Maya arrived, before Jackson made his appearance at the end of 2018.

Rob was a brilliant dad, so hands-on. When I was at work, I'd send him off to mums and toddlers play groups. And, rather than be self-conscious, he'd love it. When I got calls from other players' partners, asking if Rob was home from training, I'd have to tell them he'd been home for hours. While his teammates were doing whatever they were doing, Rob was collecting the kids from school and playing with them in the garden, before doing all the other stuff he did for his family, like delivering dinner to his Granddad Bob.

After the kids were born, Rob became a bit more cautious when it came to his rugby. If he got a knock on the head, he'd say he was fine, ask for some smelling salts and get back out there. But maybe now he was thinking, 'I will have a life after rugby, and I'll need to be there for the kids. I can't be hobbling around with a bad back or hip, or having headaches all the time.'

★

Believe me, when things started going a bit wrong with Leeds, Lindsey and my parents knew how upset I was. But however important rugby was to me, it was just a bit of fun compared to my new greatest achievement, which was producing Macy. And Lindsey's right, I did start to wonder about all the knocks and bangs I was getting – I think that happens to a lot of people who play collision or combat sports.

But despite all that, it didn't mean I was going to dial down the intensity. Rugby was how I made my living, so I had a responsibility to play it as hard as possible. And despite winning another Grand Final and Harry Sunderland Trophy, I was still pissed off about what Brian had done to me. I didn't moan or mope, that just wasn't me. But when a solid offer came in from Wigan, I came very close to leaving.

We'd had a decent start to the 2012 season, including a big win over Featherstone in my testimonial and a victory over Manly in the World Club Challenge. That was another bruising encounter, far harder than the 26–12 scoreline suggests. And I don't think I'd ever heard more noise at Headingley, it was rocking that night. Ryan Hall touched down twice in the first half and we ended up outscoring them five tries to two, but our defensive resolve was probably more impressive than our attacking flair. I was just happy to still be on the field when the final hooter went – and remember picking up my third winners' medal – having avoided being knocked out by Anthony Watmough.

The 'super-sub' label had started to bug me the previous season – I know people were trying to be nice, but if I was on the bench, that just suggested I wasn't good enough. I'd never been a confident person, had never really rated myself and had always been self-conscious about my performances. And now Brian was confirming my worst fears, or at least he seemed to be.

You might think that becoming the starting hooker (Danny Buderus had returned to Australia) would calm me down a bit. But in my mind, I was still a number seven, not a number nine. I was involved in a strange balancing act. On the one hand, my personal pride and loyalty to the team wouldn't allow me to shirk, while shirking would also have given Brian a reason to ditch me from the squad altogether. On the other hand, by putting the effort in and playing well,

I was proving Brian right. You know what? I couldn't help respecting Brian, but it was begrudging at best.

If anyone had thought we were going to coast to a defence of our title, a 46–6 mullering at the hands of St Helens, followed by losses to Huddersfield and Bradford (who were on the verge of going out of business) would have caused them to have a drastic rethink. I was in and out of the team during this period, because of an injured shoulder and broken cheekbone, before we hit a real rocky patch in May and the beginning of June, losing to Hull and Warrington (who both put thirty points on us) and to Wigan 50–8 at Headingley. That Wigan result, the first time a team had scored fifty points against Leeds for sixteen years, was particularly shocking because they were missing a load of first-choice players. When Warrington beat us 37–18 in our next game, we dropped to eighth in the table and looked in real danger of missing out on the play-offs.

It was around this time that Gary Hetherington called a meeting and read the players the riot act, something he hadn't had to do for probably a decade. Gary didn't pull any punches, said performances had been unacceptable, that he didn't care about anyone's reputation and that if anyone didn't want to be at Leeds, he'd gladly arrange for them to join another club.

It just so happened that I'd recently had a clandestine meeting with Wigan's head coach Shaun Wane and his assistant Iestyn Harris, in a coffee shop in Manchester (Cafe Enzo on the Kirkstall Road wouldn't have been a wise choice). They made me a concrete offer, for quite a lot more money than I was getting at Leeds. Throw in the fact that we were struggling in the league and a rampant Wigan side were running away with it, and it was obviously tempting.

I was still under contract at Leeds, and Wigan needed to find a way to get me out of it. So my dad, who was suddenly acting as my agent, got on the phone to Gary, told him he'd heard about his threat to offload players and asked if he wanted to let me go. He didn't mention the offer from Wigan. Gary replied, 'Rob? God no. I was angry at the team, not him. I know he's in demand and we could get a good fee for him, but he's part of the furniture.'

Looking back, had they taken the number seven shirt from me, I might well have joined Wigan. I think my dad would have bundled me in his car and driven me straight there. It might sound childish and silly, but that shirt meant so much to me, and losing it would have been the ultimate insult. But they didn't, and after some soul-searching I decided I just couldn't face leaving Leeds. Wigan weren't asking me to up sticks and move the family out of Yorkshire, but Wigan isn't round the corner from Pontefract, it's a sixty-five-mile drive. That would have meant spending a huge amount of time on the road, to and from training, when I wanted to be at home with Lindsey and Macy. But it was about much more than the practicalities, like houses and travel and money.

I didn't see why I should leave the club I loved just because the coach didn't fancy me. The way things were going, Brian might not be around much longer anyway. And if I'm being completely honest, the thought of joining another club scared me. I wondered if Wigan would have the same camaraderie as Leeds and, being naturally shy, I worried that my new teammates wouldn't take to me.

I adored my Leeds teammates, they'd been a huge part of my life for so long. The thought of not seeing them every day – playing pranks on them, taking the piss out of them, going through hell with them on the training field – made me feel sad and empty. And the thought of playing against them, while wearing a cherry and white shirt, just seemed ridiculous.

People nowadays are always going on about it being a good thing to leave your comfort zone. But why would you leave your comfort zone when it's so bloody comfortable? Headingley was like my second home. I could have strolled around the place in a monogrammed dressing gown and slippers and no one would have batted an eyelid. I was pals with all the backroom staff, the groundsmen and the girls in the office. What's more, why would you leave your comfort zone when you're still playing well and winning things? So when I say I was serious about leaving, it was never something I really wanted to happen.

*

After that loss to Warrington, we looked like a team in turmoil. JP was even getting involved in Twitter spats with Garry Schofield, who, as ever, wasn't holding back in his criticism. But a high-scoring, tit-for-tat win over Wakefield got us going in the right direction again, and we were back up to fifth after five straight victories in the league. When we beat Wigan in the Challenge Cup semi-finals, people were wondering what all the fuss had been about.

One of the reasons for our turnaround was the bedding in of young academy graduates, just like a decade earlier. Keith having hung up his boots, Zak Hardaker had started the season at centre, before switching to full-back to cover for the injured Brent Webb. Zak had a freakiness about him, could do things with a ball that other players couldn't, and was running in tries from all over the place, as was our young winger Ben Jones-Bishop.

There was also Stevie Ward, who had been compared to Kev and made his debut at the age of eighteen. His first game was against St Helens and he looked like a proper dickhead: we'd all died our hair red for Comic Relief, but he'd gone one step further and got a mohican. As if that wasn't bad enough, Saints put forty points on us. Lenny Henry would have been proud, because their fans had never laughed so much.

I loved having youngsters around the place, it kept me fresh, and I was always very welcoming of them. I thought that stuff was important, because I knew exactly how intimidating it could be for a kid coming into the first team. Imagine being Stevie Ward, walking into a changing room and seeing me, Kev, JP, Maggsy and Jonesy standing there, five blokes with God knows how many Grand Final rings between us. I'm surprised he didn't faint. But just as Big Fat Barrie Mac did with me – I'll never forget him striding over and introducing himself on my first day – I did my best to make Stevie feel at home, like the Artful Dodger with Oliver Twist. I realized that the more comfortable he felt, the better he'd perform. Aside from that, it was just the right thing to do.

Very soon, Stevie was one of my closest pals. He said to me once, 'You're my best old mate.' Meaning, 'You're actually all right for an ancient bastard.' In the normal world, you wouldn't see a thirty-year-old bloke hanging out with a teenager, but that happens in sport. We soon developed our own language, which basically consisted of communicating in quotes from *The Office*. Some of the other lads used to look at us like we were idiots. Which we were.

But it wasn't just Stevie, there were quite a few others. When Brad Singleton broke into the first team, I'd sit next to him on the bus to away games. Brad's from Barrow, so whenever the bus was driving through some decrepit estate in Wigan or Hull, I'd point out the window and say, 'Bet that's nicer than Barrow, eh Brad?' It did his head in. But the way I saw it, all those academy graduates were fresh meat to take the piss out of, and you can never have enough of that.

Gary Hetherington even used me as a plant when he was trying to sign Zak Hardaker from Featherstone Rovers. Zak had already made a verbal agreement to join another club, but Gary brought him in for a visit to try and persuade him that we were a better bet. When Gary and Zak walked into the coffee bar, me and Jonesy 'just happened' to be in there, and we spent the next half-hour telling Zak that we'd been keeping a close eye on his progress, how much we rated him and how Leeds seemed like the perfect fit (Zak was from my neck of the woods and also played for Featherstone Lions, so I had actually been aware of what a great prospect he was for quite a few years).

I'm not sure if that was what changed Zak's mind, but I know the fact that a couple of his heroes had taken the time to chat to him meant a lot. A few weeks later, I was picking Zak up and whisking him off to his first Leeds training session.

I had a couple of chats with Gary Hetherington about my

future at Headingley, while I know Gary also had clandestine meetings with Brian, at which the boss had to justify his decision to change my role in the team. I honestly don't know what was said between them, but I became a regular starter again towards the back end of that season, albeit at hooker. It's not where I wanted to be playing, and while I didn't moan, teammates knew I wasn't happy about it. But I did enjoy the process of working out how I could best influence the team. It's probably accurate to say that for the last six years of my career, I was motivated by trying to prove people wrong, all over again.

When we blitzed Wigan to reach the Challenge Cup Final – our best performance for months and the first time we'd beaten the Warriors in seven games – the double suddenly looked a distinct possibility. That went up in smoke when we were beaten by Warrington at Wembley, my fifth Challenge Cup Final defeat and Leeds's sixth since we last won it in 1999.

Maggsy missing the game with a knee injury didn't help our cause, but we were still in it at half-time. That all changed when Brett Delaney had a try controversially disallowed just after the restart, before Warrington scored three tries in ten minutes. The Wolves went on to seal a 35–18 victory and we were condemned to yet more Wembley desolation. And no, it wasn't getting any easier to take.

A fifth-place finish in the table gave us an elimination play-off against Wakefield, which we won quite comfortably, Ben Jones-Bishop scoring a hat-trick and Maggsy his 200th Super League try, breaking Keith's record. Next up was a tight game against Catalans in Perpignan, which was swung our way by two quick tries from Carl Ablett and Maggsy, midway through the second half.

Wigan, who had won the League Leaders' Shield, then chose to play us in the semi-finals. Just like the season before, when Warrington had picked us, Wigan's decision made perfect sense. The alternative was Tony Smith's Wolves, who had finished only one point behind Wigan in the table and beaten them twice that season. When Maggsy was banned for a high tackle against Catalans (the fact that Wigan head coach Shaun Wane publicly lobbied for Maggsy to be punished didn't go down well in the Leeds changing room), almost nobody was giving us much chance of reaching another final. But – and without meaning to sound cocky – you probably know the rest by now.

In Maggsy's absence, I started at seven for the first time in months. Not that I really needed to do much in the first half, because Wigan didn't show up. We were 11–0 ahead at the break and looking unruffled, but when Pat Richards scored for Wigan on the hour, followed by a brilliant conversion from out wide, we were suddenly 12–11 behind. Enter Kev, who had already knocked over three penalties and a drop-goal. First, he put up a testing bomb that their young full-back Jack Murphy spilled, giving us a great attacking position with four minutes to go. Then, after Liam Farrell was pinged for being offside, Kev popped over the winning two-pointer. On nights like that, when Kev was just so cool and calculating, you wondered whether he was a man or a machine.

This time we wouldn't be playing St Helens in the Grand Final, Saints having lost to Warrington in the semis. Maybe that gave us an edge we might otherwise have been missing, because we had revenge on our minds, following Warrington's victory over us at Wembley. Maggsy was back in the starting line-up, meaning I moved back to hooker. But it was Kev who stole most of the headlines again, after one of the most entertaining Grand Finals ever seen.

Richie Myler touched down early for Warrington, before tries from Kev and Ben Jones-Bishop sent us ahead. It was 14–14 at the interval, following a try from Wolves winger Joel Monaghan, before Ryan Atkins went over to give them the lead again. A try from Carl Ablett, a second-row who had somehow converted himself into a top-class centre, levelled the scores, before Kev kicked his fourth goal to make it 20–18 with twenty minutes remaining.

For the next ten minutes or so, the game was on a knife edge. That was until Kallum Watkins, who had an excellent game, beat a couple of defenders down the right, Maggsy fired a long pass left and Ryan Hall skipped over in the corner. Kev kicked the conversion from out wide to make it 26–18, which is how the score stayed.

Kev was deservedly awarded the Harry Sunderland Trophy after another monumental performance. Not only did he score a try and kick five goals from five attempts (making it twenty-one from twenty-one in the play-offs), but he also had to peel himself off the canvas twice, following a whack to the ribs and a knockout blow to the head. What Brian said after the game was right: toughness isn't about swinging your fists and showing off your biceps, it's about standing tall and performing at your best when the flak is really flying. Kev embodied an understated, almost old-fashioned, heroism. The tougher things got, the more he seemed to relish it. But he wasn't a noisy hero, like so many sportspeople nowadays, he was proper and unassuming. If you're reading this and have children who play sport, whatever sport that is, tell them to be more like Kev.

*

That Grand Final victory, my sixth, had people comparing us to other great sides in rugby league history, notably Wigan in the 1990s. True, that Wigan team won seven straight Championships, but that was in the days before the Super League salary cap. In contrast, and as has been said before, no one could ever accuse our so-called golden generation of buying success.

Ten of our seventeen-man Grand Final squad were home-grown, only two of them were imports, and all our big stars could have been earning more money elsewhere. I know I'm biased, but there was a romance about that Leeds side that successful teams in other professional sports couldn't touch. We weren't like Manchester City, spending billions on the best players from all over the world. And we weren't like Saracens in rugby union, who became the best team in Europe, but were later thrown out of the Premiership for breaching the salary cap. I know fans of other Super League clubs hated us, but that was simply because of our reputation as city slickers. And the fact we kept winning.

But despite all our success, I never really felt like much of a celebrity in Leeds. That's partly because I hardly ever went out in town, but also because Leeds is primarily a football city, unlike Wigan, St Helens or Warrington. Weirdly, the rise and triumphs of Leeds Rhinos coincided almost exactly with the fall and struggles of Leeds United. The year we won our first Grand Final, 2004, United got relegated from the Premier League. When we were winning three league titles in a row between 2007 and 2009, United were languishing in League One. By the time they'd got themselves back into the Premier League, in 2020, we'd won another four Grand Finals. But their attendances were always higher than ours and their players always paid more (as well as being more attractive to women, which may or may not be a coincidence).

But Leeds isn't like Wigan, where there seems to be a rivalry between the football and rugby league teams. Rhinos and United co-existed quite nicely, and most United fans were happy that we were doing so well. And anyway, playing second fiddle to football suited me down to the ground. Despite all the success we achieved with the Rhinos, I don't think any of us lads really felt like we were a big deal, important men about town. One day, I was driving through Leeds and saw my face on the side of a bus. People were tooting their horns, waving at me and pointing, and I almost crashed. I found it quite daunting.

I knew that Rhinos fans appreciated me, which was lovely. But most of the time, I just felt like a common-or-garden bloke. If TV wanted to do some filming or a journalist wanted to have a chat, I'd usually oblige. As long as they wrote what I wanted. I might say to them, 'Put, "Rob Burrow is refreshingly laid-back for a man with such responsibility."' Or, 'Put, "Burrow mused . . ."' (see footnote, p.24). If I was asked to visit a school or hospital, or attend a charity fundraiser, I'd say yes in a heartbeat (unless it involved judging gnome contests). Most of the other lads were the same. We didn't put up barriers, we were approachable. If

226

it seemed like we were normal members of the community, it's because we were.

I also started doing vocational courses in my early twenties, because even then I knew rugby would end at some point (and a career in pantomime or becoming one of Santa's little helpers in the North Pole always seemed like a long shot, whatever Jonesy used to say). I qualified as a massage therapist and me and Lindsey set up our own little business. I'm not having a pop at footballers, their fame and their money. That's too easy, and good luck to the lads. But I never wanted to be one. I had the best of both worlds, achieving bags of success on the field, flying under the radar off it, away from the hassle.

★

After the glories of the previous two seasons, 2013 was a bit of a damp squib. Melbourne beat us 18–14 in the World Club Challenge at Headingley, with their scrum-half Cooper Cronk running the show and full-back Billy Slater on top form. But had I not dropped Kallum Watkins's pass with the try-line beckoning and the score 8–6 to the Storm, things might have been different.

In Super League, we were going along quite nicely until May, when I did an interview with the *Yorkshire Evening Post* headlined, 'We're Just Hitting Our Straps'. We lost our next three games and were also dumped out of the Challenge Cup by Huddersfield, who were looking like the team to beat that season. Without meaning to sound mean, it was about time they had a run at things, because they hadn't won a league title since 1962 and the Challenge Cup since 1953, despite being the birthplace of rugby league.

Around this time, rumours flared up about me joining Castleford. I'd be massaging a customer in Lindsey's practice and he'd say, 'My mate down the pub reckons you're joining Cas.' One bloke even told me he'd seen a contract. I'd have to say to them, 'Look, either you can believe me or you can believe your mate down the pub. I'm not going anywhere.' In fact, Castleford had been sniffing around, but if I'd admitted that to any random punters, it would have been all over the town in minutes before appearing in the following day's papers. And now I was starting most weeks, it was never going to happen.

We ended the regular season pretty well to finish third in the table, before being stuffed 40–20 by Warrington in our elimination play-off. We were comprehensively outplayed, with Wolves second-row Ben Westwood scoring four tries. But things might have been very different had Lee Briers not been allowed to stay on the pitch after punching Carl Ablett, when we were 10–6 up.

We squeaked past St Helens in our next play-off game, Maggsy popping over a seventy-seventh-minute drop-goal to make the final score 11–10, before going up against Wigan in the qualifying semi-finals, Warrington having chosen to play Huddersfield, winners of the League Leaders' Shield, instead. That suited us, because we'd finished ahead of the Warriors in the league table and beaten them quite comfortably only a few weeks earlier. But it was a game too far for a creaking team, Wigan running out 22–12 winners at the DW Stadium (the Warriors went on to beat Warrington in the Grand Final to seal the double).

That was our first play-off defeat in nine games and had people talking about the end of an era. I understood why.

The spine of our team had been so many rounds over the years that it was a wonder we could still get out of bed in the morning and tie our own shoelaces, let alone put in a decent shift for eighty minutes. The physical toll was unbelievable. The day after a game, I'd feel like I'd been in a car crash.

As for JP, who was involved in more contacts than anyone, it must have felt like he'd been in a car crash before crawling out of the wreckage and having a punch-up with all five occupants of the other vehicle. And by the end of 2013, he'd been doing that at the highest level for fifteen years (he played his 500th career game during the 2014 season). But the strange thing is, you get used to the carnage. You still feel the aches and pains, but that doesn't stop you from getting behind the wheel and driving into a wall again. No wonder people think rugby players are nuts.

The mental toll was just as difficult to handle, maybe more so. Physical injuries and pain can be healed, patched up and masked. But the mental side is far more mysterious. When your team is on a losing streak, you're playing badly and cracks are appearing in your mind, you can't apply a bandage. And when you've won another trophy and people are telling you how great you are, you've got to somehow stop complacency from seeping in. It takes a unique kind of person to be able to get back on the field, day after day, week after week, year after year. So after our failure to win anything in 2013, people were naturally asking, 'Is Leeds's golden generation finally – finally! – washed up?'

★

We looked a long way from being washed up in the first few months of the 2014 season, losing only one of our first four-teen games (including a 46–6 win over Bradford, my 400th game for Leeds). Our backs were unplayable at times, with Tom Briscoe, signed from Hull, slotting in very nicely on the wing.

I broke my collarbone in a win over St Helens and was out for three months, before returning to the starting line-up for our Challenge Cup semi-final against Warrington (although I was on the bench for our weird 24–24 draw with Castleford, most notable for Kev receiving his first ever red card – for sticking the nut on Luke Dorn – and JP missing a last-gasp drop-goal attempt, after I accidentally passed to him). We went into our game against defending champions Warrington in iffy form, but clicked back into top gear at the right time, winning 24–16, the highlight a brilliant one-handed try by Ryan Hall.

Our opponents in the Challenge Cup Final were Castle-ford, my home-town team. There was a lot of pressure on both sides going into that game. For Cas, Challenge Cup Finals didn't come around very often. They hadn't won it since 1986, when Bob and Kevin Beardmore, who went to the same school as me, led them to a famous victory over Hull KR. Funnily enough, Bob and Kevin were their team's scrum-half and hooker respectively.

Meanwhile, Leeds hadn't won the Challenge Cup since 1999. It was my sixth appearance in a final and I was turning thirty-two the following month, so there was a real sense that time was running out to win what was still the most famous trophy in the sport. And the more the press banged on about us not winning it, the more the pressure built up, even though I always denied it.

I'd played a lot of rugby with two of the Tigers' players, captain Michael Shenton and winger James Clare, all of it many years earlier, on that cul-de-sac in Castleford. And I'd coached my opposition hooker, Daryl Clark, when he was a thirteen-year-old kid at Airedale, my old school. But it's not like I was going to get all misty-eyed and sentimental about playing against my home-town club and childhood friends. If anything, it made me even more determined to win.

I was chuffed for Cas and the community that they'd made it to Wembley for the first time in over twenty years – the excitement in the community was lovely to witness – but I'd always been the weird kid who supported Leeds. Nowadays, you see quite a lot of people wearing Rhinos shirts in Castleford, but back then, it was pretty much just me and my dad. And we always enjoyed getting one over the Tigers. To do it in front of 80,000 fans at Wembley would be just about the perfect way to break my cup hoodoo. Maybe if Mum still supported them, I'd have felt a bit different. But she abandoned Cas the moment I signed for Leeds as a kid.

Cas certainly didn't make it easy. And if it hadn't been for the finishing skills of Ryan Hall, it might have been yet more heartache. In the first half, Ryan shrugged off two tacklers to score in the corner and make it 16–4. His hand-off on Kirk Dixon, which drove him backwards about ten metres, was just ridiculous. I call it a hand-off, but it was more like a Darth Vader death grip.

Cas had cut our lead to six points with thirteen minutes left, but then Ryan blasted through half of Cas's team, like a bowling ball scattering ninepins, to put the result beyond doubt. No wonder Rhinos fans had started calling Ryan 'WBW', standing for 'World's Best Winger'. Ryan had developed into a freak, one of those rare players who was able to take the ball standing still and generate enough power to make the yards needed to get over the try-line. The way defenders bounced off him, it looked like a grown man playing against kids.

The overriding emotion after that victory was relief. All those Grand Final wins would have been a very nice return from a career in rugby league, but had I not won a Challenge Cup, it would have bugged me until my dying day. Hundreds of blokes had won it since the first final in 1897, many of them great players in great teams. For us lads not to be among them would have been a travesty. And I was chuffed for our fans, many of whom had made that long journey too many times for no reward. Now they could go out and paint London blue and amber, before heading back up the M1 with fond memories.

The one downside of that day was that Granddad Bob wasn't around to see it. He'd passed away earlier that year, having never seen me win the only trophy that really mattered back in his day. He was never a regular at Headingley because he was poorly towards the end and needed a mobility scooter to get around. But he never missed a Rhinos game on TV, and he never stopped serving me up steak for dinner. He was one of life's great characters, who played such a massive role in my formative years. His loss hit me hard.

Before the Challenge Cup Final, we were only four points behind league leaders St Helens and still in the hunt for the treble. But we lost our next three games, to make it five league defeats in a row, before crashing out to Catalans in the first round of the play-offs, courtesy of a last-ditch try at Headingley. There's no getting away from it, we collapsed down the stretch, as if we'd had a mental and physical breakdown. That just shows how finely tuned professional athletes are: that huge effort to win the one trophy that had eluded us, followed by the deserved celebrations, had robbed us of our edge.

That was a bit of a shame, because that team, ageing and creaking as it was, would probably never have the chance to win the treble again. But if you'd offered me the Challenge Cup and nothing else at the start of the season, I'd have bitten your arm off. Don't get me wrong, Dad, it was nice winning it in your kitchen. But doing it for real, lifting that famous old trophy at Wembley Stadium, like I'd seen so many greats do when I was growing up – including the peerless Ellery Hanley, my old coach Dean Bell and my childhood hero Iestyn Harris – was better than I could have imagined. I pictured Granddad Bob, waving and shouting, 'Lad, I think the sun shines out of your backside!'

11

God, it's good to be back. I think people were starting to think I was gone forever, what with the radio silence. For about six weeks, I was almost completely locked in, a still-sharp brain stuck inside a rusting cage. But as Lindsey likes to tell people, since getting my new Eyegaze gadget, I haven't shut up. If I ask her to fetch me one more coffee, I think she might punch me.

It's a remarkable bit of kit, like something from a sci-fi film. People from Dr Jung's assistive technology team came round the house and spent a couple of hours assessing me, before calibrating the tablet to my personal settings. As the name suggests, I operate it with my eyes. Just by looking at icons on the screen, I can turn the telly over, surf the internet, answer the door, operate my bed controls, post on social media or tell Baz how fat he's got on WhatsApp.

It also means Lindsey can cut back on her secretarial work – beforehand, she was being bombarded with texts from people wondering if I was OK, fielding requests from people asking me to post things on social media, monitoring my emails and even having to write speeches on my behalf. But the best thing about this new machine of mine is that I can speak to the kids again – ask the girls how their day was, tell Jackson how much I love him.

As well as all that, I can read about some of the progress that's being made in the battle against MND. They thought 2020 might be a breakthrough year, but coronavirus put paid to that. However, things are moving in the right direction in 2021. I've been involved in trials, and they're making a lot of noise in America about another new drug called NurOwn. NurOwn has passed the first two phases of three-stage trials, and people are fighting to get its approval accelerated by the government over here. As the medical people say, MND isn't incurable, it's under-funded. So it makes me proud that the noise I'm making and the money people are raising on my behalf are helping to make things happen. And it makes me want to keep fighting until my last breath.

★

Joanne and Claire, Rob's sisters

Joanne: I always knew that Rob would make it as a rugby player, because he was just so determined and courageous. Me and Claire would watch him every Saturday, playing for Featherstone Lions, but not have a clue what was going on. However, we knew Rob was good, because he'd be absolutely everywhere. And he had no fear. The other boys would be twice his size, but he'd tackle everything, didn't seem to care about his wellbeing.

That determination was there for all to see when he was diagnosed with MND. I made sure I was at Mum and Dad's when they got the call, because I had a funny feeling it might be bad news. The scene was every bit as bad as Mum described it: Dad fell to his knees, Mum was wailing, almost delirious. But that same night, Rob phoned me and said, 'Me and Lindsey have had a chat and decided that from now on, there's a no-crying policy. We can't have that in the house. We've got to carry on as normal for the kids.'

Claire: During my darker days – and everyone in the family has them – I have to remind myself what Rob wants, which is for everyone close to him to be positive. That's what keeps him going. So I try not to get upset in front of him. And if anyone does get upset, he'll give them a very stern stare.

In the early days after his diagnosis, I'd say to him, 'You alright, Rob? You feeling OK?' That just felt like the natural thing to ask. But I soon learned that he didn't want us to be asking that, he just wanted us to be normal around him. So when I see him now, I'll try to act as if nothing is wrong. It can be difficult, especially for people who don't see him as often, because they feel like they have to fill the silence. And sometimes when I'm talking to him, and he can't talk back to me, he'll be looking at me as if to say, 'You're not being normal, Claire, you're talking absolute rubbish.'

Joanne: Sometimes, I'll sit with Rob, chat away and feel really comfortable. Other times, I'll just sit there staring at him. Staring at people has always been a bad habit of mine, since I was a kid. But because Rob doesn't want us to talk about his MND, that's my way of working out how he's doing. I'll feel Claire looking at me and thinking, 'I wish she'd stop doing that.' And it drives Rob mad. If I stare at him for too long, he'll tell me off.

There was a period of about six weeks where it felt like Rob was slipping away, when his fingers no longer worked and he could no longer take part in conversations. But his new machine has made all the difference. My husband is on a WhatsApp group with him and apparently he's right in the thick of any banter that's flying around and still has to get the final word in, just like when he was a kid. I ask my husband, 'What sort of things does he say on there?' And he'll reply, 'I can never tell you. You'd be absolutely mortified.' Despite it all, Rob's still the same person he always was.

Claire: I'll go round to my parents' and Rob will be sat there with my dad, watching some programme and laughing their heads off. Rob obviously loves *The Office*, but Dad's favourite comedy is *Cheers*. I'll walk in and Dad will be doing that thing that people do: 'Watch this bit, Rob . . . this bit's hilarious . . . wait for it . . . wait for it . . .' When 'the bit' comes on, it's normally not that funny. But Rob will laugh along anyway, so his dad doesn't feel bad.

Rob getting MND has definitely brought the family closer together. Before, if we didn't see each other for a while, I wouldn't really think anything of it. But now, I realize I have to make an effort, see them as often as possible. That's what families should do. But Rob still doesn't like us being anywhere near him. We'll be helping him walk and holding his hands, and I'll look at him as if to say, 'You can't stop us touching you now!' Or I'll say to him, 'Come on, Rob, give us a kiss!', and he'll give me a look of pure disgust.

★

Before the 2015 season kicked off, JP announced that it would probably be his last. Some people refused to believe it, mainly because they just couldn't imagine Super League without him. The bloke had been around for almost twenty years, performing to the highest level season after season. How he'd only won the Man of Steel Award once, and never while playing for Leeds, was a mystery. He'd played in eleven of the seventeen Grand Finals since Super League's inception, winning nine of them. For rugby league fans, the thought of Super League without JP was like the thought of London without St Paul's Cathedral, or Blackpool without its Tower. As for Leeds fans, it filled them with dread.

I know Bradford have had terrible financial problems, but I don't think it's a coincidence that they suddenly stopped winning things after JP left in 2005. Just as I don't think it's a coincidence that Leeds couldn't stop winning things after his arrival in 2006. JP was the Colossus of Leeds. Just his name on the team-sheet was a message to opposition teams that none shall pass.

By the end, JP was hobbling into training every Monday morning, like a doddery old man, but he'd be magically transformed into a warrior again by the weekend. Whenever JP spoke in a team meeting or in the changing room before a game, it was like the first time I'd heard him. He had me transfixed, like a wide-eyed little kid, because he was just so passionate. But he didn't even have to open his mouth, just his presence was massively reassuring.

It's a bit of cliché when sportspeople talk about being in the trenches with teammates, but JP's the man I'd most want beside me before going over the top. He'd give you one of his stirring speeches and you'd know he wouldn't be asking you to do anything he wouldn't do himself. He'd blow his whistle, clamber up the ladder and you wouldn't see him for dust, because he'd be so up for the battle. And God help the other lot if he made it to their trenches. Other players could try to replicate what JP offered, but it wasn't possible.

Kylie had also indicated that it would be his final year in Super League (although he'd announced his retirement more times than Frank Sinatra), while several old warhorses were out of the door before the season started, including six-time Grand Final winner Ryan Bailey and Ian Kirke. Brian only made one new signing, Australian prop Adam Cuthbertson, and I know some Leeds fans were perturbed by the situation. The numbers didn't seem to add up: only one man in (who wasn't exactly a superstar down under), four men out, while five or six of the blokes who remained were ready to hang 'em up.

We had a gruelling pre-season, two months longer than usual because of our early exit the previous campaign. I was still fit as a fiddle and at the front of the pack when it came to aerobic training, but the physical stuff was becoming a real struggle. We'd do a lot of combat training, pairing off and body-bashing each other, which isn't ideal when you're only eleven stone wet through and the other bloke is fifty pounds heavier. The younger kids, especially, were so much stronger than me – and probably keener, without me even realizing.

We made a flying start to the season, winning ten of our first eleven games. Adam Cuthbertson had turned out to be an inspired acquisition, while the likes of Stevie Ward and stand-off Liam Sutcliffe were really starting to make an impression. As for me, I didn't even make the bench for a couple of those fixtures and started only two of them. But a far bigger shock was when Kev took me aside in the gym and told me he was switching to rugby union at the end of the season, to play for the Rhinos' sister club Yorkshire Carnegie.

It was difficult to get my head around as a Leeds fan, the Headingley South Stander I'd never stopped being, let alone as a teammate. Kev had been at Leeds since he was thirteen and was into his nineteenth Super League season. I fully expected him to see out his playing days with the Rhinos. It didn't make much sense to me that he'd try his hand at union, a completely different game, at the age of thirty-five. Bear in mind, I didn't even know the rules of union. And Carnegie weren't even in the Premiership. But Kev wanted a new challenge, so there was nothing I could do apart from shake his hand and wish him good luck.

Sadly, Kev's final season at Headingley was more fractious than it should have been. Brian dropped him to the bench for the game against Saints in April, the first time that had happened since 2003. And because it was a couple of weeks after Kev had made his big announcement, it was difficult not to conclude that it had played a part in Brian's decision.

It certainly didn't sit right with me, a bloke who had given so much for the club being treated like that. And it was very odd sitting on the bench next to Kev, given all the great things we'd done together. Kev is very even-tempered, not one to rant and rave. And Kev being Kev, he said all the right things, about everyone being happy as long as the team's winning (we did actually thrash St Helens 41–16).

But I know he was pissed off. Simmering might be the best way to describe him. I knew exactly how he felt, because I'd been simmering for years.

Kev was on the bench again for the game against Warrington, which was a real shame, because it was his 500th for Leeds. Kev was only introduced after the interval, when we were already well behind, and what should have been a celebration at Headingley ended in a forgettable defeat. It got worse for Kev when he was dropped from the squad entirely for our game against Huddersfield, the first time that had happened for fifteen years. When he also missed our next game against Widnes, Leeds fans were up in arms. It didn't help Brian's argument that we didn't win any of the games Kev missed, Huddersfield having come from behind to snatch a draw and Widnes having stuffed us at their place, the first time they'd beaten us anywhere since 2003.

Kev was recalled for the Challenge Cup game against Huddersfield, which we won 48–16. He created a try, kicked eight goals and won the man-of-the-match award. But Brian couldn't really lose, because some people were now calling his decision to drop Kev a masterstroke, the shake-up the team needed. I'm not sure about that, but we did keep on winning.

Against Hull KR, Kev kicked six goals to become the third-highest points-scorer in rugby league history, with 4,062. And even after Wigan beat us for a second time in July, after a classic match-up at the DW Stadium, we were still flying high at the top of the table. When we beat Hull to reach the last four of the Challenge Cup, with me and Kev starting in the half-backs, it was starting to look like it could be a special season, even by the standards of those that had come before.

It was around this time that I signed a new two-year contract, putting an end to speculation that I'd be finishing my career with Castleford. When my massage clients heard about it, they were astonished. Only the night before, their mate down the pub had seen me hoisting a Tigers flag on my front lawn.

Cas's head coach Daryl Powell, who I'd played under at Leeds, had actually tried to persuade me that it would be a great way to go out, with my home-town club. He also reckoned he could improve me as a player, probably as a scrum-half again. It was a great pitch, and Dad said I should give it some serious thought. I believed Daryl, and Cas are the only team I would have considered signing for at that stage of my career. But I just wasn't quite sold on the idea.

By July, I'd started only a handful of games, and my role in the team – as an impact substitute – was set in stone. But our second daughter, Maya, had arrived on 2 March 2015, making any sort of professional upheaval even less likely. I still wasn't content with my situation, but I wasn't getting up every morning feeling depressed or returning home after training in tears of frustration. It was what it was, and things could have been a lot worse.

I was coming up to thirty-three and playing in a team that was chasing glory on three fronts. And it's not like I was a shadow of my former self. The fans didn't see me as a decrepit old beast who should have been put out to pasture years ago, because I still had my pace and a few of those old tricks up my sleeve. And the fact that clubs were interested in signing me told me that I was still respected by my peers. As any sportsperson will tell you, that means so much.

★

Luke Robinson, Wigan, Salford and Huddersfield scrum-half

Rob's been teaching me how to play rugby since I was a kid, when he was at Featherstone Lions and I was playing for a team in Halifax. When I was picked to play for Yorkshire, I had two lads ahead of me in the pecking order: Rob Burrow and Danny McGuire. There was no chance I was ever going to take their spots, because they were both such brilliant players, but I was very happy and very lucky to be able to learn my craft under them.

I'm only an inch taller than Rob (although he'll probably tell you otherwise!), so he was a great inspiration to me, convinced me that our size could be our special power. Rob terrified opponents as a kid and he never stopped terrifying them as a professional. Terry O'Conner, the great Wigan prop who was six foot two and eighteen stone, used to say to me, 'It's not the big men who frighten me, it's people like Rob Burrow. He scares me half to death.'

Like me, Rob wasn't a street fighter, that wasn't in his nature. But something happened when he crossed that white line. It's like he forgot how small he was. Little blokes with magic feet don't normally enjoy defending, but he seemed to love it. When I coach the young lads at Huddersfield Giants, I talk about being 'rugby tough', which is what Rob was. I tell them, 'A tough guy isn't someone who punches, bites and stamps, a tough guy is someone like Rob.' And

I'm forever preaching to scouts, 'Don't just look for the big, athletic kids. Look for the small ones, because they might be harder. They might not be able to dominate opponents physically, but they're toughening up and learning skills those big, athletic kids aren't, just to survive. If we persevere with them, they might come good for us down the line.'

As Rob got older, his game progressed. He still had that speed and agility, but he relied on it less. He became better at controlling a game and particularly adept at pinning you in the corner with his left boot. And I realized just how good his ball skills were, especially the ability to pick the right pass at the right time, which is an art in itself. Whenever we played Leeds, I never felt they were that much better than us. But they had players like Rob, who could do things in the white heat of battle, when the pressure was at its greatest. Rob would make a break or slip someone a pass when it didn't look on. That's what separates the great players from the very good.

While I know it's not what Rob wanted his role to be, when they switched him to hooker, coming off the bench, he could be even more effective. The game would be in the balance, the big men would be getting flat-footed, and they'd throw him on to cause some chaos. I'd look at my teammates, the seventeen-stone props and the six-foot-three-inch second-rows, and they'd be rolling their eyes and heaving big sighs. Rob loved being in the washing machine in the middle of the park, surrounded by all those big lads, because he'd run rings round them. What a weapon for Leeds to have up their sleeve.

But here's the thing about Rob. Yes, he was an unbeliev-able player and a ferocious opponent. But it's how he went about it that people in rugby league admired most. He was a coach's dream: an exemplary teammate, never in trouble, resilient, never gave up, always optimistic. All traits, in fact, that Rob has displayed since being diagnosed with MND. On top of all that, he was one of the nicest men I've ever met – a fun, lovely, all-round top bloke.

God knows Rob caused me a lot of heartache, like he caused all his opponents a lot of heartache, but it was impossible not to like him. That's why the rugby league community has given him so much support in his darkest hour. He was and is a shining light. And that's why, when my little lads start playing rugby league, I'll say to them, 'Let me tell you about my old mate Rob Burrow. He's someone I'd like you to be like, on and off the pitch . . .'

★

We were magnificent in our Challenge Cup semi-final against St Helens, and it was probably one of my best performances off the bench. I'm not sure we'd ever started a game so fast; Saints didn't know what had hit them. Our backs were rampant in the first half, as was Adam Cuthbertson. No wonder he was being tipped as a potential Man of Steel. And after JP went on a gallop and scored under the posts, the game appeared to be up. When JP's running in long-range tries, with a sidestep thrown in for good measure, you know it's probably your day. Saints clawed their way back into it, but Kallum Watkins finished them off with a try late on. The one downside was that poor old Jonesy suffered a bad knee injury and would miss the rest of the campaign.

Super League bosses introduced the Super 8s in 2015,

to add a bit of jeopardy and keep the broadcasters happy. The Super 8s meant that – despite finishing top of the table after twenty-three regular season games – we and the other top-eight teams would have to play another seven. The points would be carried over, the team finishing top of the table after thirty games would win the League Leaders' Shield and the top four teams would advance to the play-off semi-finals. If you've ever watched that Alan Partridge sketch where he's trying to explain the World Cup draw (Google it, I promise it will make you laugh), the Super 8s are like that, utterly baffling to anyone who isn't a rugby league fan.

We hammered Warrington in our first Super 8s game, before earning a scrappy win over Wigan and seeing off Hull quite comfortably (I started at seven and scored my 199th and 200th career tries). That meant we were heading into the Challenge Cup Final with six straight wins behind us. This time, our opponents were Hull KR, who hadn't won the trophy since 1980, when they were captained by the aforementioned Roger 'The Dodger' Millward. Hull KR had finished tenth in the league table (at least after the regular season) and we'd beaten them twice, sticking almost eighty points on them. No one gave them much chance of beating us – and they were right not to. Tom Briscoe, formerly of Hull KR's arch-rivals Hull, scored five of our nine tries, the first man to do so in the competition's 114-year history, I grabbed one and we hammered them 50–0. That was one trophy in the bag, two to go.

As far as the bookies were concerned, Leeds winning the League Leaders' Shield now looked a formality. What do they know? Like the year before, we suddenly hit the skids, losing two in a row against St Helens and Catalans. The defeat by Catalans, who put forty points on us in Perpignan, was alarming, especially for the fans. You'd think we'd been on the lash for a fortnight after our Wembley triumph. Truth was, we'd only had one day off to recover, but we were coming apart at the seams. We had a few serious injuries and lots of niggles (I missed both of those games with a thigh strain). And every time a player hit the deck, you'd worry that their season was over.

When Castleford beat us at Headingley (another game I missed through injury), we were suddenly in grave danger of missing out on the League Leaders' Shield and dropping to third in the table, which would have meant an away semi-final. Heading into the final weekend of Super 8s fixtures, we were only ahead of Wigan on points difference. But while the Warriors had a home game against Cas, who had no chance of making the semi-finals, we had to travel to Huddersfield, who were one point behind us and still in with a chance of winning the League Leaders' Shield. We were like those marathon runners you occasionally see, way ahead of the field but suddenly on spaghetti legs as they enter the stadium, weaving all over the track with the finish line in sight.

Huddersfield were a bad team to be playing. While we'd lost three in a row, they hadn't lost in five, scoring a stack of points in the process. Plus, we hadn't beaten them on their patch since 2011. Oh, and Kev had suffered a severe dead leg against Cas. And I still wasn't fully fit. It wasn't looking great.

Eight points down with six minutes left, things were looking absolutely dire. I'd started the game at hooker, while Kev had also made the starting line-up. And we were two points ahead at the interval, although nowhere near in control. Early in the second half, Luke Robinson for the Giants, and Maggsy for us, both had tries disallowed by the video referee, before a Jamie Ellis try and a Danny Brough conversion made it 14–8 to Huddersfield. When Danny kicked a penalty with twelve minutes to go, Sky started showing pictures of the helicopter carrying the League Leaders' Shield, getting ready to set off for Wigan, who were in the process of gubbing Castleford. The Super 8s weren't everyone's cup of tea, but this was exactly the kind of drama the broadcasters were after.

When Tom Briscoe went over with eight minutes to go, after some magic hands from Kallum Watkins, we had a glimmer. It wasn't great for the environment, however, because apparently the helicopter was now hovering some-where over Manchester. There was a long break in play while Stevie Ward, who had busted his knee, was seen to, and when we got back to it, the Giants started hammering away at our line again. With three minutes to go, we were at the wrong end of the field, two points behind and looking like toast.

When Luke Robinson (who, and I want this placed on the record, is not taller than me) was halted just short of our try-line and the ball was turned over, the commentators thought Huddersfield had it in the bag. 'The Giants won't mind that,' said Stevo. 'Leeds have to score a hundred-metre try,' said Eddie.

Well, not quite. Huddersfield did us a big favour by conceding a penalty, which allowed Kev to boot the ball downfield and put us in a position from which to launch one last attack. And when Giants prop Craig Kopczak was penalized for a shoulder-charge on Zak Hardaker, Kev levelled the scores at 16–16 with a scruffy kick that just scraped over the bar. At that point, I thought the treble had gone and was just relieved we'd managed to secure home advantage in the semi-finals. As for the helicopter, I assumed it was back on its way to Wigan.

With ten seconds left, we were on our third tackle and still in our own half. So what does Maggsy do? Dinks a little kick over the top. If the ball bounces one way, it lands in a Giants player's hands and it's game over. If the ball bounces another way, it dribbles into touch and it's game over. Instead, it popped into the hands of the onrushing Ryan Hall, who left Giants full-back Scott Grix for dead and powered home for the winning try. Of course it was lucky. There's always luck involved in moments like that, because every little thing has to go right. But you've got to have players willing to throw the dice in the first place. And that has nothing to do with luck, that's all about balls.

Players and fans often refer to the League Leaders' Shield as the 'hubcap', because it isn't supposed to mean much. But winning it meant an awful lot in that moment, as you could tell by the celebrations. A few minutes earlier, we were nailed on to finish third in the table and play Huddersfield in the semi-finals the following week, at their place again. With that try from Ryan, we'd finished top of the table and secured a home tie against Saints. And the treble was still on.

That's why those celebrations, wild as they were, blew out quite quickly. We smiled for the photo with the trophy, which had made its way back from Wigan and must have done a lot of air miles that evening, got ourselves changed and headed back to Leeds, knowing there was still a lot of work to be done. We knew that if we didn't win the Grand Final, that game would soon become an irrelevance. Talk about the highs and lows of sport.

Our semi-final against St Helens was set to be the last game at Headingley for JP, Kev (at least under league rules) and Kylie (unless he changed his mind). And knowing that defeat would mean they'd never pull on the blue and amber again was a massive motivator for those boys and the rest of the team. It wasn't spoken about, because they wanted it to be about the team, not them. But we desperately wanted to send them out on the highest possible high, so losing that semi-final to old rivals Saints was unthinkable.

Once again, we did it the hard way. And the old fellas came up trumps when it mattered most. Saints, the defending champions, were leading 13–8 with fourteen minutes remaining, when JP put in a try-saving tackle on James Roby. Kev then produced a beautiful, pinpoint 40/20 kick to give us a head and feed at the scrum, before Ryan Hall – again – blasted over for a try. Kev nudged us ahead with the conversion, and when Kallum Watkins seized on a loose pass and slid over in the dying seconds, we were on our way to Manchester and eighty minutes away from a historic treble.

Wigan easily disposed of Huddersfield in the other semi, meaning it was Leeds versus the Warriors for the first time since the inaugural Grand Final in 1998. Wigan's 2015 vintage were very physical and very well-organized, and had romped their last two games, in stark contrast to our blood-and-guts battles against Huddersfield and Saints.

Jonesy, Stevie Ward and Liam Sutcliffe would all miss the final with injury, but I felt the rest of the lads were battle-hardened rather than on their knees.

I also didn't think Wigan could bully us like they had other teams, and I thought we had that little bit more magic. On top of that, so many of us had done it before at Old Trafford. We knew we could handle the situation, knew we wouldn't be overawed. It's not like we were arrogant or complacent, but there was a real sense that we were invincible.

It had been a frustrating year for me, despite all the glory along the way. I'd spent too much time on the bench when I was itching to be involved. But an injury to hooker Paul Aiton in August had given me a decent run in the team at the business end of the season and I was starting in the biggest game of all. I felt fresh as a daisy and desperately determined to win it for my old mates Kev, JP and Kylie. But I didn't just want to do it for them, I wanted to do it for me. I was still a greedy little so-and-so after all those years. I was like a kid selfishly shielding his pile of sweets, not wanting to give any of them away.

There were over 73,000 fans at Old Trafford, the most ever for a Grand Final. People were always saying the sport was on the wane, but it didn't look like it that day. And the man most inspired by the occasion was Maggsy, who scored two tries in the first half – making it six in eight Grand Finals – and set up another for our Aussie centre Joel Moon (we got lucky with that one, because it looked like Maggsy might have knocked the ball on in the build-up).

We were leading 16–6 at the interval, before Wigan turned the game on its head with two tries in ten minutes after the restart. When Matty Bowen knocked over a penalty, we were four points down with nineteen minutes remaining.

If you haven't been in that situation before, you're likely to be looking around the pitch, desperately searching for answers. But I didn't have to do any searching, I just knew the answers were there. I knew JP wasn't chucking the towel in. I knew Kev hadn't hung up his kicking boots just yet. I knew Kylie would still be swinging even after the fat lady had started singing. Maggsy still had a few rabbits under his hat and Ryan Hall still had it in him to run through walls, with five defenders hanging off him. If you were assembling the perfect crew to spring you out of jail, you could do a lot worse than that lot.

As it turned out, one of our unsung heroes played a big part in the escape. With sixty-three minutes on the clock, Maggsy put up a bomb, Ryan outjumped Wigan winger Dominic Manfredi and palmed the ball back to Joel Moon. Joel popped the ball inside to our German international Jimmy Keinhorst, who fed the ball to Josh Walters. Josh – only twenty years old, off the bench and appearing in his first play-off game – delivered his lines perfectly, dipping low and burrowing over from five metres out. That made the score 18–18, before Kev's conversion – his last goal kick for Leeds – clinched the treble.

Talk about mixed feelings. We'd pulled off the impossible mission and sent JP, Kev and Kylie out on a high, but now I had to deal with the fact that the heart had been removed from the team. I felt deliriously happy but sad at the same time. Empty, even. You can't replace people like that. You can bring new players in and hope for the best, but they're never going to be JP, Kev or Kylie.

Those three weren't just great players, they were enormous personalities. They were big voices, great examples and, more than anything else, bloody good mates. We'd been through God knows how many battles together, and now they were bidding farewell, shipping out and leaving me, Maggsy and Jonesy to soldier on. And how long did we have left? How much more could our bodies take? For the first time in my rugby career, I was contemplating the end. It wasn't happening quite yet, but it couldn't be long.

*

Brian McDermott, Leeds Rhinos head coach

I had great success as coach of Leeds, but there were always people who said, 'Yeah, but you had a very good team.' They're right, I did. I worked with a lot of extremely talented players at Leeds, but the biggest compliment I can give blokes like JP, Kevin, Danny, Jonesy and Rob is that they would have sailed through basic training with the Marines. And in case you were wondering, the word 'basic' is misleading. Marines basic training is the hardest in the world, and anyone who passes is an exceptional soldier.

In basic training, they put so many obstacles in the way. Recruits are constantly given seemingly impossible tasks, and the blokes who are still standing at the end are the problem solvers, people who say, 'I don't care what you put in front of me, I will get over it.'

Rob would have been one of those blokes. He would have been stood beside me on the side of a mountain, in horizontal rain and freezing cold; when we'd already been out there for a week, without food, without sleep, while being chased and watched by people ready to fail us; when the temptation to say, 'I can't carry on', even though the end is within touching distance, is enormous. Knowing Rob, he probably would have made light of it, told a joke about the size of someone's feet or cock or balls – big cock, small cock, it didn't make any difference to Rob. There was no escape. But there's no way he would have given in. That just wasn't in his DNA.

*

Success had become so normal that if we finished a season without winning anything, it was like the world had ended. But I wasn't surprised by what happened in 2016. I said all the right things in pre-season interviews, about us being as good as ever, but that was obviously a lie. How could we be, when three of Leeds's greatest ever players had just walked out of the door?

Maggsy injured his knee in the first game of the season, a narrow defeat by Warrington, before Widnes drubbed us 56–12. That disaster was closely followed by a 38–4 defeat by North Queensland in the World Club Challenge. We won only three of our first seventeen Super League games, leaving us rooted to the bottom of the table and contemplating a relegation battle. That May was one of the most traumatic months in the club's recent history. First, Huddersfield knocked us out of the Challenge Cup. Then we lost to Castleford at home 52–12, Wigan at home 40–8 and Warrington away 52–18. Things weren't great.

That was a weird season for me. Having played almost

exclusively as a hooker for the previous few seasons, I was suddenly a scrum-half again. And because Maggsy kept getting injured, I was often captain. That meant I was having to speak to the media all the time, and there's only so many times you can say, 'We're still trying hard and we'll turns things around eventually.'

In Brian's defence, our injury situation was absolutely shocking. And we didn't have a training ground for the first couple of months of the season, because of flooding over the Christmas period. That meant we were having to train on whatever field was available, which isn't ideal for a professional outfit. But that didn't stop disgruntled fans calling for Brian's head. Some seem to have decided that JP and Kev had been mainly responsible for our successes, rather than Brian. And no one would have been surprised if he'd handed in his notice. But as he's already said, Marines don't quit, however hard things get.

Even a remarkable upturn in form, which saw us win five of our last six matches (including against table-toppers Hull and eventual champions Wigan) didn't save us from the Qualifiers, which pitted the bottom four teams in Super League against the top four teams in the second-tier Championship.

The Qualifiers were designed as a bit of theatre to engineer the 'Million Pound Game', which was the teams that finished fourth and fifth playing each other for a place in Super League the following season. Thankfully, we won six of our seven games in the Qualifiers and managed to avoid any of that nonsense. Brian also named me the club's player of the season, for the first time since 2007. Ho-hum. It was like someone putting a cherry on top of a very shit cake.

★

To be completely honest, I didn't think we had a hope of winning anything in 2017. I didn't expect to be involved in the Qualifiers again, but another Grand Final appearance seemed like a pipe dream. Maggsy had always been more injury-prone than me, but by now he seemed to be made of poppadoms. He'd only managed thirteen games the previous season and hadn't scored a single try. Meanwhile, Jonesy was virtually being held together by tape and sticking plaster. On top of that, Zak Hardaker had jumped ship to Castleford, after a short spell in Australia, and Brian had only made three new signings, hooker Matt Parcell from Manly and two from the Championship. If the fans were pessimistic about our chances, it seemed they had every reason to be.

The first game of the season (my 500th in total, including internationals) ended in a narrow defeat by St Helens. And when Castleford clobbered us 66–10 a couple of weeks later – our fifth straight defeat by the Tigers and Leeds's biggest margin of defeat in Super League history – things were looking pretty bleak. A few of our key players missed the game through injury, including me, but there's only so many times you can lose in that manner before you have to admit a terminal decline has set in.

Gary Hetherington was furious after the game and seemed to suggest in an email to fans that Brian had a month to save his job. That seemed to do the trick, because we won six of our next seven league games to climb to second in the table. Unfortunately for me, I started most of those games on the bench, with Matt Parcell now the starting hooker and Joel Moon converted to scrum-half. By this point, I was really struggling to cope with Brian's mind games.

Brian had named me player of the season for 2016. I'd started 2017 back in the halves with Maggsy, and now I'd been dropped for someone who'd played most of his rugby as a centre (although, I should add, Moony acquitted himself very well at seven). Suddenly, I was starting to wonder how much more I could take. And when Maggsy announced that he was leaving Leeds at the end of the season, I started thinking that maybe I should do the same.

It wasn't the same around the place without Kev, JP and Kylie. And I'd been playing with Maggsy for almost twenty-five years, so the thought of being without him was almost incomprehensible. Who'd be there on my shoulder when I made a break? Who'd be there to give me a big hug when I scored a try? Other players, of course, but it wouldn't be the same. I imagined I'd feel like an old widower, wandering around the place, confused and pining for his soul mate.

On the other hand, I was still enjoying the changing room banter and what playing time I got. And while I was finding training – the hellish pre-seasons, the weights routines, the strict diet – more and more of a rigmarole, and it was taking me longer and longer to recover after games, my body had held up surprisingly well.

I do remember lying in bed after a game against Wakefield, wondering if I wanted to do it any more. I'd had a whack on the nose (that happens a lot when you've got one as big as mine) and felt sore all over, and I thought to myself, 'I really need to be healthy for the kids after I retire. What if I go on too long, do myself some proper mischief and can't even run around with them?' But at the same time, I felt physically able to carry on. I'd felt sharp in pre-season and still had my pace, which was always the most important part of my game. And, as they say, you're a long time retired.

If I'd still been an integral part of the team, I would have kept at it. But when you get to that age – I was almost thirty-five – you start thinking about your dignity, as well as the aches and pains. I felt like a bit left out, and I'd had enough of Brian. Mentally, he'd shot me to bits. So a week after Maggsy, I announced that 2017 would also be my last season in blue and amber. But unlike Maggsy, who'd be joining Hull KR, I'd be hanging up my playing boots and taking up a coaching role at Headingley, working with the kids. It was a role that Gary Hetherington had promised me, and he was true to his word.

When I told Mum and Dad I was quitting, they were taken aback. I didn't tell them I was doing it because of Brian, I just said my body had had enough. The media seemed surprised as well, and it was only Lindsey who knew the real reasons behind my decision. She said to me when Brian took over, 'Stuff Leeds, if that's the way they're going to treat you.' When I chose to stay at Leeds rather than join Wigan in 2012, she gave me her full support. But it must have been difficult for her, because she could see the toll it was taking on me. I was never at rock bottom, but I lost some of my passion and drive.

People often forget that playing sport is a job – a more cut-throat job than most – and I was like anyone who's unhappy at work. It takes a lot to get up for a game, in terms of physical and mental preparation, so to suddenly be sat on the bench most weeks, wondering if I was going to get ten minutes, or even get on the pitch at all, was torture. For years, I clung in there, hoping the boss would leave and his replacement might give me a new lease of life, as I'm sure people who work in offices and other kinds of workplaces can relate to. And I desperately wanted to finish my Leeds career on my own terms, rather than have someone finish it for me. Sadly, at least for me, that didn't happen.

On the bright side, mine and Maggsy's announcements gave the team a sharper focus at the business end of the season, just as we'd had in 2015 (had Jonesy decided to join us, it would have made it another triple, but I expected that lad to still be hobbling onto the field well into his forties). Castleford continued to be our bogey team, making it seven straight wins against us at Headingley in June, but we were a match for most. I missed a big chunk of our regular season run-in with a shoulder injury, which scuppered my hopes of playing 500 games for Leeds. But we finished second in the table behind the Tigers and hit the Super 8s running, easily beating Wigan in our opener.

However, when we were thumped by Wakefield in our second game (my first for a couple of months), the media consensus was that we were too inconsistent to win another title. A few weeks earlier, Hull had hammered us in the semi-finals of the Challenge Cup, and there was a feeling that our squad was too thin, our defence too porous and that we lacked the necessary flair and discipline.

But a week after the defeat by Trinity, which was one of the worst Leeds performances I'd been a part of, we squeaked past St Helens in the last game at Headingley before the famous old South Stand was demolished. It wasn't pretty – one journalist quipped that the former players paraded at half-time should have brought their boots – but it was more points in the bag.

I started against Hull – at scrum-half, glory be! – scoring one try and setting up another in a scrappy win, but was banned for our next game against Castleford, having been charged with headbutting an opponent (some commentators thought the punishment should have been harsher, some wondered how I'd reached him). Once again, Cas blitzed us. And even after we won our last two Super 8s games at a canter, securing a home semi-final (Maggsy scored a couple of beauties against Huddersfield, and I grabbed another), many in the media thought the Tigers, who had finished ten points ahead of us to win the League Leaders' Shield, already had the title sewn up.

Castleford only just pipped St Helens in their semi-final, the day before mine and Maggsy's Headingley swansong. To say our game against Hull was tense doesn't even begin to do it justice. The outcome was up in the air until the final whistle, Liam Sutcliffe having conjured a try from nothing midway through the second half, and Kallum Watkins edged us two points ahead with a conversion. I was never a sentimental, lump-in-the-throat kind of person in my playing days, but it was a little bit spooky driving out of Headingley that evening. The following day, the bulldozers would be moving in, to start knocking down the North Stand. I felt as if I was fleeing a crumbling empire.

As with the Challenge Cup Final a couple of years earlier, it was nice seeing Castleford abuzz. There were hundreds of Cas fans queuing for tickets in the town centre and the clusters of lads in their Tigers shirts – discussing how much they hated Leeds and what their boys were going to do to us in the Grand Final – had swelled to scrums.

A few days before the game, Cas's Luke Gale was named Man of Steel, ahead of his teammate Zak Hardaker (only one Rhino had won the award in the twenty-first century, Zak in 2015 – Maggsy hadn't, and neither had JP or Kev, which is ridiculous). There were six Cas players in the Super League Dream Team and only one from Leeds (Matt Parcell). Cas head coach Daryl Powell was named coach of the year, while the Tigers were named club of the year. But as everyone had worked out by now, Super League's play-off system didn't necessarily reward the best team, it rewarded the team that could best handle the biggest occasions. And our blokes had been doing that for years.

All things considered, Cas's players were under far more pressure than us. Only one of them, Zak, had played in a Grand Final, while we had forty-odd Grand Final rings between us. On top of that, Cas had never won a league championship in any era, while people were saying they had to beat us for the good of the sport. And because they'd beaten us eight times in a row stretching back to 2015 (including four times that season) and romped to the League Leaders' Shield, almost everyone expected them to beat us again.

Our chances of victory were given a significant boost when Zak was axed by Cas (we didn't know why at the time, but it turned out he'd failed a drugs test). And on the day – another wet one in Manchester, which didn't suit Cas's expansive game – it wasn't even close. Despite the 30,000 Cas fans packed into Old Trafford, which is three-quarters of the town's population, their team never really got out of first gear. Instead, they were treated, if that's the right word, to the Danny McGuire show, one last time. Far from looking ready for the breakers yard, Maggsy was like a Rolls-Royce just out of the showroom.

Maggsy's kicking game was immaculate; he had the ball on a string. He also scored his seventh and eighth Grand Final tries and set up one of Tom Briscoe's two. Oh, and there was a try-saving tackle. As well as two drop-goals. Some might have been surprised, but not me. I'd had a ringside seat for Maggsy's conjuring act since I was ten, and magic like that doesn't disappear overnight. I spent most of the game on the bench, but did get on for the last fifteen minutes. I even set up Maggsy's second try, with a horrible little deflected grubber. Cas did grab a late try to avoid the embarrassment of being nilled, but the final score on my 492nd and final Leeds appearance was 24–6 to us.

People assume I must have been overcome by euphoria when the final whistle went. Actually, I felt pretty deflated. Beforehand, I felt like I had a big performance in me, but I'd barely played a part. People in the media like to talk about the romance of sport, but professional sportspeople don't tend to be romantic. I spent those sixty-five minutes on the bench just feeling pissed off. I was no different to the little kid kicking his heels on the touchline at Featherstone Lions, almost thirty years earlier. Except I couldn't badger Brian to put me on.

Don't worry, I soon cheered up. Just before the presentations, Maggsy came over to me and said, 'Mate, I want you to lift the trophy with me.' I asked him if he was sure and he replied, 'Of course I'm sure.' He still talks about the look on my face, one of pure pride. Apparently, Maggsy had been visualizing that moment all week. Not him on his own, hogging the glory, but him on one side of the trophy and me on the other. That was typical of him, and typical of Leeds. I couldn't have scripted a better ending to my career. Fairy-tale stuff.

12

WHAT DO THEY USUALLY SAY AT THE END OF FAIRY
tales? That's right – they all lived happily ever after. Well,
for a while I did. I thought I'd miss being a rugby player.
Not the training, aches and pains, but the changing room
nonsense and piss-taking, as well as the soaring highs. And
I worried that when the new season started, I'd feel envious
and empty. But that wasn't the case. Not one bit. When JP,
who was head of rugby at Hull KR, tried to persuade me
to sign and play a season alongside Maggsy, I wasn't in the
slightest bit tempted.

A lot of ex-sportspeople struggle in retirement because
the skills they've acquired aren't much use in the real world,
or at least they think they aren't. And maybe if I'd gone
off and worked in an office it would have been different
(I imagine you get a bit of banter in an office, but I'm not
sure you'd get away with some of the things we got up to
in the Rhinos changing room – I'm guessing weeing on
each other is a no-no?). But I was still involved in the sport

I loved and took the responsibility of training the academy kids every bit as seriously as I took playing for Leeds. That was probably because I knew more than most how important those precious kids were to the future of the club.

As well as stints coaching my old school and Ackworth Jaguars, I'd also been involved with the Rhinos' Under-16s for a few years; I'd helped nurture Stevie Ward and Liam Sutcliffe, among quite a few others. I was good with youngsters, on their wavelength, and the fact I was so small (usually smaller than most of them) gave some of the less-developed kids hope. They'd see me up close and think, 'If this little bloke can survive in rugby league for as long as he has, and win all the things he's won, then maybe I've got a chance as well.'

Nothing gave me greater pleasure than seeing lads I'd worked with as schoolboys run out with the first team at Headingley. Or, in the case of Stevie and Liam, lift the Grand Final trophy. And now, producing the Rhinos stars of the future – the next Kevin Sinfield or the next Danny McGuire – was my full-time job. The future looked bright, full of possibilities, for them and for me.

As any coach will tell you, watching your charges from the touchline is far more nerve-wracking than playing. Losing is far worse as well. I'd also get frustrated, because some of the lads weren't great at taking criticism. I know retired sportsmen are always going on about things being better 'when I were a lad, in the good old days', but the kids were definitely softer than when I was at the academy. Nevertheless, I had a decent first year in charge, with the Under-19s reaching the Academy Grand Final and nine of my players featuring in the Yorkshire Academy side that gave the Australian Schoolboys a fright.

Unfortunately, and predictably, the first team had fallen apart. And after a run of seven straight Super League defeats, Brian left the club. I'm not suggesting results went downhill because me and Maggsy retired, but I sensed the ethos and principles that had been in place for the best part of two decades, and which had been integral to our success, had faded. When Kev was brought back in as director of rugby, there was some newspaper talk about me pulling on my boots again. That was never a possibility, but Kev did persuade me to join the first-team coaching set-up. I was fine with that arrangement at first, but when it spilled over into the following season, it became a problem.

My heart was in the academy and I wanted to teach the kids those lessons that had been forgotten, the lessons my old academy coach Dean Bell had taught me. And while I knew coaching would take up more of my time than playing, working with both the academy and first team soon became a bit of a grind. I'd always put family first, but now I was doing longer and longer hours. And I didn't just have two children to help look after, I now had three.

When Jackson was born, on 15 December 2018, I imagine I felt just like my dad when I came along. Like Dad, I already had two beautiful daughters, who filled every day with pure joy. But having a little boy would be different. For a start, Jackson would be able to pass the family name down. And I'd be able to throw a ball around with him and take him to Headingley when he was older (before anyone accuses me of being a sexist old dinosaur, Macy and Maya had shown almost zero interest in rugby!).

I imagined rolling around the living-room floor with him, just like my dad did with me, crashing into tables and doors and knocking things over. I'd be Eddie Hemmings instead of Ray French: 'Here's Jackson Burrow . . . ducks under a tackle . . . beats a defender on the outside . . . outstrips another . . . sells his old man a dummy! That's a brilliant try under the posts!'

The situation with work festered as the 2019 season progressed – and then came that awards dinner, when I couldn't say the word 'consistency'. You know the rest. There's a lesson there for everyone. There I was, letting work niggle away at me, letting it get me down, and suddenly this great big boulder fell on top of me. I was supposed to be Road Runner – 'Little Beep Beep' – not Wile E. Coyote. You never know what might fall out of the sky and flatten you or when that might happen. And then you'll think to yourself, 'Blimey, why was I wasting my time worrying about that? Or arguing with him? Or trying to earn this much more money?' And all you'll want to do is surround yourself with family and friends and make the most of however long you've got left.

Having gone public with my diagnosis, I was quite uncomfortable with all the attention and fuss. And some of the media coverage felt too much like pity. But after my meeting with Doddie, and messages galore from well-wishers and fellow MND sufferers, I knew I needed to put myself out there and try to make a difference. To do that, I needed my head to be right. That's when my rugby experience came in handy, because this was the biggest game of my life.

I had always been an underdog, always overcome

adversity – that was one of my 'things' as a rugby player. That was mainly to do with my size, but it was also to do with all those games and trophies Leeds won that we weren't really supposed to. I'd spent my entire rugby career trying not to show any weakness, and I was determined not to show any weakness now.

It was impossible for me to imagine what I was up against. And you don't know how much spirit and grit you really have until something like MND hits you. But I actually surprised myself, was tougher than I thought I might be. I suppose it's like soldiers: one day they're working in a factory, the next they're doing the most incredible things on a battlefield. Things they never thought they had in them.

When you're diagnosed with an incurable disease, of course you search for answers. And, at least in my case, plenty of people tried to provide them. One guy got in touch and said he'd received a message from God, saying he wanted to heal me. I had a vague belief in God, but had never gone to church apart from for christenings, weddings and funerals. And I know Lindsey was thinking, 'If there is a God, why has he let this happen to Rob?' But I thought to myself, 'What's the worst that can happen? I might as well keep my options open. Science can't help, so let's see what God can do.' I went along to church once, and then the first coronavirus lockdown kicked in. If God really did want to heal me, he obviously wanted to do it in the comfort of my living room.

Neil Verner, the inventor from Wakefield who said he was going to cure the both of us, died of MND in January 2021. Whether it was down to his gadgets or not, he'd hung around for a lot longer than he was supposed to. But much as I loved him and admired his resolve, I couldn't be like Neil, spending my final days on earth engaged in battle with MND. I was fully committed to raising money and awareness, so that future MND patients wouldn't have to go through the same as me. And I'd get frustrated when I learned about treatment available in other countries but not the UK. But I was what my neurologist Dr Jung might call a more typical MND patient, intent on spending what time I had left wallowing in love and kindness, rather than scouring the internet for miracles.

★

Barrie McDermott, Rhinos teammate

I don't enjoy crying, I'm not one of those people who thinks it's good to get it all out of your system. I suppose you'd call me a man of a certain era. But I spent a lot of time crying in those early days after Rob's diagnosis. I'd sit back and think, 'How cruel is life, that a lovely fella everyone likes, a man who's never done anyone a bad turn, can end up with something like this?' I'd pay Rob a visit, or give him a call, and I wouldn't be able to help it. However, in the end I thought, 'I've had enough of this. It's not helping anyone.' And me, Kev, JP, Keith, Maggsy, Jonesy and a few others got together and said, 'Right, let's see what we can do to make sure Rob and his family are secure.'

That's when we started ploughing our efforts into raising money and awareness. I found that helped me as well, because it felt like I was involved, rather than sitting helplessly on the sidelines. Soon, we had WhatsApp groups set up with forty or fifty people in them. And whenever someone asked for help, whether it was donating a signed shirt for a charity event or accompanying one of us on a run, my phone would be like a fruit machine, pinging, buzzing and vibrating as messages flew in one after the other.

What people have to understand about Rob is that while he was the life and soul of the dressing room, he was always a private person. Put him in a room full of strangers and he'd be looking for the back door the whole time, because he wouldn't be comfortable. And it would have been easy for him to do the same when he was diagnosed with MND. I wouldn't have been surprised if he'd said, 'Right lads, I'm just going to spend all my time from now on with Lindsey and the kids, away from the public glare.'

Instead, he put himself front and centre, whether it was doing interviews, writing books or having documentaries made about him. He's amazed me, and I'm so proud of him for doing that. He's shown that you can have a dignified and fulfilling life with MND, and he's jolted people into action, inspired people like me to do whatever they can do to stand up to that terrible disease.

Rob's a humble man, finds all this praise and help difficult to deal with, but it must give him great comfort to know that he's so loved and admired. And the reason he's so loved and admired is because he's made a difference. Every time he played a game of rugby, he made a difference. And now he's making a difference by shining a light on MND, so that maybe what's happened to him doesn't happen to too many more people in the future.

People often ask me, 'Who's the toughest you played with or against?' I mention people like Jamie Peacock and Adrian Morley, stereotypically hard rugby league players. But anyone's list of toughest players has to have Rob on it. And he wasn't just one of the toughest, he was also one of the bravest. He didn't care that he was giving five or six stone away, he didn't care how hard opposition players were meant to be, he was going to get stuck in.

I often think about that disagreement he had with Hull's Epalahame Lauaki, when Rob started swinging punches at that mountain of a man. Everyone was laughing apart from Rob. He was deadly serious. He thought someone was taking liberties and he was going to do something about it. He never walked away, never backed down, just like he's not backing down now.

But it's not just Rob who deserves the utmost respect and admiration, it's the whole Burrow family. Rob wouldn't be able to do what he's doing without Lindsey. To play rugby league, we had to be brave. But spend a bit of time around Lindsey and you'll see what bravery really is. When I ask her how she's doing, she'll reply, 'Fine. I'm a tough old bird.' And I'll think to myself, 'I can't believe the strength she's got.' As for Rob's mum and dad, the hurt they feel and the pride they have for their son – they're just so overwhelmed by how much he's loved – makes that big lump in my throat appear again.

Then, of course, there are the kids, who mean everything to Rob. And while Macy and Maya's memories of their dad might fade as they grow older, and Jackson might have no memories at all, people like me will make sure to tell them what an incredible man he was. I'll be talking to people about Rob for as long as I can, because everyone should know his story.

★

Baz tells me that I've helped bring some of the old gang back together, which is lovely to hear. It's not like they fell out or anything, but old workmates drift apart – even old teammates who won so much together – and before you know it, you haven't spoken to each other for years.

On 12 January 2020, me and some of the boys played together for one last time at Headingley. The game against Bradford was originally meant to be Jonesy's testimonial, but Jonesy being Jonesy, he wanted to make it a joint event. That was an emotional afternoon, to put it mildly. For starters, Baz, who was doing punditry for Sky (he'd got far too fat to play), kept hugging me and crying. In the end, I had to tell him to leave me alone! And when I walked out before kick-off, behind Macy and Maya and with Jackson in my arms, Headingley erupted. The place was packed to the rafters, a 20,000 sell-out, and I'm told there was barely a dry eye in the house. Imagine how I felt.

JP, Kev, Maggsy, Keith and Kylie had a runaround in the second half and gave a few glimpses of what Leeds had lost. JP's (very grey) head was dripping blood and bandaged up after about two minutes, Keith went on a couple of rampaging breaks, Maggsy and Kev showed off a few of their silky touches, and Kylie forgot it was a friendly and kept trying to whack people into the following week. And with five minutes to go, I got to have a little trot.

That's when the emotion really hit me, like an uppercut that almost took my head off. I'd been lucky enough to play in plenty of big games with huge, passionate crowds, but nothing had made me feel like I felt that day. Alas, I didn't have it in me to do a repeat of the 2011 Grand Final (I could barely see for the tears in my eyes), but it was just beautiful to share a pitch with my old mates again. And it was wonderful to know how much people appreciated me.

★

JP recently gave an interview in which he suggested you've got to have a screw loose to play rugby league, given what it takes out of you physically. I know what he means. If you went to a rugby dinner and saw all the ex-players hobbling along on knackered hips and knees, bent double, unable to straighten their arms and with fingers like Twiglets, you'd be forgiven for thinking rugby league was some kind of madness. A very brutal madness at that. And ever since my MND diagnosis, I've thought a lot about whether it was rugby that caused it. Did I work my muscles too hard because I was always striving to be the strongest, pound for pound? Or did I take too many bangs to the head?

I was knocked out about twenty times during my career, plus hundreds of minor concussions during training and games. The authorities got wiser to the dangers as my career progressed, cracking down on high tackles and introducing concussion assessments, but you can never make any collision sport completely safe. Look at what's happening in rugby union, with lots of ex-players, many of them still young, revealing they've got dementia. But while the link between concussions and brain damage has been proven, the medical experts don't know if head knocks or extreme physical activity cause MND.

I can understand if parents reading this don't want their kids to play rugby, but if Jackson wants to give it a crack, he has my blessing. And if he ever runs out in the blue and amber at Headingley, I'll be the proudest dad in the world, beaming from ear to ear, wherever I happen to be.

Rugby league gives much more than it takes. Just look at my story. If you'd told a ten-year-old me, a shy little lad from a working-class town in Yorkshire, that I'd win one trophy with Leeds, I wouldn't have believed you. If you'd told me I'd be part of the most successful team in Super League history, I'd have thought you were mad or on drugs. But it happened. I've got eight Grand Final rings to prove it, as well as a head crammed with wonderful memories.

But Jonesy's right, while rings and medals are nice, they're a small part of the story. In fact, you don't have to win anything for rugby league to benefit you. It's bloody good fun, and it keeps you fit as a fiddle. But it's also an education, in that it instils discipline, self-confidence, toughness, resilience and perseverance. If you're lucky enough to make it as a pro, you'll have the opportunity to bring great joy to your community (unless you're from Castleford and you play for Leeds, in which case you'll just annoy people). And you'll inspire the younger generation to go on the same great journey as you.

Of course I'm biased, but there is no greater sport than rugby league, anywhere in the world. Never mind what happens on the pitch, the way it rallies around players who fall ill or suffer serious injuries is unmatched. When former St Helens and Hull full-back Steve Prescott announced he had stomach cancer in 2006, the rugby league family was there for him. When Hull KR's Mose Masoe suffered a life-changing spinal injury in 2020, the rugby league family was there for him. That phrase 'rugby league family' might sound a bit trite, but as someone who's been wallowing in its love and kindness for the best part of a year and a half, that's exactly what it is.

Rugby league hasn't always helped itself. It's 2021 and people still associate it with old blokes with whippets in tow, fags in the corners of their mouths and rolled-up *Racing Posts* tucked under their arms. That's an out-of-date stereotype. But there's no getting away from the fact that rugby league is primarily a working-class sport played in a few pockets of the North, invisible to most people who don't live in those communities.

People call rugby league 'parochial', and they mean it as an insult. But I don't think being parochial is necessarily a bad thing. It's why rugby league is so down to earth. It's why its players are real and part of their communities. It's why fans see us as them. It's why, when I'm being wheeled through Castleford town centre, people take a break from calling Leeds scum and try to stuff money into my pockets. It's why rugby league is such a loving family.

★

Clare Balding, Rugby Football League president

I'm not meant to have favourites, either as a presenter or in my role with the RFL, but I've always had such a soft spot for that great Leeds Rhinos side. I spent enough time with that gang to know how decent and honourable they were, and they played a big part in me falling in love with rugby league, Rob in particular.

If you were creating a rugby league comic strip hero, he'd basically be Rob. He was no bigger than a jockey (if he'd grown up anywhere near my dad's yard, he would have been snapped up in a heartbeat) and one would have assumed that rugby league was not the game for him. So whenever I interviewed him, or we showed some of his highlights, I wouldn't be able to stop smiling, because he was just so inspirational. And I'd often imagine some little kid watching at home and thinking, 'If he can do it, why can't I?'

It wasn't just Rob's bravery and talent that I admired, it was also the fact that he seemed to love the game so much. And everything he did, he did it for the honour of Leeds and the appreciation of his teammates.

Rugby league in England has always felt ignored and misunderstood, ever since it broke away from the Rugby Football Union in 1895, and there are still rugby league people who feel slightly bitter about that. But I think its northernness is its strength, what makes it so special. Rugby league is about so much more than big, hard men battering each other. It has a strong moral code. It takes its responsibilities very seriously. It's about lots of individuals feeling part of something bigger. So instead of constantly worrying about how other people view it, rugby league should be confident enough to say, 'We're not going to change for anyone, because we're already good and strong enough.' The response to Rob's diagnosis, from inside and outside Leeds, has proved that.

Like everyone who knows Rob, I was devastated when I heard about his diagnosis. But watching him cope, with such outstanding dignity and bravery, has been even more inspiring than anything he did on a rugby pitch. And watching teammates and opponents, tough northern men like Kevin Sinfield and Barrie McDermott, showing their vulnerabilities and emotions, showing that it's OK to cry and let other people know just how much you care about a mate, has been wonderful to witness. Heart and soul, that's what rugby league has. And Rob has brought it out for all to see.

★

Whenever I was at a rugby dinner in my playing days, I'd look at all the ex-players – old fellas with silver hair, bent noses and limps – sharing old stories and giggling like children, and think to myself, 'That'll be me and the lads in twenty or thirty years, all sat around a big table, reminiscing about the good old days.' Keith would suddenly be that much faster than he really was. Baz would suddenly be that much thinner. Jonesy would suddenly be the most skilful player in Super League history. I imagined we'd laugh so hard that tears would stream down our faces. I imagined we'd still be glowing with pride at everything we achieved. I imagined we'd still feel lucky that we got to play a sport we loved with such special individuals. That dinner will never happen. Well, it might, it's just that I won't be there. But I reckon I've experienced something just as great: too many people die not knowing how much the folks they held most dear loved and appreciated them. That won't happen to me.

So many people wanted to help, I soon ran out of words to describe how much it meant to me. I probably used 'overwhelmed' too much, but it fitted the bill perfectly. One day, Stevie Ward turned up at my house with his laptop, opened it up and said, 'If you could think of one person you'd most want to get a message from, who would it be?' I immediately replied, 'Michael Jackson', because he'd been a hero of mine since I was a kid. Stevie was good, but he couldn't perform miracles. Instead, he'd somehow managed to get

Ricky Gervais to post a video message on Twitter, which was the next best thing.

Me and Stevie watched it together and wept with laughter. The best part was the comments underneath, from people slagging Ricky off for being horrible. I didn't want him to be nice to me, that would have been a bit weird. I wanted Ricky Gervais to be Ricky Gervais, just like I wanted everyone to be themselves around me. People shaking my hand and wishing me well in the Co-op was lovely, but I didn't always know how to react, because niceness can feel a bit too much like pity. But Ricky's video was perfect and made my week.

A few weeks after my last game at Headingley, there was a fundraising dinner at the club, with 400 guests. Among them was England football coach Gareth Southgate, Leeds boxing world champion Josh Warrington, Olympic triathletes Alistair and Jonny Brownlee and quite a few famous rugby union players from England and Scotland. That's when it dawned on me that I was raising awareness of MND far beyond the confines of the rugby league family.

Barely a day went by without another heart-warming story in the papers, about charity rugby matches, clubs donating gate receipts to the MND Association and people walking, running and cycling all over the country to raise money. When Leeds played Wigan, each Warriors player wore a special shirt, stitched with a word they thought best described me. And after the game, the shirts were auctioned off. The rivalry between Leeds and Wigan is fierce, so that meant a lot to me.

One young Rhinos fan called Holly Beaumont walked almost 300 miles, Keith and some other lads rode their static bikes non-stop for over a day, JP ran a fifty-five-kilometre ultra-marathon across Exmoor, Barrie and his gang completed the Three Peaks Challenge, Castleford legend Oliver Holmes cycled 700 kilometres in seven days and another former player, Craig Forsyth, rowed 3,000 miles on his own across the Atlantic. Apologies if I've forgotten anyone, but the love poured in so thick and fast that it was difficult to keep up.

Of course, it's impossible to forget what Kev did for me and my fellow MND sufferers, smashing out seven marathons in seven days. During one of his runs, I met Kev in front of a huge mural that a street artist called Akse had painted of me, on the side of a building in Leeds. Can you imagine how overwhelming that was? Kev's target was £77,777, but he raised £2.7 million. I loved what he said afterwards: 'One of our mates hit a rough patch and we did what we could to help.' That was Kev all over, making his incredible feat seem like the most natural thing in the world.

Then there was the racehorse that me and a few of my old Rhinos teammates bought, called Burrow Seven (my 'manesake', as one of the tabloids put it). We gave fans the chance to part-own him, with any profits and prize money being donated to MND research. Meeting him for the first time at his training yard in Leyburn was a magical moment. There's a great photo of him looking slightly nonplussed and me and Barrie looking giddy with excitement.

He's just such a beautiful horse, a powerful, majestic grey with a white splash on his nose. And he reminded me of my Granddad Bob. Not to look at, that would be weird. But Granddad Bob was such a big fan of racing, so a horse being named after me would have made him so proud. When Burrow Seven finally gets a run out, I'm sure Granddad Bob will be having a flutter in heaven.

What made all the support even more remarkable was the fact that we were in the middle of a pandemic, which had made life so challenging for so many people. Sometimes, all the attention I was getting, when there were so many others having a hard time of things, made me feel a bit guilty. And after my BBC documentary was broadcast, I felt the need to post a tweet, pointing out that there were some MND sufferers getting no help at all. I kept having to remind myself that me putting myself out there might make that less likely.

When Leeds reached the Challenge Cup Final in October 2020, they wanted me to lead them out at Wembley. Unfortunately, coronavirus restrictions and the logistics of a long trip from Yorkshire to London put paid to that. Instead, I watched the Rhinos do battle with Salford at home with the family.

Luke Gale, our new number seven, kicked the winning drop-goal with a few minutes to go. And when the final whistle went, I had a grin so wide it was almost falling off the sides of my face. The boys, many of whom I'd played with or coached, said some lovely things about me afterwards. And whether I'd inspired them to victory or not, I was certainly with them in spirit – living every pass, kick and tackle and going through the same old emotional wringer.

After Kev ran all those marathons, there were calls for him to be made rugby league's first ever knight. I certainly wasn't arguing. Official honours for rugby league players are too thin on the ground, which is why I almost fell out of my wheelchair when I discovered I'd been given an MBE. Thankfully, I'd also been inducted into Leeds Rhinos' Hall of Fame only a few weeks earlier, so Lindsey's speech-writing skills were pretty polished by then.

I was obviously as proud as punch, but that honour wasn't just for me. It was for the whole of rugby league – small in the grand scheme of things, but with a bigger heart than any other sport – my Rhinos teammates and my family, who made me the person I am and have displayed such strength and dignity since my diagnosis. But most of all, it was for Team MND. I hoped it showed that their plight wasn't being ignored, that MND was still on the radars of the powers that be, and that influential people were still fighting hard on their behalf.

★

Lindsey Burrow, Rob's wife

Even at the height of Rob's career, we were very private people. So being thrust into the spotlight has been quite overwhelming. There was always a shyness about Rob, especially when he moved out of his comfort zone. I could even see that he was doubting himself when he started coaching.

As for me, I was just a normal girl, flying under the radar, and suddenly I was being interviewed for TV, newspapers and podcasts. It was surreal and difficult at times. In the early days, I'd worry about saying the wrong things and coming across as stupid (which is why I often asked Rob's dad to do them instead!). But me doing an interview is nothing compared to what Rob's going through, while raising awareness of MND has given us all a purpose. I suppose it could be described as another coping mechanism. So whenever I'm asked to do something now, I say yes in a heartbeat.

When Rob's cousin organized for a few of us to do the Yorkshire Three Peaks, Rob kept telling me I was going to struggle without any training. I'd say to him, 'How am I supposed to train, Rob? I'm looking after you and the kids, as well as trying to hold down a job.' Then Rob bet me £1,000 I wouldn't do it. As soon as he did that, I knew I would (although I'm not sure he ever paid me). As time went on, I started waking up at 5.30 in the morning and going for a run, before getting the kids up for school. It was so nice to have an hour to myself, pounding the roads and clearing the mind of clutter.

The support we've had has given us so much to smile about, although I worry people are fed up hearing about us and that I'm unable to express how thankful I am. Rob's last game at Headingley, when he walked onto the pitch with Macy, Maya and Jackson, was particularly emotional, a special moment we'll always treasure. But the small gestures, away from the cameras, are just as touching. The person in the supermarket who asks us how we're doing, even though they don't know us from Adam. The treats from family and friends, some of whom I haven't seen for years. The calls from Rob's old teammates, asking if there's anything they can do to help.

Despite all that, Rob's still my main sounding board. The person I moan at, in other words. I sometimes feel sorry for him, because he can't escape. But he knows he helps me just as much emotionally as I help him physically. We still annoy each other, like when we were kids. Even when Rob's voice went, I'd know when he was mad at me. And when he got his Eyegaze machine, he was suddenly barking orders and driving me potty.

But, and I can't stress this enough, we've had plenty of happy times as well. I can be quite officious, simply because I've got so many things to fit into my days. And while Rob has more fun when he's at his parents, we do manage to laugh. When he started losing his voice, he'd tell me something, I'd repeat it back to him and he'd start giggling, because I'd have got it completely wrong. I almost knock his head off every time I get him in the car. And when Leeds Beckett University made Rob an honorary doctor of sport science, I said to him, 'I studied at university for three years and no one took a blind bit of notice; you were there for a month and they've made you a doctor.' There were pictures of him in his cap and gown all over the internet.

But most of the laughs are to do with the kids. Like when they see Rob and Doddie on TV together – Doddie in his yellow tartan trousers and Rob about half his size. Or the time we rented a mobility scooter for Rob and the kids spent all day riding on it, as if it was a bumper car. Or the trips to the seaside. Or the birthday parties and the Christmases that we're desperate to make as special as possible, because we don't know how many more Rob will share with them.

Maya is probably the closest to Rob in terms of personal-ity. She's a cheeky monkey and likes to play jokes, but she's also stubborn and does whatever she wants. Macy is more like me, sensitive and takes things to heart. She's also that bit older, so better understands that Rob won't be getting better. One day, she said to me, 'Mummy, for my birthday, my wish would be to go on holiday with Daddy, because it might be the last one we get to go on together.' Another time, she said, 'I'd give my voice to make Daddy better.' That broke my heart, and I worry about the long-term effects it will have on her and Maya. But at least they'll have memories of their dad, unlike Jackson. I know that gets to Rob, because it's never been about what he can't do for himself, it's always been about what he can't do for me and the kids.

People sometimes ask me what advice I'd give to someone who has a loved one with MND. I'd just want to give them a big hug. What do you say to someone who's faced with that? I'm still struggling to come to terms with it myself, which is why I get embarrassed when people call me Superwoman.

When I heard what Barrie said, about learning what bravery really is from spending time around Rob's wife, I thought, 'Is he really talking about me?' Maybe it's the Yorkshire gene, or maybe Rob's determination has rubbed off, but the only thing I can do is try to stay positive and crack on. If there was anything I could do to change our situation, I'd do it. If I could give my life to save Rob's, I would. But there's no point wasting time thinking about what I'd like life to be like, I have to deal with things as they really are.

Rob's illness has changed my perspective completely. Looking back, I was guilty of taking a lot of things for granted. But since life became unrecognizable almost overnight, I've better understood that I need to make the most of every opportunity and live it to the fullest. I also understand exactly how lucky I am, to have three beautiful children with such a wonderful man. I've ended up as Rob's carer, as well as his wife. And MND does its best to take a person away from you. But Rob has never stopped being the heart and soul of the family, and I love him more than ever.

When the kids grow up, I hope they're as kind, generous and loving as their dad. I hope they'll always be able to draw inspiration from his determination and dignity. I hope they'll be able to see the light, however desperate and devastating a situation might seem. And I hope they'll always be proud of how we fought this horrible disease as a family, raised awareness, and maybe saved others from experiencing the same suffering.

It's hard to think about life without Rob, and I worry about how everyone will handle it. Not just the kids, but also his parents, sisters and teammates. But I just have to treasure what time we have left together and make as many memories as possible. One thing I do know: when I look back, I won't be saying, 'I wish we'd done this or done that.' Instead, I'll be saying, 'You know what? We ticked more boxes than most. What a wonderful time we had together. It was an honour and a privilege to be that man's wife.'

★

My dad always said I should write a book. I wasn't so sure, because most of the rugby league books I'd read contained lots of stories about boozing, fighting and various other shenanigans, which wasn't really my thing. It was only after the BBC got involved, and I started feeling all that tremendous love and warmth from the public, that I thought, 'Maybe I do have an interesting tale to tell.' People love an underdog story, and I've been battling against adversity my whole life. I was never meant to play rugby league, and now I'm tackling this horrible disease. Maybe by putting pen to paper, I can inspire a few people. Give them some hope. Make them say, 'Wow, what a top fella. If he can remain positive, despite everything he's going through, maybe I can, too.'

Having written it, I realize it's more of a love letter than a book. Albeit a long one. I hope it's been a sweet love letter, rather than a bitter one. I hope it's been uplifting, rather than bleak. And I hope you don't feel sorry for me, because that's the last thing I wanted. Why would a man like me need anyone's pity? As Kev put it, I hit a rough patch, that's all. It hasn't been ideal, I'll give you that. But MND isn't the worst thing in the world. I'm not trying to portray myself as a hero, but I'm glad I got it rather than my beautiful wife and kids. And what a lucky life I've had overall. No regrets, I wouldn't change a thing.

Ever since my diagnosis, it's hit me like a dose of smelling salts just how great humanity is. All that misery you see when you turn on the news doesn't have to be real life. And it's opened my eyes to how blessed my life has been. Unlucky blokes don't get to play a game they love – the best game in the world, no doubt – and pretend it's a job. They don't get to be part of one of the most successful rugby league teams in history, win stacks of trophies and make grown men cry. What better way to earn a crust than making people happy?

Imagine yourself in that Leeds changing room: Jamie Peacock in full throttle, more stirring than Shakespeare; Barrie McDermott, the kindest tough guy there's ever been, with an arm around your shoulder; Keith Senior, who'd never let a man take a liberty, staring back at you; Danny McGuire, a magician who could spring you from the stickiest situation, wearing a small, confident smile; Jamie Jones-Buchanan, the ultimate warrior, strapping up for battle;

Kevin Sinfield, that great leader of men and everyone's big brother, at the heart of it all. Painted the picture? Now tell me how unlucky I am.

With those lads around you, like a ring of steel, rough patches feel a lot smoother. And there's plenty more where they came from. You'll even find them in rugby union. Wearing yellow tartan trousers, like my mate Doddie.

Dr Jung said something that made me think: 'What MND patients want most is to be surrounded by love.' Why? Because we know we haven't got as much time as we'd want. But everyone's dying, when you think about it. From the moment you're born, you've only got so long left. So why not surround yourself with love all the time, like I've tried to? Why wait for the rough patch?

Maybe you're reading this and thinking, 'That's all well and good, but some people aren't as fortunate as you.' Well, I kind of hope you are! I totally agree, fortune is having two sisters who spend their whole lives trying to kiss you. Fortune is having a mum and dad who believe in your dream, however mad it might seem, and do everything in their power to make it come true. Fortune is having a beautiful, super-smart partner who could have had the pick of the bunch but chose you instead.

I've been batting above my average since that first date at the pictures, when we were only fifteen. And I still pinch myself some mornings, to make sure I'm not dreaming and Lindsey's really my wife. There are times when I feel bad that Lindsey has to do what she does. But there's something beautiful about being cared for by the only girl you ever loved. In truth, Lindsey's been mothering me from the day we met, which is why I know our three children can't go wrong. If they turn out like their mum, which I'm sure they will, the world will be a far kinder, more special place.

But hold your horses, Granddad Bob. We'll be reunited sooner than I thought, but I'm not ready for your steak just yet. There are still things to do and memories to make. Does that sound like an unlucky way to spend your days? Maybe keep it warm in the oven. I've got too many reasons to live.

Acknowledgements

Having decided that it might be a good idea to write a book, following my diagnosis and the attention triggered by my appearances on the BBC, I didn't really know how to go about it or whether it would even be possible. It was the literary agent Ruth Cairns (a Featherstone girl originally) who convinced me that my story could – and should – be told. In September 2020, Ruth and the writer Ben Dirs visited me, Lindsey and my dad in Pontefract. After our chat, Ben went away and knocked up a proposal. And a few weeks after that, Robin Harvie of Pan Macmillan snapped up the book. It really did happen that fast.

Ben had written autobiographies with lots of famous sportspeople, so I was overwhelmed that he'd been asked to work with me on mine. He had to overcome the fact I couldn't speak, but his talent shone through in how he was able to pull all the different strands together to tell my story. Thank you, mate, for giving me a legacy that Lindsey, the kids and the rest of the family can enjoy forever. I can never repay you, but I'm so proud of what we did together. Thank you, Ruth, for seeing what was possible when I wasn't so sure. And thank you, Robin, and everyone at Pan Macmillan, for providing the platform. By publishing my story, you're doing sterling work in the fight against MND.

Fittingly, the writing of this book was a team effort, with lots of people pitching in to help. Here's the gang who filled in the detail (besides those whose direct quotes appear): the magnificent Doddie Weir, who provided chapter and verse of our first fateful meeting; Tanya Arnold of BBC Look North, who relayed her memories of my first post-diagnosis interview; Stacey and Lee Hicken, producers of the brilliant Leeds Rhinos documentary *As Good As It Gets?*; BBC Breakfast's Claire Ryan (big props also to the rest of the team – you've been so understanding and kind); Sky Sports's Stephen Owen; Leeds Rhinos' Phil Daly (if Lindsey has been my PA, Phil has been Lindsey's very own media man); and rugby league writer Phil Caplan. Huge thanks to all of you, this book would not have been possible without your generous contributions.

Other sources included an interview between me and my old mate Stevie Ward, which took the form of a *Mantality* podcast; my appearance with Will Perry and Jon Wilkin on the *Out Of Your League* podcast; Lindsey's appearance on Natalie Anderson's *The Capsule* podcast; and literally thousands of archived newspaper articles, written by good, upstanding journalists fighting to keep the great sport of rugby league and MND in the public eye. Also credit to Leeds Rhinos' Leanne Flynn, who furnished us with quotes from a host of old Rhinos faces – Carl Ablett, Daryl

Powell, Gary Hetherington, Brad Singleton, Ryan Hall, Liam Sutcliffe, Willie Poching, Danny Ward and Gareth Ellis – some of which came in very handy indeed.

Finally, a big shout-out to the transcribing team of Rob Murray, Luke Reddy and Neil Matheson, as well as Fran Hewitt of the Leeds Teaching Hospitals NHS Trust, who kindly facilitated Ben's interview with Dr Jung.

That's just the people who helped me write this book. Thanking everyone who has helped me throughout my life, especially with my rugby career and since my diagnosis, would fill another hundred pages. Rest assured, you're never far from my thoughts and we'll keep marching on together.

Picture Acknowledgements

All pictures in the first photo section are courtesy of Rob
  Burrow. For the second photo section:

Rob in wheelchair © Allan McKenzie/SWpix.com

Rob with Jamie Peacock © Allan McKenzie/SWpix.com

Rob with Kev Sinfield after his marathons © Allan McKenzie/
  SWpix.com

Rob v. St Helens 2011 © Simon Wilkinson/SWpix.com

Rob v. Manly 2012 © Vaughn Ridley/SWpix.com

Rob v. Wigan with Kev 2015 © Alex Whitehead/SWpix.com

Rob v. Bradford 2004 © John Clifton/SWpix.com

Rob and teammates v. Warrington 2012 © Vaughn Ridley/
  SWpix.com

Rob with Tony Smith © Vaughn Ridley/SWpix.com

Rob in 2008 World Cup © Vaughn Ridley/SWpix.com

Rob v. Castleford 2017 © Alex Whitehead/SWpix.com

Rob lifting trophy with Danny McGuire © Alex Whitehead/
  SWpix.com

Rob v. North Queensland 2016 © Allan McKenzie/SWpix.
  com

Rob with Kev and Brian McDermott © Allan McKenzie/
  SWpix.com